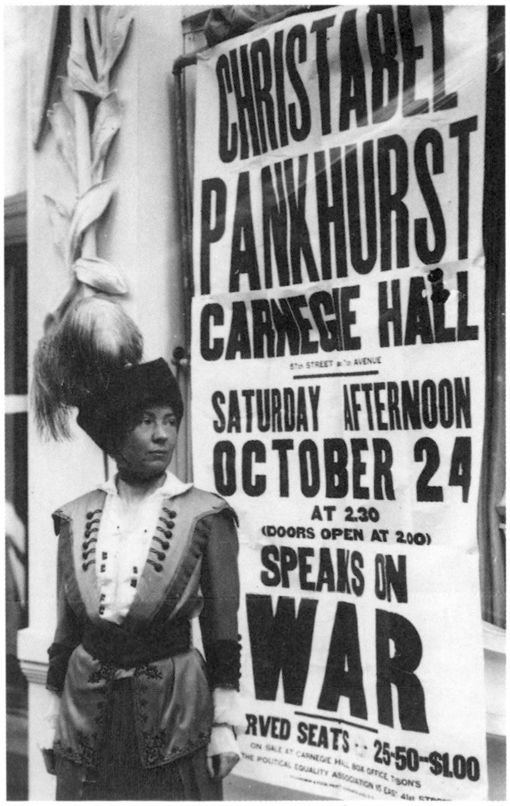
CHRISTABEL
PANKHURST
CARNEGIE HALL
SATURDAY AFTERNOON
OCTOBER 24
AT 2.30
(DOORS OPEN AT 2.00)
SPEAKS ON
WAR
RVED SEATS 25-50-$1.00

WHO'S WHO of WOMEN in the TWENTIETH CENTURY

General Editor · Jean Martin

Crescent Books
New York/Avenel, New Jersey

This 1995 edition published by Crescent Books, distributed by Random House Value Publishing, Inc., 40 Engelhard Avenue, Avenel, New Jersey 07001

Random House
New York · Toronto · London · Sydney · Auckland

Produced by Brompton Books Corporation, 15 Sherwood Place, Greenwich, Connecticut 06830

ISBN 0-517-12027-5

8 7 6 5 4 3 2 1

Printed and bound in China

PAGE 1: *Amelia Earhart.*

PAGE 2 *(top) Emma Goldman; (center left) Rigoberta Menchu; (center right) Winnie Mandela; (bottom left) Takako Doi; (bottom right) Christabel Pankhurst.*

PAGE 3: *(left to right): Carol Moseley Braun, Barbra Streisand, Steffi Graf.*

THESE PAGES: *Thousands of women campaigned for "Votes for Women" in the early twentieth century.*

Picture Credits

The Bettmann Archive, New York, NY: pages 7, 18 (bottom left), 25 (bottom right), 31 (top left), 32 (left), 37, 38 (top left), 40, 45 (bottom right), 46 (bottom left), 47 (bottom right), 50 (top left), 51 (bottom right), 59 (both), 62, 74, 75 (top center), 76 (left), 82 (both), 84, 88, 90 (top center), 93, 94 (top left), 97 (top center), 99 (top left), 100 (bottom), 104 (both), 106 (bottom right), 107, 111 (top left), 119, 120, 121 (bottom left), 134, 136, 143, 148 (top right), 155 (bottom right), 156 (bottom left), 158.

Brompton Picture Library: pages 13 (top), 15, 42, 44 (top left), 60 (bottom left), 61 (top left), 68, 71 (top right), 85 (right), 98, 109 (top left).

Hulton Deutsch Collection Ltd., London: pages 6 (top right), 8 (bottom left), 17 (top right), 19 (both) 23 (bottom right), 24 (top left), 79, 95 (top right), 139 (both), 154 (top left).

National Archives, Washington, D.C.: page 16 (top right).

National Portrait Gallery, London: page 131.

Newsweek/© Shel Secunda: page 123 (bottom left).

Reuters/Bettmann Newsphotos, New York, NY: pages 2-3, 9 (both), 11, 12 (top right), 18 (top left), 21, 22 (top center), 25 (top center), 26 (top center), 27, 30 (top left), 35 (top right), 39 (bottom right), 44 (bottom center), 46 (top right), 48 (top left), 49, 53 (bottom left), 55 (top right), 56, 57 (bottom), 61 (bottom right), 63 (bottom center), 64 (top left), 71 (bottom left), 83 (bottom right), 92 (top left), 101 (bottom right), 102, 106 (top left), 112 (bottom left), 115, 116 (top right), 125, 127, 144 (top center), 145 (top left), 147, 151, 153 (bottom right).

Springer/Bettmann Film Archive, New York, NY: pages 57 (top right), 69 (bottom right), 122.

UPI/Bettmann Newsphotos, New York, NY: pages 1, 6 (top left), 8 (top right), 10 (both), 12 (bottom left), 13 (bottom), 14, 17 (bottom right), 20, 22 (bottom center), 23 (top left), 24 (bottom right), 26 (bottom left), 28, 29, 30 (bottom right), 31 (top right), 32 (bottom right), 33, 34 (both), 35 (bottom left), 36, 38 (bottom right), 39 (top left), 41, 43 (both), 45 (top left), 47 (top left), 48 (bottom right), 50 (bottom center), 51 (top center), 52, 53 (top right), 54 (top center, bottom right), 55 (bottom right), 58 (both), 60 (top center), 63 (top left), 64 (bottom center), 65, 66-67, 69 (top left), 70, 72, 75 (bottom right), 77-78, 80-81, 83 (top left), 85 (top left), 86-87, 89, 91, 92 (top right, bottom), 94 (bottom center), 95 (top left), 96, 97 (bottom right), 99 (bottom right), 100 (top left), 101 (top right), 103 (all three), 105 (both), 108, 109 (bottom right), 110, 111 (bottom right), 112 (top left, bottom right), 114, 116 (bottom left), 117 (both), 118, 121 (top center), 123 (top right), 124, 126, 128-29, 130, 132-133, 135, 137, 138, 140-41, 142, 144 (bottom right), 145 (bottom right), 146, 148 (bottom left), 149, 150, 153 (top left), 154 (bottom right), 155 (top center), 156 (top right), 157, 159 (both), 160.

University of Georgia Public Information, Athens, GA: page 76 (bottom right).

Westchester County Historical Society Picture Collection: page 152.

Picture research by Sara Dunphy.

Design by Sue Rose.

The Contributors

Kate F. Jennings is a graduate of Columbia University. She has contributed to a number of magazines and newspapers in her native Connecticut, and is the author of several books, including *Grant Wood*, *Winslow Homer*, and *John Singer Sargent*.

Midori A. Lockett is an arts administrator and producer. She earned a Master's degree in Arts Administration from Drexel University and a B.A. degree in Theatre Arts from Brown University. Midori has worked as a publicist and copywriter for radio and television. She presently resides in Philadelphia.

Elizabeth Miles Montgomery studied history and art history at Hollins College in Virginia, and has since worked in advertising, fund-raising, and publishing. She lives with her husband in Norwalk, Connecticut. She has written a number of books, including *The Best of MGM*, *Norman Rockwell*, and *Georgia O'Keeffe*.

Janey Skinner is a writer and activist based in San Francisco. An honors graduate of Brown University, she studied Comparative Literature. She has worked in Latin America as a human rights monitor and trainer for three years, and also leads workshops in the United States and Canada.

Sande Smith is a writer and dancer who is a graduate of Brown University. She has been the editor of *Listen Real Loud, News of Women's Liberation Worldwide* for the American Friends Services Committee in Philadelphia, and she is the author of two books: *The Life and Philosophy of Malcolm X*, and *Martin Luther King*.

Robin Langley Sommer studied art history and aesthetics at Loyola University and became a writer and editor in New York City. She has written over a dozen books, including *Frank Lloyd Wright*, *Toys of Our Generation*, and *Native American Art*. She lives in Old Greenwich, Connecticut.

A

Bella Abzug served three terms as Democratic congresswoman for New York's Nineteenth District beginning in 1970.

ABBOTT, Berenice
1898-1991
American photographer

A socially committed documentary photographer whose 1937 volume of images *Changing New York* secured her reputation, Berenice Abbott studied fine art in New York and Europe. In Paris she worked as a technical assistant in the studio of the modernist photographer, Man Ray, from 1923 to 1925. She opened her own studio there, photographing some of the most famous artists of the day including James Joyce, Edna St. Vincent MILLAY, Jean Cocteau and André Gide. Her work was shown at the Salon des Independents de Photographie in Paris in 1928. She rescued the work of Eugène Atget from obscurity, raising funds to purchase his negatives and prints which she brought to the attention of American collectors when she returned to New York in the 1930s.

In the 1930s Abbott documented the architectural structures of old New York in a style offering austere, objective immediacy. She was a member of the Photo League which was founded in 1936 as an offshoot of the Federal Arts Project sponsored by the Works Progress Administration. Abbott taught at the New School of Social Research from 1934 to 1958, and later wrote several technical treatises and developed photography to illustrate the laws of physics.

ABZUG, Bella
1920-
American lawyer, feminist, human rights activist

A New Yorker through and through, Bella Abzug is known for her dashing hats and brash leadership in the women's movement. Born Bella Savitsky in the Bronx, she was educated at Hunter College and Columbia Law School. Admitted to the New York bar in 1947, she specialized in labor and civil rights law, often defending clients for free. In 1961 she founded Women Strike for Peace, later becoming active in the anti-Vietnam war movement, for which she came under surveillance by the CIA. A staunch Democrat, she served three terms as a congresswoman for New York's Nineteenth District beginning in 1970, and in 1975 she served one year as a co-chair of President Carter's National Advisory Committee on Women, then served on the Democratic National Committee. In the 1980s she practiced law, wrote, taught, and worked as a television commentator. In 1991 she co-chaired the Women's Environmental and Development Organization, bringing together women's issues with environmental security and economic justice.

ADAMSON, Joy
1916-1980
Austrian conservationist

Joy Adamson at the filming of her book Born Free *in Kenya in 1971. Her work stimulated African wildlife conservation efforts.*

Joy Adamson left her native Austria to spend almost 30 years in Kenya. As wife of the Senior Game Warden of Africa's Northern Frontier District, she explored some of the continent's most inaccessible regions. A gifted painter and photographer, she undertook in the 1950s to make a record of the vanishing tribal way of life, published as *The Peoples of Kenya*. Her best known works are those on her friendship with the lioness Elsa and her cubs: *Born Free*, *Living Free*, and *Forever Free*. Her dedication to African wildlife and its conservation increased world awareness of Africa's natural heritage and encouraged other conservationists in their efforts to breed endangered species and return them to the wild.

ADDAMS, Jane
1860-1935
American pacifist, suffragist, social reformer

A powerful vocal opponent to World War I, pacifist Jane Addams never allowed public criticism to deter her sense of purpose.

In 1887 she observed the work done at Toynbee Hall, a settlement house in London's East End. With Ellen Gates

Starr, she co-founded Chicago's Hull House, the first major settlement house in the United States, in 1889. Serving Chicago's immigrant enclave, Hull House became the model for settlement houses throughout the country.

During World War I, she actively participated in the suffrage movement and denounced the United States' involvement in the War. In 1915 she organized and chaired the Women's Peace Party. That same year, along with Emily BALCH, she founded the Women's International League for Peace and Freedom (WILPF).

An advocate of free speech, she helped found the American Civil Liberties Union in 1920 and served on its national committee for ten years. Her commitment to world peace and justice for all was recognized in 1931 when she became the first American woman to receive the Nobel Peace Prize.

Jane Addams became the second woman to win the Nobel Peace Prize, in 1931.

AKHMATOVA, Anna
1889-1966
Russian poet

Acclaimed as Russia's greatest woman poet, Akhmatova was raised near St. Petersburg. She first published her poetry in 1907 and with the writer Nikolai Gumilyov, whom she married in 1910, launched the Acmeist Movement, which emphasized Russian traditions in opposition to the contemporary symbolist style. Her collections from this period include *Evening* (1912), *Beads* (1914) and *The White Flock* (1917).

Akhmatova divorced Gumilov in 1918 and three years later he was shot for his counterrevolutionary politics. After producing the volume *Anno Domini MCMXXI* (1922), which dealt frankly with women's passion and won her great fame, Akhmatova was forced out of the public arena, and did not publish again until 1940. By then she had been exiled to Tashkent and was formally censured in 1946. She was finally reinstated to the writer's union after Stalin's death but her more somber, Christian poetry describing the pain of a survivor and social and political issues failed to win public popularity in Russia. Her best works, "Requiem" and "Poem Without a Hero", were published abroad. Her collected *Poems of Akhmatova* were published in 1973. She received an honorary degree from Oxford University in 1965 and won the Etna-Taormina poetry prize in Italy in 1964.

ALEXANDER, Jane
1939-
American actress

Born Jane Quigley in Boston, the actress was educated at Sarah Lawrence College and the University of Edinburgh, where she divided her interest between mathematics and the stage. After roles in summer stock and off-Broadway, she made her Broadway debut in 1963 in *A Thousand Clowns*. She joined the Arena Stage Company in Washington, D.C., where she and James Earl Jones first starred in *The Great White Hope*. They repeated the roles on Broadway, for which Alexander won a Tony and a Drama Desk Award in 1969. For her performance in the movie the following year, she received her first Academy Award nomination. She has been nominated three times since, for *All the President's Men* (1976), *Kramer vs Kramer* (1979), and *Testament* (1983). Equally at home on television, she received Emmy nominations for both parts of *Eleanor and Franklin* (1976, 1977), and *Malice in Wonderland* (1985). She has won Emmys for *Playing for Time* (1980) and *Calamity Jane* (1984). In 1993 she was appointed Chairman of the National Endowment for the Arts by the Clinton administration.

ALEXANDER, Madame
1895-1990
American doll manufacturer

Beatrice Alexander was born in Brooklyn, New York, where her father operated a doll hospital, which he would open in the middle of the night to repair toys on an emergency basis. This made her want to make an unbreakable doll. During World War I, when German dolls became unobtainable, she and her father designed and produced a rag doll, dressed as a Red Cross nurse. In 1923 she founded the Alexander Doll Co., and by 1925, the factory in Harlem, New York, was producing dolls made of cloth with faces of pressed fabric, a more durable substance than the usual bisque or composition. After World War II, she used a hard-surfaced plastic. In the 1930s she began to manufacture portrait dolls, many of them based on characters from children's books, including the well-known Little Women, and the first curly-haired baby dolls. Madame Alexander was one of the first to create a wide variety of clothing, accessories and furniture for her dolls. She stressed that her dolls were made as playthings, but they are much sought after by collectors today.

A

ALLENDE, Isabel
1942-
Chilean novelist

With her novels *The House of the Spirits* (which became a 1994 film), *Of Love and Shadows*, and *Eva Luna* widely translated, Isabel Allende is among the most popular South American authors today.

The dramatic events of her own life spawned her fantastical stories and family sagas. Born in Peru, she worked as a journalist in Chile until the military coup of 1973 that toppled her uncle, President Salvador Allende. She fled to Venezuela, and while her uncle and thousands more Chileans died in the coup and its aftermath, she began to write *The House of the Spirits*, weaving political events and Chilean culture through the lives of a fictional family. Now living in California, Allende's most recent novel *The Infinite Plan* confronts the cross-cultural tensions that Allende has experienced in her 22 years of exile.

ANDERSON, Elizabeth Garrett
1836-1917
British physician

The first woman to qualify as a physician in England, Elizabeth Garrett first trained as a nurse. She attended lectures given to the medical students at London's Middlesex Hospital, until the male students insisted upon her leaving. Unsuccessful in all her applications for university courses, she eventually studied privately with professors, took a course in midwifery, and was qualified by the Society of Apothecaries. This enabled her to run a dispensary for women, which eventually grew into the New Hospital for Women. She took her final medical examination in Paris and was allowed to practice as a doctor from 1870. In 1883 she was elected dean of the London School of Medicine. She moved to her native town of Aldeburgh, Suffolk, with her husband, James Anderson, in the early 1900s. He was elected mayor of Aldeburgh and she was asked to complete his term upon his death in 1907. Subsequently, she was elected mayor in her own right – the first woman in the United Kingdom to achieve this distinction.

Dr. Elizabeth Garrett Anderson, England's first female physician and mayor.

ANDERSON, Margaret
1886-1973
American editor, publisher

Born in Indianapolis, Margaret Anderson moved to Chicago in 1908. In 1914 she founded *The Little Review*, one of the first magazines in the United States to specialize in publishing the work of the modernists, especially writers of the Chicago School such as Carl Sandburg, Sherwood Anderson and Ben Hecht, as well as such poets as William Carlos Williams and Amy LOWELL. In 1917 she hired Ezra Pound as foreign editor, and began to include European authors such as W.B. Yeats, T.S. Eliot and James Joyce. When the magazine, by then published in New York, serialized *Ulysses* in 1918, issues were seized and destroyed by postal authorities under charges of obscenity. The trial became a landmark case in the history of the freedom of the press, although, at the time, the charges of obscenity were sustained. Margaret Anderson moved the magazine to Paris in 1924 where she championed many of the important artistic movements of the time, including Cubism, Dadaism and Surrealism until *The Little Review* ceased publication in 1929. Anderson also wrote three volumes of autobiography.

ANDERSON, Marian
1902-1993
American contralto

Anderson began singing at the age of six in the Union Baptist Church in her native Philadelphia. She was the recipient of the first scholarship from the National Association of Negro Musicians, and toured black college campuses. She made her London debut in 1930 and her first European tour in 1933, singing in London, Germany (including Salzburg) and Scandinavia. Anderson signed a contract with impresario Sol Hurok on 1935, and made her long-awaited New York debut the following year. In 1939 she sang at the Lincoln Memorial in Washington, D.C., before 75,000 people, after the Daughters of the American Revolution refused to schedule a concert at Constitution Hall. She subsequently sang at the White House, and made her long-delayed debut at the Metropolitan Opera in 1955, as Ulrica in *Un Ballo in Maschera*, the first performance by a black in a leading role. After a long and successful career, she made a farewell tour in 1965 and retired. She also worked for the civil rights movement and was a U.S. delegate to the United Nations in 1958. Her extraordinary voice, with a range of three octaves, was described by conductor Arturo Toscanini as "a voice such as one hears once in a hundred years."

Contralto Marian Anderson was the first black singer to sign a contract with the Met.

ANGELOU, Maya
1928-
American writer

A prolific and inspiring poet, writer, performer, and educator, Angelou was born Marguerite Johnson in St. Louis, Missouri, and studied dance with Pearl Primus in New York City. She later taught modern dance at the Rome Opera House and at the Habimah Theatre in Tel Aviv. Active in the civil rights movement, she is

Maya Angelou reads her "On the Pulse of the Morning: The Inaugural Poem" at President Bill Clinton's inauguration in 1993.

best known for her poetry and for her serial autobiography, which began with *I Know Why the Caged Bird Sings* (1970). The four companion volumes, spanning 35 years of her life, are remarkable for their depiction both of a black woman's discovery of her identity and of the community that helped to shape her. In 1993 she wrote and read "On the Pulse of Morning: The Inaugural Poem" at the inauguration of President Clinton. She has received several honorary degrees and has taught at a number of colleges and universities.

ANNE, The Princess Royal
1950-
Princess of Great Britain

The only daughter of Queen Elizabeth II, Princess Anne broke tradition by attending school (Benenden) rather than being educated at home. An accomplished sportswoman, she has won many awards for her prowess in riding. In 1973 she married Mark Phillips, then a lieutenant in the Queen's Dragoon Guards. They separated in 1989, and later divorced. In 1992 she married Timothy J.H. Laurence, a naval commander. She is president of the Save the Children Fund, which fosters health care for mothers and small children and seeks to alleviate problems in famine-stricken areas and among refugees. Combining her love of riding with her love of children, she works with the Riding for the Disabled Association teaching disabled children to ride horses. She was created Princess Royal in 1987. In 1990 she travelled to the former USSR on the first official visit by a member of the British royal family.

AQUINO, Corazon
1933-
Filipino president

Corazon Aquino had only spent two months in the political arena when she became president of the Philippines in 1986. Maria Corazon Cojunangco was born into one of the wealthiest Chinese-Filipino familes in the country, and she received a crash course in politics and insurgency when her husband Benigno Aquino was imprisoned in 1972. After he was assassinated in 1983, Aquino agreed to run for president if then-president Ferdinand Marcos, under international pressure to restore democracy, called a snap election. When she won, Marcos tried to keep her from her seat, yet with the support of members of the military and millions of marching people, she became president. Although unable to keep her promises of agrarian reform, an end to corruption, and improved economic health, she did make sure that her successor was democratically elected.

ARBUS, Diane
1923-1971
American photographer

Known for her haunting images of society's outsiders, Diane Nemerov grew up in an affluent Jewish family in Manhattan. She married photographer Allan Arbus at 18 and spent the next 20 years producing fashion layouts for magazines and newspapers with her husband. An encounter in 1959 with Lisette Arnold, a master of strange caricatures, convinced her to pursue her own vision – close-up, unsparing, black-and-white portraits of transvestites, prostitutes and disenfranchised people with peculiar miens and distorted expressions. She won a Guggenheim grant in 1963 and again in 1966, and her work was part of a critically acclaimed show at the Museum of Modern Art in 1967. She was also part of a New Documents show there in 1969 and was given a posthumous solo retrospective in 1972. The last works she exhibited before her suicide in 1971 were inmates at a mental hospital dressed up in formal attire for a party. In the year following her death, she was honored at the Venice Biennale, the first American photographer to be included in that international exposition.

Philippine president Corazon Aquino gives the Laban (Fight) sign in 1986.

ARDEN, Elizabeth
1878?-1966
Canadian cosmetics entrepreneur

Florence Nightingale Graham was born in Woodbridge, Ontario, but chose a new name for herself in 1909 when her partnership with the early cosmetics entrepreneur Elizabeth Hubbard broke up, and she went into business for herself. She was a pioneer in the use and advertising of beauty aids for "ladies" at a time when make-up was thought of only in connection with women in the theatre or other "low" professions. Arden also sought to improve the safety of cosmetics by eliminating unhygienic practices and dangerous ingredients. She was one of the first to hire chemists to produce her face creams and astringent lotions. She established salons throughout the United States, Canada and Europe which introduced a regimen of scientific beauty treatment and preparation, teaching women how to improve and tone their bodies through diet and exercise, especially at the spas she opened in Maine and Arizona. Her success in the field of cosmetics allowed her to indulge in horse racing, and one of her horses, Jet Pilot, won the Kentucky Derby in 1947.

Elizabeth Arden was one of the first to popularize the use of cosmetics.

Hannah Arendt is best known for her writings on the "banality of evil".

ARENDT, Hannah
1906-1975
German–American political philosopher

One of the most highly regarded political philosophers of the postwar period, Hannah Arendt was born in Hanover, Germany, and received her doctorate in philosophy in 1929. She left Berlin after a brief internment by the Gestapo in 1933 and was again imprisoned, in southern France, before escaping to New York in 1941. Her early essays appeared in *Jewish Frontier*, the *Partisan Review* and the *Nation* while she taught at Brooklyn College in New York.

Her treatise *The Origins of Totalitarianism* was published in 1951, the year she acquired United States citizenship. A major, influential study of anti-Semitism, imperialism and totalitarian governments, the book also traced the decline of nation states in eighteenth-century Europe. She received a Guggenheim Fellowship and produced *The Human Condition* in 1958, which discussed man's political capacities in action and speech. In 1963 she covered the trial of Adolf Eichmann in Jerusalem for the *New Yorker* and wrote a controversial book about the experience.

Arendt was the first woman to be a full professor at Princeton University and also taught at the University of Chicago. Her final work *The Life of the Mind* was published posthumously in 1979.

ARNOLD, Eve
1913-
American photojournalist

Eve Arnold originally studied medicine before switching to photography classes at the New School of Social Research in 1947. Her instructor was Alexey Brodovitch, the art director for *Harper's Bazaar*, and her early efforts were freelance assignments for *Vogue* and the *Sunday New York Times*. She made several important studies of Harlem as well as political events in New York, and while working in Hollywood portrayed famous actors and actresses of the era such as James Cagney, Clark Gable, Marilyn MONROE and Paul Newman.

In 1951 Arnold became the first woman member of Magnum, a highly respected photographers' cooperative in New York. She captured images of the civil rights movement during the 1960s and produced a film about harems in Arabia called *Behind the Veil* (1973). Her feminist volume of photographs, *The Unretouched Woman*, was published in 1976, and she produced *Flashback, the Fifties* in 1978.

Arnold's China compositions of the 1970s focused on women performing menial tasks with quiet dignity. She also sought out unusual individuals – wrestlers, members of the militia and religious fanatics. These images were collected in a 1980 volume *In China: Photographs of Eve Arnold*. Her later books include *Marilyn Monroe: An Appreciation* (1987), *The Great British* (1990) and *All in a Day's Work* (1991).

ARZNER, Dorothy
1900-1979
American film director

A native of San Francisco, Arzner began her career in film by typing scripts. She later became a cutter and chief editor at Paramount. After editing 52 films, including *The Covered Wagon* (1921) and *Blood and Sand* (1922), for which she filmed the bullfight scenes, Arzner was given her first directing assignment, *Fashions for Women* (1927) with Esther Ralston. Her subsequent silent films included *Get Your Man* with Clara Bow. The first woman director in Hollywood, Azner was reportedly the first to develop and use the boom mike. She was still the only female director in the 1930s, when she made such films as *Christopher*

Strong (1933) with Katharine HEPBURN and *The Bride Wore Red* (1937) with Joan CRAWFORD. She left the film industry in the mid-1940s after a serious bout of pneumonia and started the first film-making course at Pasadena Playhouse. She subsequently taught film at UCLA and made 50 commercials for Pepsi-Cola with Joan Crawford, who was then chairman of the board.

ASH, Mary Kay
1920?-
American cosmetics entrepreneur

Mary Kay Wagner was born in Hot Wells, Texas, and was a student at the University of Houston when she married her first husband during World War II. After their divorce, to support her family she went to work for the Stanley Home Products Company where she subsequently became manager. She moved to the World Gift Company in Dallas in 1952, and in 1963 after being refused a promotion and salary equivalent to her male co-workers, she started Mary Kay Cosmetics with only $5000. Using door-to-door sales, and the concept of hostesses inviting friends to join in a sales party, she established a network of over 185,000 independent saleswomen, working in areas distant from department stores, whom she encouraged with incentive prizes of mink coats, diamond pins and her trademark pink Cadillacs. The company went public in 1967 and by the late 1970s the company had a market value of $50 million. Ash and her son recovered ownership of the company in the mid-1980s, and with greater incentive programs increased sales by 60 percent. In 1988 the company was valued at $400 million.

ASHCROFT, Dame Peggy
1907-1991
British actress

Edith Emily Margaret Ashcroft was born in Croydon, south London and trained at the Central School of Drama there. By the late 1930s she was regarded as one of the leading Shakespearean actresses of her time and the finest Juliet of the century. A member of the first Old Vic Company in 1932, Ashcroft starred in Komisarjevsky's famous productions of *Fraulein Else* in 1933, and *The Sea Gull* in 1936. After the war she continued to appear in Shakespeare and other classic plays, as well as the occasional modern one, including Samuel Beckett's *Happy Days.* She became familiar to a larger audience in the 1980s when she appeared in the 1984 BBC dramatization of *The Jewel in the Crown* and in *A Passage to India* (1984), a role for which she won the Academy Award for Best Supporting Actress. She was created a Dame Commander of the British Empire in 1956.

ASHFORD, Evelyn
1957-
American track and field athlete

Born in Shreveport, Louisiana, Evelyn Ashford was the only girl invited to join her high school track squad. She was awarded a track scholarship to UCLA and competed in the 1976 Montreal Olympics when she was a freshman, placing fifth in the 100 meter dash. By 1978 Ashford was the top United States sprinter and left college to train full-time. She was considered an odds-on favorite in the 1980 Moscow Olympics, but the US boycott of these games prevented her from competing. At the 1984 Olympics held in Los Angeles, she won the gold medal in the 100 meter event and was a member of the gold medal winning 4 × 400 meter relay team. Against East German rival Marlies Gohr in a Zurich track meet after the Games, she won the 100 meter dash in a world record time of 10:76. She won her fourth Olympic gold medal in the 1992 Olympic Games in Barcelona in the 4 × 100 meter relay.

ASHLEY, Laura
1925-1985
British textile designer, entrepreneur

Born in Merthyr Tydfil in Glamorgan, Wales, and educated in London, Laura Mountney began her extensive business with her husband Bernard Ashley at her own kitchen table, silk screening cushion covers after she gave up her job as a designer when pregnant with her first child. She also designed smocks and aprons which were the foundation of a romantic style of clothing for women and children and continues to be popular. Using natural fabrics, especially cotton, often woven and printed in Wales, and patterns and motifs based on 18th and 19th century sources, she also developed an entire line of furnishing materials which led to coordinated wallpapers, borders, tiles, quilts and paints. These were designed to combine patterns and colors in a simple yet sophisticated way which allowed people to create rooms of a certain traditional style suited to modern taste without a decorator. The business, originally Ashley Mountney Ltd., became Laura Ashley Ltd. in 1968 and has since spread throughout the world.

ASHRAWI, Hanan
1946-
Palestinian political leader

In 1987 Hanan Ashrawi became one of the main voices of the Palestinian people in the international news media. Through her calm arguments, well-modulated tones, and Western dress, she was able to make the plea for Palestinian self-determination in a language that Westerners understood. During the Middle East Peace Talks between Israel and the Palestinian Liberation Organization (PLO), she was one of the PLO's spokespersons. After the agreement made between Israel and the PLO, she resigned from the PLO to start her own organization, the Palestinian Independent Commission of Human Rights, that will monitor and protect human rights in the Israeli-occupied territories once the PLO takes charge.

Palestinian spokeswoman Hanan Ashwari has effectively communicated the needs of the Palestinian people to the Western world.

ASQUITH, Countess Margot
1864-1945
British political personality

A "woman of unrestrained candor," this fashionable debutante earned a reputation throughout England for her sparkling parties attended by the intellectual, politically savvy and powerful alike. Margot Asquith selected her friends based upon their character, not their political worth, and as wife of the Prime Minister Herbert Henry Asquith (1908-16) this sometimes proved to conflict with his interests. A member of The Souls, a group of intellectuals and artists, conservatives and liberals, Asquith is credited with nurturing England's aesthetics and influencing fashion for years after her death. An author, she published her autobiography, travelogues, essays and a novel.

ASTOR, Lady Nancy
1879-1964
American-born British politician

Born in Virginia, Nancy Witcher Langhorne left the U.S. in 1906 for England, where she met her second husband, Waldorf Astor, a descendant of America's first millionaire family. Waldorf Astor was a British citizen, and a member of the House of Parliament. When he succeeded his father, the first Viscount Astor, in the House of Lords in 1919, Nancy Astor replaced him in the House of Commons as Conservative MP for Plymouth, becoming the first woman to take a seat in Parliament. She was reelected for over two decades. Famous for a dry wit and dramatic flair, and passionate about children, she worked to regulate child labor, create day care centers, and prohibit youth under 18 from frequenting pubs – a controversial stance at the time.

Virginia-born Lady Nancy Astor became the first woman in Britain to hold a seat in Parliament, in 1919.

ATWOOD, Margaret
1939-
Canadian writer

Margaret Atwood was born and raised in Ottawa, Ontario. As a child, she accompanied her father, an entomologist, on extensive journeys into the remote northern reaches of Quebec and Ontario, and experience which flavors much of her writing. She graduated from the University of Toronto, published a book of poems, *Double Persephone*, in 1962, and received a master's degree from Radcliffe College.

For several years thereafter, Atwood taught in the English departments of several Canadian universities, during which time she published several volumes of verse, including *The Circle Game* (1966). Her first novel, *The Edible Woman*, was published in 1969. She has continued to develop her central theme of female self-discovery and emancipation in her distinctive style in such novels as *Surfacing* (1972), *Lady Oracle* (1976), *Life Before Man* (1979), *The Handmaid's Tale* (1986), *Cat's Eye* (1988), *Wilderness Tips* (1989), and *The Robber Bride* (1993).

AUNG SAN SUU KYI
1945-
Burmese politician

This winner of the Nobel Peace Prize in 1991 continues the legacy of her revolutionary father, Bogyoke Aung San. A leader in the Burmese struggle for independence from Britain during the late 1940s, he was killed when she was 2. Aung San Suu Kyi was educated at Oxford where she studied politics, philosophy and economics. In 1988 she returned to Burma (now Myanmar) to nurse her dying mother, and was swept up into the movement against the military dictatorship. Calling her a "dangerous subversive," the government placed her under house arrest in 1989. Even though she was confined, her party, the National League for Democracy, won elections hands down, but the military government refused to give up power. As of 1994, international pressure on the government may result in her release. Writings by and about her have been published in *Freedom From Fear and Other Writings* (1991).

Burmese opposition leader Aung San Suu Kyi speaks in 1989 in defiance of martial law before being placed under house arrest.

AYLWARD, Gladys
1903-1970
British missionary

London-born Gladys Aylward was a maid-of-all-work who saved for years from her meagre earnings for the fare to China, where she felt called to be a missionary. In 1932 she finally reached Yangcheng, where she assisted an elderly Scottish missionary for several months before being left on her own by the older woman's death. She soon won the love and respect of the local people and became a naturalized Chinese citizen.

Aylward did heroic work among the victims of the Japanese invasion of 1936. In 1940 she led more than 100 homeless children out of the war zone in an epic journey that was dramatized in the film *The Inn of the Sixth Happiness*. Despite failing health, she returned to the East to work with the poor for the rest of her life.

B

BACALL, Lauren
1924-
American actress

A native New Yorker, Betty Joan Perske worked as a model while attending the American Academy of Dramatic Arts. Her film career began when director Howard Hawks spotted her photograph on the cover of *Harper's Bazaar*, and signed her to a seven-year contract. Her first role, opposite Humphrey Bogart in *To Have and Have Not* (1944), brought her instant stardom. Her husky voice and intelligence were perfect for the heroines of the new, somewhat cynical films of the period. Bacall and Bogart were married in 1945, and subsequently appeared together in *The Big Sleep* (1946), *Dark Passage* (1947) and *Key Largo* (1948). After Bogart's death in 1957, and several less successful films, Bacall returned to Broadway in *Goodbye Charlie* in 1959. Her other Broadway appearances include *Cactus Flower* (1967), *Applause* (1970), for which she won her first Tony, and *Woman of the Year* (1981), for which she won her second Tony. Her later films include *Harper* (1966), *Murder on the Orient Express* (1974), *The Shootist* (1976), *Mr. North* (1988) and *Misery* (1990). She has written two autobiographies, *By Myself* (1978) and *Lauren Bacall Now* (1994).

Lauren Bacall was one of Hollywood's most popular actresses in the postwar period.

BADEN-POWELL, Dame Olave
1889-1977
British Girl Guide organizer

Olave Soames was born in Dorset, England, and lived in 17 different households as a child. In 1912 she accompanied her father on a cruise to the West Indies, and met Robert Baden-Powell, founder of the British Scouts. Despite the 32-year difference in their ages, they married the same year.

Olave began recruiting Girl Guides during World War I in Sussex and became Chief Guide in 1918. After fortifying the organization over the next decade she was elected Chief Guide of the World in 1930. She flew 487,777 miles between 1930 and 1970, earning the title of the world's most travelled woman, and she was greeted warmly by diplomats and heads of states in many countries. She was created a Dame of the British Empire in 1932 and received the Order of the White Rose from Finland and the Order of the Sun from Peru. At the time of her death, the World Association of Girl Guides and Girl Scouts listed 6.5 million members. Her 1973 autobiography was entitled *Window on My Heart*.

Girl Guide organizer Olave Baden-Powell.

BAINBRIDGE, Beryl
1933-
British novelist

With wicked humor and sharp naturalistic portraits of the English working class, Bainbridge has universalized her own childhood to examine the link between violence and the search for love.

Comedy and horror pepper her novels, including the award-winning *The Bottle Factory Outing* and Booker Prize nominee *The Dressmaker*. Bainbridge has said she writes to heal herself from the bruises of poverty and violence in the Liverpool home of her childhood. She worked as an actress for radio and theater before taking up writing. Her most recent novel *The Birthday Boys* (1994), an unheroic account of Scott's 1910-12 expedition to the South Pole, reflects Bainbridge's scope as a mature writer, and the surety of her elegant wry language.

BAKER, Ella
1903-1986
American civil rights and labor activist

From neighborhood development, to leadership development, to civil rights organizing – Ella Baker brought it all together. Raised in Littleton, North Carolina, she moved to Harlem, New York, in 1927. In 1932 she joined with George Schuyler, a black writer with the *Pittsburgh Courier*, to organize the Young Negro Cooperative League that promoted consumer cooperatives. During the 1930s she was employed with the Workers Education Project (WEP) of the Works Progress Administration and helped workers acquire basic literacy and political insights. In the early 1940s she worked as national field secretary for the NAACP. With a group of Southern ministers, she founded the Southern Christian Leadership Conference in 1957. A key mover in the sit-ins of the 1960s, she helped students form the Student Nonviolent Coordinating Committee in April 1960. Throughout her life, she worked to create organizations that nurtured the leadership of all the people rather than the leadership of a few.

BAKER, Dame Janet
1933-
British mezzo soprano

Janet Abbott Baker was born in Hatfield, Yorkshire, and sang in local choirs before turning to the serious study of voice in London where she took a master class with Lotte LEHMANN, and later attended the Mozarteum in Salzburg. She made her operatic debut as Rosa in Smetana's *The Secret* with the Oxford University Club in 1956, the same year she joined the chorus at Glyndebourne and won the Daily Mail Kathleen FERRIER Prize. She returned to Glyndebourne in 1965 as Dido in Purcell's opera *Dido and Aeneas*, and later sang with the English National Opera and at Covent Garden. As a concert singer, she was a noted interpreter of Mahler and Elgar, and in the opera house her repertoire ran from the early Italian works of Monteverdi to Benjamin Britten, who wrote the role of Kate Julian in *Owen Wingrave* for her. She was presented with the CBE in 1970, and created Dame Commander of the British Empire in 1976. She made her final appearance at Covent Garden in 1981 as Alceste, and coming full circle (the title of her autobiography) sang her last Glyndebourne in 1982 as Gluck's Orfeo, a role that she had made her own.

BAKER, Josephine
1906-1975
American entertainer

Josephine Baker was born in St. Louis, Missouri, to poor parents. At 13 she joined a vaudeville company, and her dancing and comic talents attracted attention, landing her a role in Eubie Blake's Broadway show *Shuffle Along* and appearances at the Plantation Club in New York. She went to Paris in 1925 with *La Revue Nègre* and her routine was picked up by the director of the Folies Bergére. She became known for her exotic looks, risqué costumes, and skill as a comedienne.

Baker lived luxuriously, married a Jewish industrialist, and worked for the French Resistance during World War II, earning high military honors. With her second husband, Jo Bouillon, she converted her French estate, Les Milandes, into a village for refugee children.

When she was refused service because of her race at the Stork Club in New York in 1951, she criticized the columnist Walter Winchell for not coming to her aid. He then lambasted her in print as a Communist, an accusation that affected her career thereafter.

BALCH, Emily Greene
1867-1961
American pacifist, social reformer

Affluent and well-educated, Emily Greene Balch was a member of Bryn Mawr College's first graduating class in 1889. From 1896 to 1915 she taught economics and sociology at Wellesley College.

Later dismissed from her teaching post because of her liberal views, she worked in a Boston settlement house. During this period she promoted child welfare reforms in Massachusetts and served on the Massachusetts Commission on Immigration and the Massachusetts Commission on Industrial Relations. Much of her work was influenced by Jane ADDAMS, with whom she founded the International Women's League for Peace and Freedom.

An ardent pacifist, she sought out potential areas of political unrest and urged the United States government to outlaw war. She advised President Woodrow Wilson on which points to incorporate into the League of Nations covenant. During World War II, she worked for the rights of Japanese-Americans interred in camps. For her efforts on behalf of world peace, she received the Nobel Peace Prize in 1946.

BALL, Lucille
1911-1989
American actress, television producer

Born in Jamestown, New York, Lucille Ball went to New York City at the age of 15 to join the theatre. She subsequently traveled to Hollywood, and became one of the Goldwyn Girls, appearing in a number of B-movies, before landing her first billed role in *Carnival* (1935). Her best-known early role was in *Stage Door* (1937), but she also starred in *Room Service* (1938), *DuBarry Was a Lady* (1943) and *Sorrowful Jones* (1949). A pioneer performer in the new medium of television, she created the wildly successful situation comedy *I Love Lucy*, with her husband Desi Arnaz. The show, which made full use of her brilliant timing (and was one of the first to deal with pregnancy) outlasted their marriage. A shrewd executive, Ball kept the production rights of the show in her own hands, starting Lucille Ball Productions in 1968, at the Desilu Studios, which was still owned by Ball. It was eventually sold to Gulf and Western for $17 million. Ball returned to Broadway in the musical *Wildcat* in 1960, and made her final film, *Mame*, in 1973.

BANDARANAIKE, Sirimavo Ratwatte Dias
1916-
Sri Lankan prime minister, politician

Sirimavo Bandaranaike, the first woman in the world to become prime minister, has described herself as a reluctant politician. While she focussed on the traditional duties of home, she also supported women's social welfare movements, and advancing her husband Solomon Bandaranaike's political career. In 1956 he be-

Sirimavo Bandaranaike, Sri Lankan prime minister from 1960 to 1965 and 1970 to 1977.

came prime minster of what was then Ceylon, but was assassinated in 1959. She began to campaign, speaking out for the party he formed, the Sri Lanka Freedom Party. During her two terms as prime minister (1960-65 and 1970-77), she made Sinhalese the official language and declared Ceylon the Republic of Sri Lanka, enacting a new constitution. An economic recession and her monopoly on power in the government resulted in her loss of popularity, and even though she was no longer prime minister, she maintained leadership of the Sri Lanka Freedom Party until 1993.

BANKHEAD, Tallulah
1903?-1968
American actress

Tallulah Brockman Bankhead was born in Huntsville, Alabama, the daughter of the Speaker of the House, William Bankhead. Against her parents' wishes she became an actress in New York, appearing in her first play, *Squab Farm*, in 1918, the same year she made her first film, *When Men Betray*. She was a star in New York and London in the 1920s, working with Gerald DuMaurier in *The Dancers* in 1923, and playing Iris March in *The Green Hat* (1925). She returned to the United States in the 1930s and appeared in a series of films, in summer stock and on Broadway in *Rain* in 1935. She won the Critic's Circle Award for *The Little Foxes* in 1939, and again for *The Skin of Our Teeth* in 1944, the year after making her best (and best-known) film, *Lifeboat* (1943). She continued to appear on Broadway throughout the 1940s, and actively campaigned for Harry Truman's reelection in 1948. Best known for her distinctive drawl and wit, she is remembered for her presence rather than her performances, which also included roles in Tennessee Williams' *A Streetcar Named Desire* and *The Milk Train Doesn't Stop Here Anymore*.

BARA, Theda
1885-1955
American actress

She was born Theodosia Goodman in Cincinnati, Ohio, and acted in a touring company and on Broadway before going to Hollywood. Although she appeared in several earlier films, including the 1915 version of *The Two Orphans*, and *Carmen*, she became famous overnight as the vamp who tries to destroy the good-hearted young hero in *A Fool There Was* (1915). She played similar roles in 40 pictures over the next three years. An early example of studio hype reinvented her life, claiming that she was the daughter of a French artist and his Arab mistress, born in the shadow of the Sphinx, and that her name was an anagram for Arab Death. The publicity overkill destroyed her career, and in her last movies made in the mid-1920s, she burlesqued the roles that had made her famous. She retired in 1926.

BARBARA, Agatha
1923-
Maltese president, politician

The first woman to be president of Malta, Agatha Barbara entered politics in 1947 when elected as the first woman Member of Parliament of Malta. She held her seat as MP until 1982. While MP she served as Minister of Education (1955-58 and 1971-73). From 1974 to 1981 she was Minister of Labour, Culture and Welfare, and in 1982 became president of the Republic of Malta, a post she held until 1987. Deeply concerned with the social welfare of her people and the advancement of women, she is founder and chair of the Executive Committee of the Malta Labour Party Women's Club. Since 1988, she has been the chair of the Samaritans–Malta.

BARDOT, Brigitte
1934-
French actress, animal rights activist

Born in Paris, Bardot was educated at ballet school and became a model, appearing on the cover of *Elle* at 15. She met Roger Vadim, then an assistant director, and was married to him from 1952 to 1957, the years that saw the establishment of her screen persona as the "sex kitten" in his movies such as *And God Created Woman* (1956). Critic Pauline Kael called her "the distillation of all those irresponsible, petulant teenagers", but her physical appearance was copied across America. Her later films, such as *Viva Maria* (1965), were dismissed at the box office by the changing taste of the public. Bardot herself had said years before, "I am now spending my life trying to erase the Bardot legend." Bardot is now best known for her work with animal rights organizations, especially those opposed to the culling of seals. She was created a Chevalier of the Legion of Honor in 1985.

Brigitte Bardot, a "sex symbol" in the 1950s, now campaigns for animal rights.

BARKER, Ma (Arizona Donnie Clark)
1872-1935
American outlaw

As head of the United States' last great outlaw band, Ma Barker, along with her four boys, were notorious criminals during the 1930s. Through her example, her sons garnered a disrespect for the law. The reputed mastermind of the Barker gang, Ma allegedly planned all their kidnappings, murders and robberies down to the most minute details. It is speculated that during their heyday, the Barkers netted more than $3 million but because of their notoriety were forced to remain in poverty.

Alvin Karpis, a Barker gang member, refuted the Federal Bureau of Investigation's notion that Ma was the mastermind. He painted her as an excessively doting mother whose sons were pathologically devoted to her. Ma Barker and her son Fred were killed during a four-hour shootout with the FBI in Florida.

BARRYMORE, Ethel
1879-1959
American actress

Ethel Barrymore was born into the theater. Her mother Georgina Drew was a member of the great theater family centered in Philadelphia, and her father Maurice Blythe joined the company, taking the stage name Barrymore. It was the name that all three of his children used. Ethel attended the Convent of the Sacred Heart in Philadelphia, and made her debut at the age of 14 in a production of *The Rivals*, starring her grandmother, Mrs. Louisa Drew, and her brother Lionel. In 1901 she took Broadway by storm in the role of Madame Trentoni in Charles Frohman's production of *Captain Jinks of the Horse Marines*. She had another triumph in 1911 in *Trelawny of the Wells*. From that time until her retirement in the 1940s she was considered one of the "first ladies" of the American stage.

Her other major appearances included *Declassée* (1919); *The Kingdom of God* (1928), the production that opened the Ethel Barrymore Theatre in New York; and her final role as Miss Moffat in *The Corn Is Green* (1942). She made films throughout her career, including *Rasputin and the Empress* (1932), in which she starred with her brothers John and Lionel, and *None But the Lonely Heart* (1944), for which she won the Academy Award for Best Supporting Actress.

BARTLETT, Jennifer
1941-
American artist

Jennifer Bartlett is a dynamic modern painter whose unique, room-scaled, interpretative landscapes borrow from a range of styles: impressionism, pointillism, abstract expressionism and minimalism. She is noted for her "Garden Series" of paintings. One of these was a 153-foot work called *Rhapsody*, which consisted of 988 12-inch-square steel plates painted with Testor enamels to elucidate concepts of mountain, ocean, tree and house. Another Bartlett artwork, *Sea Wall*, combined wall canvases with real wooden dinghys placed on the gallery floor. *In the Garden* was a diptych assimilated from 200 drawings based on her living experience in a country house in southern France. She has had solo exhibitions in Europe and across the United States.

Founder of the American Red Cross and president of the organization until 1904, nurse Clara Barton gained fame for her work on the battlefield during the Civil War.

BARTON, Clara
1821-1912
American nurse, founder of the American Red Cross

Whether it was recalling the skills she used to found New Jersey's first public school or the resilience she demonstrated as one of the first female federal employees, Clara Barton contributed an invaluable service "to bring humanity to the battlefield."

During the American Civil War, she established a network for procuring goods, converted her home into a storehouse and provided mule-driven teams to transport supplies. She also compiled information on missing soldiers and personally marked the graves.

In 1869 she went abroad and became involved in the Franco-Prussian War (1870-71), distributing supplies in the battle zone under the auspices of the International Red Cross of Geneva.

Upon her return to the United States, she campaigned for eight years to establish the Red Cross in the United States. Her appeal to the American people included plans for relief for domestic crises. In 1881 Barton's determination was rewarded with the organization of the American Association of the Red Cross, which she presided over until 1904.

BAUSCH, Pina
1940-
German dancer, choreographer

The artistic director and chief choreographer of the Wuppertal Dance Theatre, Bausch is known for the dark and often pessimistic interpretations of the human condition portrayed in her imagistic psychodramas. A gifted dancer at an early age, she entered the Folkwangschule for music, dance and speech in Essen in 1955, whose founder, Kurt Jooss, was a German expressionist choreographer. In 1959 Bausch received a stipend to attend the Juilliard School in New York where her instructors included Antony Tudor and José Limon. She returned to Germany to dance with Jooss's Folkwang-ballet and began designing her own ballets. She became director and choreographer of the Wuppertal Opera Ballet in 1973, and renamed it Wuppertal Dance Theatre. Her programs included contemporary works such as Jooss's anti-war ballet *The Green Table*, Agnes DE MILLE's *Rodeo* and her own *Fritz*, about childhood fears.

Bausch's *The Rite of Spring* had a premiere at the Olympic Arts Festival in Los Angeles in 1984. In 1985, Bausch's avant-garde work *Arias* was presented at the Brooklyn Academy of Music, and since then she has presented several American premieres there.

BAY, Josephine
1900-
American financier, philanthropist

Born in Anamosa, Iowa, Josephine Holt Perfect moved to Brooklyn, New York, as a child. After college, she joined the Brooklyn Junior League, and took over the League's debt-ridden bookstore, which she managed to sell in a deal which paid off its debts and gave the League a percentage of the profits. In 1942 she married Charles Ulrick Bay, a senior partner of the brokerage firm of A.M. Kidder, and began to attend meetings and business lunches, at her husband's instigation. She accompanied him to Norway when he was named ambassador in 1946. After their return, she joined the Kidder firm as a limited partner in 1955, and on her husband's death the following year, became president and chairman. As such she was the first woman to head a member concern of the New York Stock Exchange. She was also the chairman of the executive committee of the American Export Lines Corporation.

BAYLIS, Lilian
1874-1937
British theatrical manager and impresario

Born in London, Lilian Baylis was taken to South Africa by her parents in 1890, and later taught music in Johannesburg. She returned to England in 1898 and joined her aunt Emma Cons in the management of the Royal Victoria Hall, known familiarly as the Old Vic. In 1912 she became sole manager on her aunt's death and turned to presenting opera and Shakespeare, producing all of his works between 1914 and 1923. In 1926 she hired Ninette DE VALOIS to direct the dancing in both the plays and operas, with the promise of a permanent home for de Valois's ballet school, and in 1931 she acquired Sadlers Wells Theatre for the exclusive presentation of opera and ballet. The companies she started evolved into the Royal Ballet and the English National Opera, while the Old Vic continued to produce Shakespeare until 1963. Lilian Baylis was made a Companion of Honour for services to the arts in 1929.

BEACH, Sylvia
1887-1962
American editor, publisher

A native of Baltimore, Nancy Woodbridge Beach worked as a volunteer farmhand in France and for the Red Cross in Belgrade, Serbia, during World War I. Like many other Americans at that time, she didn't return home, but stayed in Paris, where she opened a bookstore. Located on the Left Bank, Shakespeare and Company was also a lending library and a meeting place for many of the French and American intellectuals in the city. Setting up a press with money loaned by Harriet Weaver, Beach published many of them, including Gertrude STEIN. In 1922 she agreed to publish James Joyce's *Ulysses*, a long and painstaking procedure complicated by the numerous mistakes made by the non-English-speaking typesetters. She also enlisted the aid of Ernest Hemingway to smuggle the books into the United States via Canada. In 1938 the French presented her with the Legion of Honor for services to literature. Shakespeare and Company lasted, with occasional financial support from friends, until the Nazi occupation when it was forcibly closed and Beach was interned. In 1959 she helped organize an exposition at the American Cultural Center, "The Twenties – American Writers in Paris and Their Friends."

Lilian Baylis, founder of the Old Vic and Sadlers Wells theatres in London.

Sylvia Beach at her famous Paris bookstore, Shakespeare and Company.

B

BEATRIX, Queen
1938-
Dutch monarch

Daughter of Queen Juliana who reigned for 31 years, and granddaughter of Queen Wilhelmina who reigned for 50 years, Beatrix ascended to the throne in 1980. She earned her Ph.D. from the University of Leiden in 1961, and married Prince Claus von Amsberg in 1966, a controversial match at first because of Amsberg's history of being a member of the Hitler Youth and with the German Army during World War II. Considered steely like her grandmother, Queen Beatrix has shown herself to be concerned with issues of social welfare and conditions of third world peoples.

BEATTIE, Mollie
1947-
American conservationist, government official

In 1994 Mollie Hanna Beattie became the first woman director of the U.S. Fish and Wildlife Service. Experience with Outward Bound beginning in 1973 led to her decision to get a master's degree in forestry from the University of Vermont in 1979, and in 1985 she was appointed Vermont commissioner of forests, parks, and recreation. She expanded state parks and forests, and advocated local community decision-making. With a master's degree in public administration from Harvard, she became in 1991 executive director of the Snelling Center for Government, a public policy institute, and three years later she moved to Washington, D.C. to take up the challenge of national ecosystem management.

BEAUVOIR, Simone de
1908-1986
French philosopher, writer

A champion of the feminist movement and leader of modern existentialism, Simone de Beauvoir was born in Paris. She graduated from the Sorbonne in 1929 and took second in the philosophy finals there to Jean-Paul Sartre, who became her lifelong partner and associate.

De Beauvoir promoted the principles of humanism, where in absence of absolute moral law, people devised their own values and were responsible for their actions. De Beauvoir's dedication to improving women's lives led to her highly popular though controversial two-volume text *The Second Sex* (1949). Its central theory, demonstrated through complex literary and historical analysis, was that women were perceived to be inferior and were maintained in that role by a male-dominated society. The deplorable status of the elderly who face similar prejudice, neglect and discrimination was examined in De Beauvoir's 1972 volume *The Coming of Age*. Her novel *The Mandarins* (1954) won the Prix Goncourt. Her noteworthy autobiography was produced in four volumes.

Simone de Beauvoir with Jean-Paul Sartre (left) and Claud Lansman at Giza.

BEECH, Olive Ann
1903-1993
American aircraft industry executive

Olive Ann Mellor was born in Waverly, Kansas, grew up in Paola, and attended the American Secretarial and Business College in Wichita. In 1925 she took a job as a secretary-bookkeeper at the Travel Air Manufacturing Company, which had been founded that year by Walter Beech. She married Beech in 1930, and in 1932 assisted him in the setting up of Beech Aircraft. When he contracted encephalitis, she became acting chief executive, just as the company was expanding into the military field. Under her guidance the firm supplied the planes on which 90 percent of all American bombardiers and navigators were trained during World War II. After Walter's death in 1950, Olive Ann became president, and helped the company's worth rise from $75 million in 1963 to $267 million in 1975. Although she retired in 1968, she remained active in day to day operations, and became a director of the Raytheon Corporation when that organization bought Beech Aircraft in 1980.

Gertrude Bell, Middle East advisor to the British during and after World War II.

BELL, Gertrude
1868-1926
British adventurer, Arabist

Granddaughter of Sir Lowthian Bell, a pioneer in iron and steel technology, Gertrude Bell was remarkable for exploring the uncharted regions of the Middle East alone and advising the British government on Middle East policy. The first woman to obtain a first in history at Oxford (1888), Bell first travelled to Persia in 1892 and began learning Persian. An accomplished linguist, she learned Arabic while staying in Jerusalem in 1899 and travelled in Palestine before setting off for the Syrian interior in 1905, the subject of her book *The Desert and the Sown*. She joined several archaeological digs, and travelled through the Syrian desert to Iraq (1910-11) and to central Arabia (1913-14). In 1919 she was appointed Oriental Secretary in Baghdad, and campaigned for the independence of the Arab states.

BELL, Vanessa
1879-1961
British painter

A member of the Stephens family which was the core of the Bloomsbury Group of writers, artists and intellectuals in London in the early 1900s, Vanessa Stephens studied at the Royal Academy of Art and travelled in Italy. She married the art historian Clive Bell in 1907 and was an associate of the critic and curator, Roger Fry, who organized exhibitions of post-Impressionists in London. Fry recruited Vanessa Bell as an innovative designer for his Omega Workshops which produced decorative screens, mosaics, embroideries, carpets and pottery.

Bell's style was influenced by the post-Impressionists and her portrait of the biographer, Lytton Strachey, is rich with Fauve color and a loose line as uninhibited as her famous Bloomsbury social gatherings.

Bell had a long affair with the modern British painter Duncan Grant, who embraced the patterning schemes of Matisse. Together they painted murals on the walls of her house in Sussex, which is now a national monument.

BENETTON, Giuliana
1938-
Italian designer, entrepreneur

Born near Treviso, Italy, Benneton became a skein winder at the age of 13 in a small knitting company in Treviso, and later sewed sweaters together for a local manufacturer. In 1955 she bought a home knitting machine, and began to design and make brightly colored sweaters which her brother Luciano sold to local shops. Her first collection of 18 pieces was the foundation of the company. In 1965 they built a factory in Ponzano, near Treviso, and opened a shop in Belluno three years later. Her bright designs became popular in Italy and led to an expanding export business, with the first non-Italian shop opening in Paris in 1969. The first five U.S. shops opened in 1979. By 1993, there were 6400 outlets in almost 100 countries. The company is still directed by members of the Benetton family.

The largest manufacturer of knitwear in the world, Benetton was also the first Western retailer to open shops in Eastern Europe.

BENNETT, Louie
1870-1956
Irish trade unionist

The first woman president of the Irish Trade Unions Congress, Louie Bennett combined issues of women's suffrage with Irish nationalism and the rights of workers. Not politically active until her 40s, she helped form the Irishwomen's Suffrage Foundation in 1913 and its affiliate the Irish Women's Reform League, which spotlighted the social and economic conditions of women workers. She also worked with Francis Sheehy Skeffington on the *Irish Citizen*, and joined the International Women's League for Peace and Freedom to campaign for peace in World War I. In 1916 she began restructuring the Irish Womens' Workers Union into a very powerful union, of which she became General Secretary until 1955. President of the Irish Trade Unions Congress from 1931 to 1932 and 1947 to 1948, she also served on the Irish-Labour Party administrative committee.

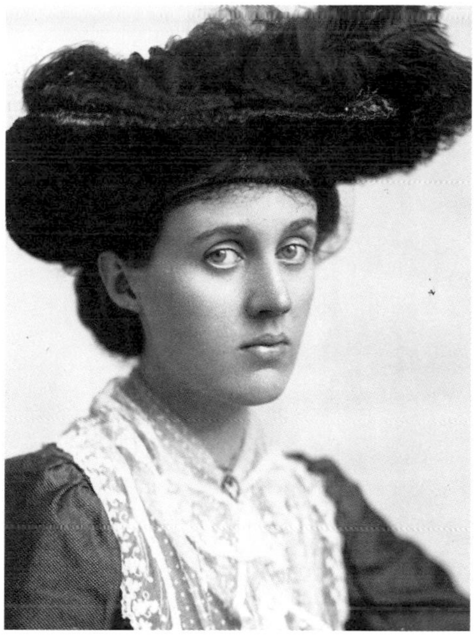

Artist Vanessa Bell (the sister of Virginia Woolf) was a member of the famous Bloomsbury Group in London.

BERGMAN, Ingrid
1915-1982
Swedish-born actress

Ingrid Bergman was born in Stockholm. Orphaned young, she enrolled at the Royal Theatre of Dramatic Art in her native city in 1933. Three years later she starred in the Swedish film *Intermezzo*, directed by Gustav Molander. Her performance as the young violinist was so striking that she was hired by Hollywood to play the role again in the 1939 American remake, co-starring Leslie Howard. In 1943 she starred with Humphrey Bogart in *Casablanca*. The following year she won her first Academy Award, for her performance as the wife being driven mad by her husband in

Gaslight. She made a series of great films, including Alfred Hitchcock's *Spellbound* (1945) and *Notorious* (1946), before her career was interrupted in 1949 when she left her husband and child for Italian director Roberto Rossellini. Eventually Hollywood and the public forgave her, and she returned to films, winning a second Academy Award for *Anastasia* in 1956, and a third in 1974 for *Murder on the Orient Express*. She gave her final performance in the TV movie *Golda*, the year of her death.

BERNHARDT, Sarah
1844-1923
French actress

Henriette Rosine Bernard was born in Paris, and after some initial training entered the Comédie Française in 1862, making an early impact in a production of Racine's *Iphigenie*. A staunch French patriot, she organized and ran a field hospital during the Franco-Prussian War, as well as a hospital in Paris during the Siege and the Commune which followed it. She returned to the theatre and became famous for her expressive acting in roles which ranged from the classic French drama of Racine and Cornielle to those plays written for her, including *La Dame aux Camellias, Tosca, Lorenzaccio* and *L'Aiglon*. She was renowned for the clear purity of her voice. Bernhardt also played Hamlet quite successfully, including on the nine tours she made of the United States. She managed several theaters, including the Theatre de la Renaissance and the Theatre des Nations, which was renamed the Theatre Sarah Bernhardt in 1899. She appeared in several early films, even after she had a leg amputated in her seventies. She was created a Chevalier of the Legion of Honor in 1914.

The great dramatic French actress "Divine Sarah" Bernhardt set the standard for actresses of her time.

BESANT, Annie
1847-1927
British social reformer

Born in London to Irish parents, Annie Wood married the Reverend Frank Besant in 1863 but lost her religious faith during her infant son's serious illness. In 1872 she began to write for the free-thinking *National Reformer* and published a pamphlet on birth control with *Reformer* publisher Charles Bradlaugh in 1877. This led to a sensational trial for obscenity during which she lost the custody of her daughter. Thereafter, she worked in a variety of reform causes, including George Bernard Shaw's Fabian Society, which addressed the dangerous working conditions in factories, and the Theosophical Society, which fostered international brotherhood. In this capacity she settled in India and conducted schools for Hindu girls. In 1917 she chaired the Indian National Congress.

BETHUNE, Mary McLeod
1875-1955
American educator, civil and women's rights activist, government official

Committed to the advancement of black people, especially of black women, Mary McLeod Bethune established a small school for young African-American women which, through her ingenuity and perseverance, became Bethune-Cookman College.

The director of the Federal Council on Negro Affairs during Franklin D. Roosevelt's presidency, she worked for better educational and employment opportunities for blacks. Her appointment made her the first black woman to hold a major federal office. She was president of the National Association of Colored Women (NACW), and in 1935 she founded the National Council of Negro Women, an umbrella organization for the major black women's organizations which facilitated their participation in socio-political life.

In recognition of her contributions to the advancement of all African-American people, she received the Spingarn Medal in 1935, the highest honor bestowed by the National Association for the Advancement of Colored People (NAACP).

BHUTTO, Benazir
1953-
Pakistani prime minister, politician

Elected the first female prime minister of Pakistan in 1988, Bhutto was born into a wealthy land-holding family and was educated at Oxford. In 1979 her father, Zulfikar Ali Bhutto, Pakistan's first democratically elected prime minister, was executed after a miitary coup. Vowing to help her country regain civilian rule, Bhutto spoke out against the government. From 1981 to 1984, she spent almost all her time under arrest. She left the country in 1984, and returned in 1986 after nominal civilian rule had been restored. Advocating a socialist program, she became co-chair of the Pakistani People's Party. After two years as prime minister, she was ousted by the president and the army in 1990 on charges of corruption and nepotism. In 1993 she was reelected as prime minister. Her autobiography *Daughter of Destiny* was published in 1989.

BINH, Nguyen Thi
1927-
Vietnamese politician

Vice-president of Vietnam, Binh was deeply influenced by her parents, who were nationalist leaders. From 1951 to 1954 she was jailed by the French for her anti-colonialist organizing, and later, she and her husband joined the underground opposition to U.S.-supported President Diem. From 1963 to 1966 she served as a council member of the Union of Women for the Liberation of South Vietnam, and later became a member of the Central Committee of the National Liberation Front, known pejoratively as the Viet

Pakistani prime minister Benazir Bhutto was first elected to the post in 1988.

Cong. From 1969 to 1976 she was Minister for Foreign Affairs of the Provisional Revolutionary Government of South Vietnam, and signed the 1973 Paris Peace Accord that ended the war between Vietnam and the United States. From 1976 to 1987, she was Minister of Education of the Socialist Republic of Vietnam, and in 1992 she became vice president of Vietnam.

BISHOP, Elizabeth
1911-1979
American poet

Bishop was born in Worcester, Massachusetts, and raised by grandparents in Nova Scotia. She attended Vassar College, where she and Mary McCarthy founded the magazine *The Conspirato*. After Vassar, she travelled to California, Massachusetts and Brazil. Poems included in the volumes *North and South* (1946), *Questions of Travel* (1965) and *Geography II* (1976) reflect the disparate climates, the force of nature, and the emotional pulls she experienced in different places.

Bishop had a long affair with the South American intellectual Lota de Macedo Soares, with whom she lived outside Rio de Janiero for 15 years from 1951 to 1966 until Soares's suicide. Bishop returned to the U.S. and taught at the University of Washington, and was a poetry professor at Harvard from 1969 to 1977. She lectured that she was "opposed to making poetry monstrous or boring"; the qualities she sought for her poems were accuracy, spontaneity and mystery.

Though she wrote fewer than 100 poems in her lifetime, she received the Pulitzer Prize in 1955 and the National Book Award in 1969.

BISHOP, Hazel
1906-
American chemist, cosmetics manufacturer

Born in Hoboken, New Jersey, Hazel Gladys Bishop attended Barnard College, receiving her BA in 1929. A pre-med student, she was forced by the Depression to shift from Columbia to night classes. From 1935 to 1942 she worked as a research assistant to Dr. A. Benson Cannon, a well-known dermatologist. During the war, she was a senior organic chemist with Standard Oil, experimenting on aviation fuel. After the war she did petroleum research for Socony. At the same time, she was experimenting at home with formulas for lipstick. Bishop made 309 experiments, followed by two years of testing, before she introduced the first "no-smear" lipstick at a Barnard College Club fashion show in 1949. The following year she founded Hazel Bishop, Inc. She continued to experiment, creating other beauty products. She became the head of the cosmetics marketing program at the Fashion Institute of Technology in 1978, and was the first person to occupy the Revlon Chair at FIT.

BISSELL, Emily
1861-1948
American welfare worker, founder of Christmas Seals

Born in Wilmington, Delaware, Bissell organized the first chapter of the American Red Cross for Delaware, and was actively involved in other charities including creating the first public playground and first free kindergarten in Wilmington. However, her most noted first was designing and printing Christmas Seals.

The idea of selling a Christmas stamp to collect funds to fight tuberculosis was first conceived by a Danish postal worker. Bissell persuaded the American Red Cross to mount a campaign to sell the Christmas Seals, whose proceeds were used to provide a hospital for tuberculosis sufferers.

The creation and sale of the stamps was later taken on by the National Tuberculosis Association. For her contribution to the welfare of tuberculosis sufferers, Bissell was the first lay person awarded the Trudeau Medal of the National Tuberculosis Association in 1942.

BLACK, Shirley Temple
1928-
American actress, diplomat

Hollywood's hottest child star, Shirley Temple danced and sang her way into the hearts of America during the 1930s. She became famous at the age of five in the 1934 movie *Stand Up and Cheer*. Between 1935 and 1938 she was Hollywood's top box office attraction, making $300,000 a year from films, and thousands more from sales of Shirley Temple dolls and accessories. Yet poor financial management left Temple with little money. Her last movie was made in 1949.

In 1969 she became a delegate to the United Nations, beginning a highly respected career in international diplomacy and volunteer work. In 1974 President Gerald Ford named her ambassador to Ghana, and in 1989 she became ambassador to Czechoslovakia during the Bush administration. She tells her story in *Child Star: An Autobiography* (1988).

BLAIR, Bonnie
1964-
American speed skater

At the Olympic Games in Lillehammer, Norway, in 1994, Bonnie Blair became the winner of the most Olympic gold medals ever by an American woman, surpassing Janet Evans in swimming, Pat McCormick in diving and Evelyn Ashford in sprinting. She has won five golds overall: the 500 meters at the Calgary 1988 Olympics, the 500 and 1000 meters at the 1992 Albertville Olympics, and the 500 and 1000 meter events in 1994. Including the bronze medal Blair won at Calgary in the 1500 meters, she is the most decorated American winter Olympian, male or female, surpassing another

American speed skater Bonnie Blair won five gold medals at the 1994 Olympics.

speed skater, Eric Heiden, who swept five events in 1980.

Blair was born and raised in Champaign, Illinois, where she trained as a speed skater at Centennial High School. She was the U.S. sprint champion from 1985 to 1992.

BLANKERS-KOEN, Fanny
1918-
Dutch track and field athlete

The first woman to win four Olympic gold medals and one who did so with two toddlers in attendance at the 1948 Games in London, Francina Blankers-Koen was born in Baarn, the Netherlands. Although her father was an expert shotputter and discus thrower and she grew

Fanny Blankers-Koen wins the 80-meter hurdles at the 1948 Olympics.

up with four brothers, her interest in sports did not develop until she met a trainer, Jan Blankers, whom she later married. She qualified for several events for the 1936 Berlin Games but the Dutch did not participate in the Olympics until the 1948 Games.

She was skilled in more events than she could enter in the 1948 Olympics but she won her three individual events, the 100 meter- and 200 meter dashes and the 80 meter hurdles, and was a member of the winning 400 meter relay team. She also established world records in the long jump and the high jump before she retired in 1952.

BLAZEJOWSKI, Carol
1957-
American basketball player

Blazejowski was the first woman awarded the Margaret Wade Trophy in 1978 for her college basketball career, during which she amassed a total of 3,199 points for Montclair State University in New Jersey. Born in Cranford, New Jersey, she was a veteran of street ball. At Madison Square Garden, she set a game record for her college team by earning 52 points.

A member of the silver medal-winning U.S. team at the World University Games in Bulgaria in 1977, "The Blaze" missed the 1980 Summer Olympics in Moscow, which were boycotted by the United States. She then played for the New Jersey Jems, and when the Women's American Basketball Association was formed in 1984 she joined its New York club. She was inducted into the Basketball Hall of Fame in 1994.

BLUM, Arlene
1945-
American mountaineer

Arlene Blum was a member of the first all-woman ascent of Alaska's Denali, the highest peak in North America, and she participated in the 1976 Bicentennial Expedition to Mount Everest, a mixed expedition intended to demonstrate women's stamina at high altitudes.

Blum was born in the Midwest and began climbing while a student at Reed College in Oregon, where she received a Ph.D. in chemistry. She later taught and carried on research concerning environmentally hazardous chemicals.

Inveterate American mountaineer Arlene Blum with fellow climber Hugh Swift at Lamayuru during the Great Himalayan Traverse in August 1982.

Blum's greatest achievement was her organization of the 1978 American Women's Himalayan Expedition. She raised funds for the $80,000 journey costs by selling a T-shirt with a mountain logo and the caption "A Woman's Place Is On Top . . . Annapurna". No woman or American had ever reached the top of this avalanche-prone peak, the 10th highest in the world. Two expedition climbers, Irene Miller and Vera Komarkova, mastered the summit with two sherpa guides.

In 1980 Blum led the Indian-American Women's Expedition to the Gangotri Glacier near the border of India and Tibet.

BLYTON, Enid
1897-1968
British children's writer

Born and raised in Beckenham, England, Blyton took a teacher certification course in 1916 and became governess to a family in Surrey. She soon opened her own children's nursery school and began contributing to the magazine *Teacher's World* and the journal *Sunny Stories.*

Blyton's first book of poetry *Child Whispers* was published in 1920. During the 1920s and 1930s she edited teachers' texts and developed a children's encyclopedia. She began writing school stories for girls, which became immediate best-sellers, and soon took up writing adventure stories with a wider appeal, of which *The Famous Five* and *The Secret Seven* series are the best-known. She produced over 400 titles which have been translated into 165 languages, making her the most frequently translated British author after Shakespeare and Agatha CHRISTIE.

At one time librarians imposed a ban on her works because of her limited vocabulary and what they deemed racist attitudes held by her main characters. The author was incensed and the controversy brought the issue of curtailing children's reading by censorship into the public forum.

BOOTH, Evangeline
1865-1950
British-born American Salvation Army commander

Evangeline Booth was inspired by her parents who co-founded a Christian charitable organization in 1865. It operated on a military pattern with evangelism as its foundation. The organization evolved into the Salvation Army (as it would be called from 1878) and established mission stations throughout England to house and feed the poor.

She moved to the United States in 1896 to work with the American Salvation Army. In 1904 she took over the leadership, becoming the first woman commander of a Salvation Army. For thirty years under her guidance, it expanded its evangelical efforts, established social services and provided emergency disaster relief.

In 1919, Booth received the Distinguished Service Medal for her years of service with the Salvation Army.

Evangeline Booth became commander of the U.S. branch of the Salvation Army in 1904.

Britain's first female Speaker of the House of Commons, Labour MP Betty Boothroyd.

BOOTHROYD, Betty
1929-
British politician

In 1992 Betty Boothroyd became the first female Speaker of the House of Commons. Daughter of union activists, as a girl she was more interested in dance than politics, and toured with a dance group called the Tiller Girls. She credits that experience with teaching her teamwork, a skill she put to good use when she entered politics. In 1950 she became an assistant to several Members of Parliament in London, and later traveled to the United States and campaigned for John F. Kennedy. She returned to London in 1962. After a series of unsuccessful runs for MP within the Labour Party, she won in 1973. She became Deputy Speaker in 1987 and then in 1992 won election as Speaker in a landslide victory supported by Labour and Conservative MPs alike.

BORDEN, Lizzie
1860-1927
American accused murderer

The subject of a macabre children's nursery rhyme, this quiet New Englander gained notoriety when her father and stepmother were found savagely murdered in the family home in 1892. Her father, a thrifty merchant, was cold and distant to his spinster daughter who lived at home. Allegedly frustrated by his indifference and resentful of her stepmother, Lizzie Borden took an ax and hacked them both to death while they napped.

This case had one of the first sensationalized murder trials as reporters flocked to the small Massachusetts town of Fall River. The case challenged notions that well-off "ladies" could not kill. At one point, the Borden's Irish maid was accused and reporters exploited the prejudice which existed between old-time New Englanders and the recent Irish immigrants. Despite the strong evidence against her, Lizzie Borden was acquitted and remained in Fall River the rest of her life.

BOULANGER, Nadia
1887-1979
French composer, teacher, conductor

Parisian-born Nadia Juliette Boulanger received her first music lessons from her Russian mother, and could read music at the age of five. She won many prizes by the time she was 16 and studying at the Paris Conservatoire. She won the Prix de Rome for her cantata *La Sirène* in 1908, but abandoned composition in 1912, believing that her younger sister Lily (1893-1918) was the better composer. She turned to teaching at the École Normale, the Paris Conservatoire and the American Conservatory at Fontainebleau where she taught and influenced a generation of young Americans, including Walter Piston, Aaron Copland and Virgil Thomson, as well as Dinu Lipatti and Jean Françaix. During the 1930s and 1940s, she taught at Wellesley, Radcliffe and Juilliard. During this time, she also became the first woman to conduct the Boston Symphony in 1938, and the New York Philharmonic in 1939. She was also the first woman to conduct the Halle Orchestra in 1936. She was instrumental in the revival of early music, and was created a Commander of the Legion of Honor.

BOURGEOIS, Louise
1912-
French sculptor

An abstract sculptor whose vernacular employs elements of the surreal and haunting sexual imagery, Bourgeois was born in Aubusson, France, where her family had a tapestry business. She worked as a child restoring beautiful textiles, and at 25, left Aubusson to attend the École des Beaux Arts in Paris. She married art historian Robert Goldwater in 1938, and served as an apprentice to Fernand Léger. Bourgeois and Goldwater went to New York in the 1940s, where she attended the Arts Students League and became friends with Max Ernst,

Nadia Boulanger was the first female conductor of the Boston Symphony Orchestra and the New York Philharmonic.

Marcel Duchamp and Salvador Dali. Her works include *Femme Couteau* (Knife Woman), *Garden at Night* (a series of black-and-white painted organic bulb forms) and a group of hanging cocoons called *Lairs* that symbolize the womb. Her *Confrontation* of 1978 was a feminist statement that evoked disembodied body parts. Bourgeois had a solo retrospective of her work at the Museum of Modern Art in 1983, and her 1994 solo exhibition "Locus and Memory" travelled from the Brooklyn Museum to the Corcoran Gallery in Washington, D.C.

BOURKE-WHITE, Margaret
1904-1971
American photojournalist

A photojournalist noted for her distilled images of the Depression era, Margaret Bourke-White's work graced the first cover of *Life* magazine on November 23, 1936. Bourke-White trained at the Clarence H. White School of Photography at Columbia. She worked for *Fortune* magazine from 1929, and for *Life* from 1929 to 1957.

A social activist sensitive to the dispossessed during the Depression, Bourke-White was inspired by photodocumentaries provided for the Works Progress Administration's Farm Security Administration. With her second husband, the writer Erskine Caldwell, she produced the 1937 publication *You Have Seen Their Faces*, which focused on Southern tenant families; its images were influential for policymakers.

As a foreign correspondent for *Life*, Bourke-White was the first U.S. reporter allowed into Russia after the revolution, capturing glimpses of a hitherto largely unknown society. During World War II, she accompanied the American army on its invasion of Europe and was present at the liberation of the Buchenwald concentration camp. She was afflicted with Parkinson's Disease in the 1950s, of which she later died.

BRAUN, Carol Moseley
1947-
American lawyer, politician

In 1992 Carol Moseley Braun became the first black woman elected to the U.S. Senate. She was also the first woman from Illinois to hold a Senate seat. The Chicago native, who received her law degree from the University of Chicago, served as assistant U.S. attorney (1973-77) and state legislator (1979-88), and in 1988 became Cook County Recorder of Deeds. A divorcee, Braun is the only single mother in the Senate, and she has defined her top priorities as senator as the development and support of young people and the education system in Illinois. Her victory coalition joined blacks and whites, urban and rural people, resulting in the defeat of the previously unbeaten Alan Dixon. In her acceptance speech she praised the constituents for voting their hopes, not their fears, and showing that racism and sexism can be transcended.

Carol Moseley Braun, Democratic senator from Illinois, became the first black woman elected to the U.S. Senate in 1992.

BRAUN, Eva
1912-1945
German mistress of Adolf Hitler

Eva Braun first met Adolf Hitler in 1929 at the studio of his official photographer, Hoffmann, for whom she worked as an assistant. Smitten with the future German Chancellor, she became Hitler's lover in 1932. Although he often treated her cruelly (she filled many diaries with complaints about his mistreatment or indifference) Braun remained loyal to him.

During World War II she worked as Hitler's secretary and remained with him in Berlin during the waning days of the War. It is reputed that she married him in his bunker the day before they committed suicide.

BRINKLEY, Christie
1953-
American supermodel, artist

In a highly competitive business with resounding emphasis on youth, Christie Brinkley has maintained a successful career for two decades.

This Los Angeles native radiates California blonde beauty. She is best known as the Cover Girl cosmetics model, but has also appeared on *Sports Illustrated* covers and in numerous posters and calendars. An accomplished painter, she studied art in Paris and married there for the first time. Her modelling career began in the mid-1970s. Although she never aspired to model, her curvaceous figure set her apart from the other waif-like models. In 1985 she married singer-songwriter Billy Joel. She appeared in his "Uptown Girl" video and painted the cover of his album *River of Dreams*.

Despite traumas (she divorced Joel and survived a fatal helicopter crash), Brinkley continues to project a down-to-earth public image.

Eva Braun's diaries have made fascinating reading for those interested in the life of her paramour, Adolf Hitler.

BROOKS, Gwendolyn
1917-
American poet, novelist

A major name in twentieth century poetry, Gwendolyn Brooks was the first black writer to win the Pulitzer Prize for poetry, for *Annie Allen* in 1950.

Born in Kansas, where her mother predicted she would be the "lady Paul Laurence Dunbar," Brooks attended school in Chicago, where she still lives. The poems of *A Street in Bronzeville* (1945) and *Annie Allen* contain carefully crafted portraits of black people fighting off the relentless depersonalization of poverty. This dignity and rebellious flair mark all her books, and especially her later, more overtly political poems.

In 1985 Brooks was named the first black woman Poetry Consultant to the Library of Congress, and a decade later she was honored as the National Endowment for the Humanities 1994 Jefferson Lecturer. She recently completed *Report from Part Two*, her second volume of autobiography, to be published in 1995.

Helen Gurley Brown, author of Sex and the Single Girl, *made* Cosmopolitan *one of the best-selling magazines in the United States.*

Editor-in-chief of The New Yorker, *Tina Brown was a playwright and journalist before transforming the British magazine* Tatler *in 1979 and* Vanity Fair *in 1984.*

BROWN, Helen Gurley
1927-
American magazine publisher, author

Born in Green Forest, Arkansas, Helen Gurley studied at Texas State College before she moved to New York and entered advertising. She worked as a copywriter and account executive and married David Brown before writing *Sex and the Single Girl*, the best-selling book which celebrated the independence in all things of young working women. In 1965 she published the sequel, *Sex and the Office*. The same year she became editor-in-chief of *Cosmopolitan*. In the succeeding years she has made it one of the five highest selling magazines in the United States, and made the "Cosmo Girl" a recognizable icon. Her subsequent books, which include *Outrageous Opinions* and *Having It All*, have not been as successful. Since 1972, she has also acted as editorial director of *Cosmopolitan*'s foreign editions. In 1985 she won the New York Women in Communications Award and established the Helen Gurley Brown Research Professorship at Northwestern University.

BROWN, Tina
1953-
British magazine editor

Christina Hambley Brown was born in Maidenhead, Berkshire, and was educated at St. Anne's College, Oxford, where she took her degree in English in 1974. The previous year, her first play *Under the Bamboo Tree* had been produced and won the *Sunday Times* Drama Award. She became a journalist, working for the *Sunday Times*, as well as an occasional contributor to *Punch*. She became editor of the British magazine *Tatler* in 1979, and transformed it from a society journal into a more current publication, featuring celebrity interviews and unusual visual flair.

When she became editor-in-chief of the new *Vanity Fair* in 1984, she made similar changes, instigating unusual cover shots of celebrities, saying, "They look wonderful and they sell." While in this position she won the Magazine Editor of the Year Award from *Advertising Age* in 1988. In 1992, with a good deal of controversy, she became editor-in-chief of *The New Yorker*, making distinct changes in its format and contributors, and introducing color and photography, in an attempt to make the magazine more topical.

BRUNDTLAND, Gro Harlem
1939-
Norwegian prime minister, politician

In 1981 Gro Harlem Brundtland became the first woman to be prime minister of Norway, but lasted only eight months. Five years later, she was re-elected Prime Minister. A doctor, she served in various health care organizations, acquiring a reputation as a woman with very strong views and a sharp mind. In 1974 she was appointed Minister of Environmental Affairs, and in 1975 became the Labor Party's vice chairman. She was elected to the Parliament in 1981, and then became Prime Minister. On her re-election as Prime Minister in 1986, she filled many many Cabinet posts with women, and facilitated the election of more female

Former Norwegian prime minister Gro Harlem Brundtland in a 1989 photograph.

MPs. Her economic plan helped Norway relieve much of its economic decline. As chair of the U.N. Commission on the Environment, she has led the discussion on how to make global corporations responsible for environmental health.

BRYANT, Lane
1879-1951
American designer, entrepreneur

Lena Himmelstein was born in Lithuania and emigrated to the United States as a young girl. She began working as a seamstress, specializing in fine lingerie and maternity clothes, at a time when pregnancy kept many women at home. One upper-class client asked her to design a dress that the client could wear to a dinner party without shocking the other guests. From this request grew the idea of making such clothes for the general public. In 1910 she opened her first shop, which catered to women who were pregnant, and women who were overweight. The following year, she advertised in the *New York Herald*, and her complete stock of clothing was sold out by the next day. Catering especially to women who were ignored by the finer department stores, the Lane Bryant stores managed to sell over a million dollar's worth of merchandise by 1917. The company continued to expand and is now owned by The Limited, Inc.

BUCK, Pearl
1892-1973
American writer

The first American woman awarded the Nobel Prize for literature in 1938, Pearl Buck won the Pulitzer Prize in 1932 for her novel *The Good Earth* (1931), a saga of Chinese peasant farmers. Its adaptation into a Broadway play and Hollywood film, and its international success, made Buck, the daughter of Presbyterian missionaries, into a millionaire sought out by the media.

Born Pearl Sydenstricker in Hillsboro, West Virginia, she was raised in China on the Yangtze River and returned to the United States to graduate from Randolph-Macon College in Virginia in 1914. She married John Buck, an agriculturalist missionary, in 1917 and moved to Nanking, China, where she taught English and literature at the university there. She divorced Buck in 1934 and married her editor, Richard Walsh, and settled in Bucks County, Pennsylvania.

Buck wrote over 100 books and published many articles in her lifetime, including two works about China during World War II called *Dragon Seed* and *The Promise*. In 1949 she founded Welcome House for the adoption of Asian-American children, and from 1958 to 1965 she was president of the Authors' Guild.

BUMBRY, Grace
1937-
American mezzo soprano, soprano

Bumbry was born in St. Louis, Missouri, and was a member of a church choir when she was introduced to Marian ANDERSON. In 1954 she won a scholarship to the St. Louis Institute of Music, but the laws of segregation would have required her to attend separate classes. She appeared on the Arthur Godfrey Talent Scouts on national television and was offered scholarships at several northern schools. She chose Northwestern University, where she attended master classes with Lotte LEHMANN and became her protégé. She subsequently studied in Europe where opera houses offered more opportunities for a black singer. She made her debut as Amneris in *Aida* at the Paris Opera in 1960, and the following year she sang Venus in *Tannhaüser* at Bayreuth, a performance which earned her 42 curtain calls. She made her American debut as Venus at the Chicago Lyric in 1963, and her Metropolitan Opera debut as Princess Eboli in *Don Carlo* in 1965. A regular member of the company, she also appeared as Bess in the Met's revival of *Porgy and Bess* in 1985.

BURTON, Beryl
1937-
British cyclist

The foremost female cyclist of the twentieth century, Beryl Burton had a 20-year unbroken reign as the Women's Best British All-Rounder (BBAR) from 1958 to 1978 and racked up 80 English titles and seven world championships in pursuit cycling and road racing.

She was born in a poor Yorkshire family and lured to the sport when she married cyclist Charles Burton. In 1967 her 12-hour race distance of 277.37 miles beat the men's best distance cyclist by 10 miles. In 1980 she raced 100 miles in a little over four hours, competing in the heat and humidity of August.

BUTCHER, Susan
1954-
American dogsledder

The second woman to win the Iditarod Trail Sled Dog Race (see RIDDLES, Libby), Susan Butcher accomplished the feat in a record time of 11 days, 15 hours and 6 minutes in 1986. Her first-place finishes in 1987 and 1988 made her the first person ever to win the gruelling 1100-mile Alaskan race in three consecutive years.

Butcher was born in Cambridge, Massachusetts, and got her first dogsled when she moved to Colorado in 1972. She began training for the Iditarod in earnest a few years later, spending the long winters in the Alaskan wilderness with her dog team. When she ran her first Iditarod in 1978, she finished nineteenth, the first woman to finish the race in the top twenty. After that, she finished in the top ten every year through 1994, except for 1985, when she withdrew from the race after a pregnant moose mauled her dogs on the trail. She won the race in 1990 and set a new record. She has also set speed records in several other dogsled events. She and her husband own a large kennel in Alaska where they breed huskies for speed and endurance.

C

CABALLÉ, Montserrat
1933-
Spanish operatic soprano

Born in Barcelona, Montserrat Caballé learned to sing at the Convent where she was a pupil, and was accepted as a student at the Liceo Conservatory when she was 8. In 1954, she won the Conservatory Gold Medal, the highest singing honor in Spain. She made her operatic debut with the Basel Opera in 1957 as Mimi in *La Boheme*, and her American debut in a concert performance of *Lucrezia Borgia* with the American Opera Society, substituting at the last moment for Marilyn Horne. The same year she joined the Metropolitan Opera's roster, making her debut as Marguerite. Her repertoire includes all the usual soprano roles, the *bel canto* ones of Donizetti and Bellini, and some of the more difficult modern ones including Salome, Elektra and Marie in *Wozzeck*. She is also known for the recitals she performs with her husband, tenor Bernabé Marti.

CABLE, Mildred
1878-1952
FRENCH, Evangeline
1869-1960
FRENCH, Francesca
1871-1960
British missionaries

This triumvirate of Christian missionaries preached the gospel throughout the hostile, sparsely inhabited regions of the Gobi Desert.

Evangeline French was born in Algiers and her sister, Francesca, was born in Belgium. After attending school in Geneva, their family moved to England. Eva French converted to Christianity after hearing the China Inland Mission lectures in 1893 and sailed to Shanghai to become a missionary. Mildred Cable was born in Guildford and like Eva Cable, was inspired by the China Inland Mission. She met up with French in China in 1902 and they became lifelong companions.

Sarah Caldwell conducts a dress rehearsal of La Traviata *for her Met debut.*

Francesca French joined her sister in China and the three women ran a school for girls while planning a journey to spread the word of the Bible throughout the Gobi. They departed from the City of Prodigals (Suchow) and ultimately arrived at the City of Seagulls (Chuguchak). Taking with them only three sleeping bags, a tent, a kettle, a frying pan and a good supply of Bibles, they made their way safely across this immense territory, encountering bandits, lamas and revolutionary generals along the way. Their 1942 narrative *The Gobi Desert* is a lively account of their daring exploits as Christian pilgrims.

CALDERONE, Mary S.
1904-
American physician

Born in New York City, the daughter of photographer Edward Steichen, Calderone studied chemistry and then drama before taking up the study of medicine in her thirties. She was a pioneer in the dissemination of information about sex and birth control, helping to found the Sex Information and Education Council of the United States despite the hostility she encountered. In 1950 she became medical director of Planned Parenthood/World Population and lectured extensively on the problems of overpopulation, ignorance, and sexual bigotry.

CALDWELL, Sarah
1924-
American conductor, opera impresario

Sarah Caldwell was born in Marysville, Missouri, and went east to study violin and viola at the New England Conservatory in Boston. In 1947 she joined the New England Opera Company as the assistant to the director, Boris Goldovsky. She established an opera workshop at Boston University in 1952, and subsequently became the first chairman of the Music and Theatre Department. In 1958 she founded the Opera Group of Boston, which became the Boston Opera Company in 1965, acting as its artistic director and conductor. Her company is known for its productions of rare operas

Soprano Maria Callas takes one of her numerous curtain calls following her performance in *Tosca* at the Metropolitan Opera House in 1965.

and premieres, both world and American, as well as clever productions of the usual repertoire. She has an astonishing ability to attract great talent for low wages, and many of the best singers of today, including Beverly Sills and Placido Domingo, have sung for her. Caldwell frequently acts as producer, administrator, scenery designer and publicity manager for her company as well as conductor and stage director. In 1976 she became the first woman to conduct at the Metropolitan Opera.

CALLAS, Maria
1923-1977
American operatic soprano

Cecilia Sophia Anna Maria Kalogeropolous was born in New York, but returned to Greece, her parents' homeland, in 1936 to study at the Royal Academy of Music in Athens. She made her debut at the Athens Royal Opera in *Cavalleria Rusticana* in 1939, as a student, and went on to sing in all the major international opera houses, including the Metropolitan, Covent Garden and La Scala. Her voice was noted for its dramatic power, and its versatility which allowed her to sing both dramatic and lyric roles. She is also considered one of the great singing actresses of the mid-twentieth century, and this talent and her remarkable voice guided by conductor Tullio Serafin were responsible for a revival of interest in the early operas of Rossini, Donizetti and Bellini. However, her temperament and recurring vocal problems led to lengthy feuds with rivals and opera house management. She was dismissed from the Metropolitan by Rudolf Bing, though later reinstated. In 1973-74, she made her farewell concert tour with tenor Guiseppe de Stefano.

CALLIL, Carmen
1938-
Australian publisher

Callil was born in Melbourne and educated at Melbourne University. She settled in England in 1963, and worked as a buyer's assistant at Marks and Spencer before entering publishing. She worked for several firms, including Hutchinson, Batsford and Andrew Deutsch before founding her own company, Carmen Callil Book Publicity, in 1972. She also founded Virago Press the same year. Dedicated to publishing works by female authors, Virago was most successful with its line of Modern Classics begun in 1978, a list "dedicated to the celebration of women writers and to the discovery and reprinting of their works." Although the company first concentrated on English authors, such as Antonia White, Margaret Kennedy and Emily Eden, the list broadened to include works from different centuries and cultures. Callil was also a Managing Director of Chatto and Windus and the Hogarth Press and is a member of the Board of Directors of Channel 4.

CAMPBELL, Naomi
1971(?)-
British supermodel, singer, novelist

Caribbean-born Naomi Campbell wanted to follow in her mother's footsteps and become a contemporary ballet dancer; however, her lithe figure and distinctive face destined her for a more high-profile career in fashion modeling. Discovered at school as a teenager, she was the first black woman to grace the covers of both British and French *Vogue*. She delighted fashion audiences everywhere and was voted one of "The Most Beautiful People in the World." Not willing to limit her talents to the runway, she launched a singing career in 1993, and in 1994 published her first novel, *Swan*, whose protagonist is a white supermodel.

Jane Campion holds the Oscar for Best Original Screenplay for The Piano *(1993).*

CAMPION, Jane
1954-
New Zealand film director

Born in Wellington, New Zealand, Jane Campion studied at the Sydney College of the Arts and the Australian Film, TV and Radio School, known for allowing its students the freedom to experiment. Campion's early works, all short subjects, include *Peel* (1982) and *Passionless Moments* (1984). The same year she began working with the Women's Film Unit, a group founded with the aim of promoting careers for women in the traditionally male-dominated Australian film industry. In 1985 Campion was granted the funding by the Australian Film Commission to make a full-length feature. Before this film, which ultimately became *The Piano*, was started, Campion had produced several other works, the made-for-television film *Two Friends* (1986), the short *Tissues*, and *Sweetie* (1988), the story of a dysfunctional family. Her reputation outside Australia was determined by the rapturous reception of *An Angel at My Table* (1990), a biography of author Janet Frame. *The Piano* (1993) earned her the Palme D'Or at Cannes (the first woman so honored) and two Academy Awards.

CANNON, Annie Jump
1863-1941
American astronomer

A native of Dover, Delaware, Cannon was educated at Wellesley and Radcliffe and joined the Harvard College Observatory in 1911 as curator of astronomical photographers. She spent her entire career at Harvard, where she was appointed William Cranch Bord Astronomer in 1938. She classified some 400,000 stars in her lifetime – more than any previous astronomer – and in 1918-24 published *The Henry Draper Catalogue.* It classified the spectra of all stars from the North to the South Poles as studied by photographing their light through a refracting prism. (See also Fleming, Williamina.) Between 1925 and 1949, she published *The Henry Draper Extension*, which classified the faint stars.

CARAWAY, Hattie Ophelia Wyatt
1878-1950
American politician

The first woman elected a U.S. Senator, Hattie Caraway was a farm woman who spent most of her life taking care of her children and her politician husband. In 1931 her husband died, and in line with an Arkansas custom she was appointed senator to complete his term. Surprisingly she decided to run, and with Senator Huey Long's assistance, won election to the Senate on an egalitarian platform in 1932. She advocated Prohibition, farm relief, the New Deal and in 1943, became the first woman member of Congress to endorse the Equal Rights Amendment. She won a second term in 1938. From 1945 to 1946 she served on the Federal Employee's Compensation Commission and from 1946 to 1950 on the Employee's Compensation Appeals Board.

CARSON, Rachel
1907-1964
American ecologist, writer

Rachel Carson is best known for her controversial book *Silent Spring* (1962) that protested pesticide pollution and offered diatribes against the irresponsible industrial community in America. She was born in Springdale, Pennsylvania, and educated at the Pennsylvania College for Women and Johns Hopkins University. She studied genetics and zoology and became editor-in-chief for the American Fish and Wildlife Services in 1949. Her research into offshore life was carried on at the Woods Hole Marine Biological Laboratory in Massachusetts.

Her other published works include *Under the Sea Wind, The Edge of the Sea* and *The Sea Around Us.* Among the many awards she has won for scientific and literary acheivement are the Literary Award of the Council of Women of the USA (1956), the Schweitzer Prize for Animal Welfare (1963) and the Conservationist Award from the National Wildlife Federation.

American astronomer Dr. Annie Jump Cannon in her laboratory in 1930.

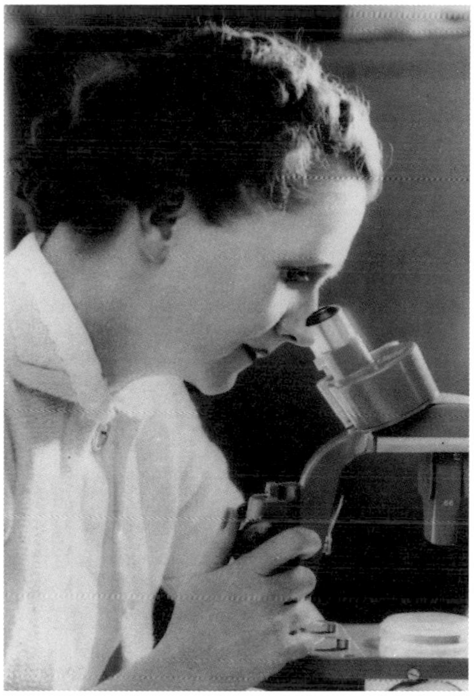

Rachel Carson's Silent Spring *(1962) provoked anti-pollution activism in the U.S.*

CARTLAND, Dame Barbara
1901-
British novelist

With over 600 million copies of her novels in print, Barbara Cartland has made a great success out of romance. The Guinness Book of World Records lists her as the best-selling author in the world, despite naysayers who point out that her plots are repetitive, or highly unrealistic. Her loyal readers know they'll get a well-told story of fairy book love, gorgeously set in the nineteenth century and filled out with authentic details. She published her first novel *Jigsaw* in 1922, and she writes an average of 23 books a year. When she's not travelling the world in search of exotic settings or dictating a new novel, Cartland speaks for a number of charitable causes and for the Conservative Party in her native England. She was created Dame of the British Empire in 1991.

CASLAVSKA, Vera
1942-
Czechoslovakian gymnast

One of the finest women gymnasts in the world to date, Caslavska won 22 World, Olympic and European titles between 1959 and 1980 including seven Olympic gold medals. Born in Prague and trained as an ice skater, Caslavska first competed internationally in the 1958 World Championships where she won a silver medal. At the 1964 Tokyo Olympics, Caslavska won gold medals in the balance beam, the vault and the combined individual title, defeating the legendary Soviet gymnast Larissa LATYNINA.

At the 1968 Olympic Games in Mexico City she won four gold medals, in uneven bars, floor exercises, vault and all-around, and two silver medals in the balance beam and team event. Her victory was poignant in light of the Soviet invasion of Czechoslovakia two months prior to the Games.

CASSATT, Mary
1844-1926
American painter

Renowned for her sensitive Impressionist portraits of women and children, Cassatt was born in Allegheny City, Pennsylvania, to an upper-class family who took her to Europe on several occasions in her childhood. She showed a precocious facility for painting and graduated from the Pennsylvania Academy of Fine Arts. Thereafter, she travelled to Europe to study the old masters in Italy, Spain and Holland, and in the early 1870s her canvases were shown at the National Academy of Design in New York and the Paris Salon.

Cassatt soon settled in Paris where her style was influenced by Edouard Manet and Edgar Degas, whose encouragement and advice was crucial to her development. She took part in five Impressionist shows in Europe and Degas painted her image on several occasions.

A technical virtuoso, Cassatt used many of her relatives and their young children as models. She produced genre scenes as well, such as *The Modern Woman*, a large mural displayed at the 1893 World's Columbian Exposition in Chicago. She urged American patrons to collect Impressionist paintings and was instrumental in their acquisition by museums in the United States.

For her dedication and talents, Cassatt was awarded the Legion of Honor by the French government in 1904. She earned a measure of international recognition unusual for a woman of her era and she was a passionate advocate of women's suffrage. In her later years, her eyesight deteriorated and she abandoned painting in 1914.

Barbara Castle in 1949. Labour MP from 1945 to 1979, she has remained a force in British politics.

CASTLE, Barbara
1911-
British politician

Even in her eighties, Barbara Castle maintains the strength and forthrightness that has earned her the distinction of being one of the most influential politicians of the British Left. During World War II, she worked as an administrative officer for the Ministry of Food (1941-44), followed by a stint as a journalist for the *Daily Mirror*. Active in local government from 1935 to 1945, she became a Member of Parliament (MP) in 1945, and served until 1979. While MP she was Minister of Transport (1954-58), and Secretary of State for Employment and Productivity (1968-70). In 1970 she guided passage of the Equal Pay Act through Parliament. She left the House of Commons for the European Parliament. From 1979 to 1985, she was leader of the British Labour Group. Her autobiography *Fighting All the Way* was published in 1993.

Suffragist leader Carrie Chapman Catt founded the League of Women Voters in 1919.

CATHER, Willa
1873-1947
American writer

A novelist whose characters are the pioneer emigrants who settled the American West, Willa Cather was born in Virginia and moved with her family to the windswept plains of Red Cloud, Nebraska, when she was nine. Educated in Latin and the English classics by her family, she graduated from the University of Nebraska in 1895 and wrote for the Lincoln newspaper.

Cather lived in Pittsburgh for ten years where she edited *Home Monthly* magazine, wrote for the *Pittsburgh Daily Leader*, composed verse and published a short story collection, *The Troll Garden*. In 1906 Cather moved to New York and joined the staff of *McClure's* magazine. She shared an apartment on Washington Square with her companion Edith Lewis and the couple travelled to the Southwest, trips which furnished material for her novels. Her heroes in *O Pioneers!* (1913), *My Antonia* (a strongly autobiographical work published in 1918) and *A Lost Lady* (1922) conquered the prairies by overcoming natural obstacles with spiritual resources. Other works included *House*, a war novel *One of Ours*, which won the Pulitzer Prize in 1922, and *Lucy Gayheart* (1940).

CATT, Carrie Chapman
1859-1947
American suffragist, peace activist

A leading force in obtaining women's right to vote in the United States, even as a child Carrie Chapman Catt stood up for girls' equality with boys. When her father refused to send her to college, she worked her way through Iowa State College by teaching and housekeeping. In 1883 she became superintendent of schools of Mason City, Iowa. In 1885 she became assistant editor of the *Mason City Republican*, owned and edited by her husband Leo Chapman. He died the following year. In 1887 she joined the Iowa Women Suffrage Association, soon becoming a national representative. Active in the National American Women Suffrage Association, she quickly became a leading organizer, and travelled the country rallying support and resources for women's right to vote. She served as president of NAWSA from 1900 to 1904, and 1915 to 1920. A brilliant tactician and organizer, her leadership culminated in the 1920 ratification of the 19th amendment that granted women suffrage. In 1919 she founded the League of Women Voters. She went on to do international organizing calling for an end to war and women's political participation in their countries.

CHADWICK, Florence
1918-
American distance swimmer

When Florence Chadwick decided to challenge the currents of the English Channel, she had no world records or Olympic medals. She was born and raised in San Diego, California, where she swam in competitions in San Diego Bay, but her best finish was only a fourth in the 1936 Olympic team trials. She took a job with the oil company, Aramco, and practiced in the Persian Gulf. She succeeded in her swim on August 8, 1950 from France to Dover in a record time of 13:23. On September 11, 1951 she became the first woman to swim the Channel against the tides from England to France, which she accomplished in 16 hours, 22 minutes. By October 1955, she lowered her time to 13:55. She was also the first woman to swim across the Catalina Channel, from Catalina Island to the California coast, which she accomplished in 13:47, and she set a record beating all prior attempts by both men and women in her swim across the Straits of Gibraltar with a time of 5:06.

Coco Chanel's chic designs are still widely copied and are perennially popular.

CHANEL, Gabrielle (Coco)
1883-1971
French designer

Coco Chanel began her career in fashion as a milliner in Deauville. She opened her first shop in Paris in 1914, selling simple dresses in wool jersey, a fabric that had never before been used for women's clothing. But it was after World War I, when a new sense of freedom revolutionized fashion, that Chanel came into her own. She created a simple, straight silhouette, with short skirts and low waistlines. She adapted men's styles to women's use, combining tailored clothes with her signature chunky costume jewelry, as well as putting women into bell-bottomed sailor pants and pea jackets. She also introduced bobbed hair and made tanned skin fashionable. Her best-selling perfume, Chanel No. 5, first appeared in 1922. Her couture house closed in September 1939 and did not reopen until 1954. Her postwar collections were best known for her suits of jersey and fine tweed with collarless jackets, and certain trademark accessories like quilted handbags, multiple strands of pearls and gold chains and beige slingback pumps with black toes. Her basic black dress and suit, copied everywhere, made it possible for anyone to appear in fashion at a reasonable cost.

CHER
1945-
American singer, actress

A singer and actress whose cool, hippie appeal as Sonny Bono's singing partner during the 1960s developed into a mature, independent film and musical career in the 1980s and 1990s, Cher was born Cherilyn Sarkisian in El Centro, California. A starstruck youngster who took part in local plays and musical events, Cher drew notice from Sonny Bono, one of Phil Spector's record producers. Bono asked her to join him in club date duets, and their song "I Got You Babe" hit the top of the Billboard charts in 1965. Cher continued to sing and record on her own after her breakup with Bono in the mid-70s. She married Greg Allmann in 1977 and had a hit with her song "Take Me Home."

Cher's acting career took off with a Broadway role in *Come Back to the Five and Dime, Jimmy Dean, Jimmy Dean* and film appearances in *Good Times, Charity* and the movie version of the play. Her first major recognition was for her part in *Silkwood* (1983), for which she received an Oscar nomination for Best Supporting Actress. She won an Oscar for her starring role in the offbeat romantic film *Moonstruck* in 1988, and had a 1988 hit record "I Found Someone". Her album *Love Hurts* (1991) and starring role in *Mermaids* (1990) ensured her continuing popularity.

CHICAGO, Judy
1948-
American feminist artist

An ardent feminist whose collaborative artworks focus on issues of women's rights, Chicago was born Judith Cohen and took the name of her native city. After graduating from UCLA, she and a colleague, Miriam Schapiro, established the first feminist arts program in 1971 at the California Institute of the Arts.

Together they are best known for an extensive project called *Woman House*, an environmental piece of 1972 that renovated an abandoned building in Los Angeles into an all-female arts center. With 400 female artists, Chicago went on to devise *The Dinner Party* over five years (1974-79). A huge table in the form of an equilateral triangle (each leg was 48 feet long) was laid out with 39 place settings designated for female trailblazers such as Earth Mother Gaea, Georgia O'KEEFFE, and Emily Dickinson. Their porcelain plates were painted with sexual imagery and the names of 999 other female role models were inscribed in gold on white floor tiles.

Chicago's art confronts sexual discrimination and used gender media such as embroidery and china to underscore her feminist agenda. She wrote about sexual iconography in *Womanspace Journal* in the 1970s and created shock value pieces such as *Red Flag*, connoting menstruation.

Feminist artist Judy Chicago employed over 400 female artists over 5 years to produce her monumental piece The Dinner Party.

CHILD, Julia
1912-
American cook, author

Born in Pasadena, California, Julia McWilliams attended Smith College and joined the OSS during World War II, where she met her husband Paul Child, who was also in the OSS. After the war, he was sent to Paris, where his wife entered the Cordon Bleu Cooking School. She met Louisette Bertholle and Simone Beck at this time, and in 1951 the three of them opened L'École des Trois Gourmands in Paris. On the Childs' return to the United States in 1961, they moved to Boston and Julia, in collaboration with Bertholle and Beck, wrote her first cookbook, *Mastering the Art of French Cooking*. She appeared on television during the publicity campaign for the cookbook, and WGBH in Boston decided that she would be an excellent host for a cooking program. *The French Chef* had its premiere in 1963, and won a Peabody Award in 1965 and an Emmy in 1966. In various guises under various titles it has continued to run into the 1990s. Child is also the author of several other cookbooks, including *The French Chef Cookbook*, and *The Way to Cook*.

CHISHOLM, Shirley
1924-
American politician

"Unbought and unbossed," Shirley Chisolm, the first African-American woman to be elected to the U.S. House of Representatives, was not always interested in politics. For years she ran a nursery school, only becoming politically active after joining the Seventeenth Assembly

Shirley Chisholm (D-NY) in 1972, the year she became the first black woman to run for the Democratic nomination for president.

District Democratic Club in the 1940s showed her how little representation black people and women had in Democratic party politics. In 1960 she formed the Unity Democratic Club in order to run black candidates, won election to the New York State Assembly in 1964, and made history in 1968 when she won election to the U.S. House of Representatives. She held her seat from 1968 to 1983 and advocated for civil rights and women's rights, and in 1972 became the first black woman to run for Democratic nomination for president. In 1984 she started the National Political Congress of Black Women to mentor prospective political candidates. President Clinton appointed her ambassador to Jamaica in 1993.

CHI'U CHIN
1879?-1907
Chinese revolutionary

Years after her early death, Chi'u Chin is still revered in China as a freedom fighter. Deeply upset by the splendor maintained by Manchu rulers while the population lived in poverty, she renounced her own sheltered middle-class upbringing. In 1903 she left her husband and children and went to Tokyo where her ideas of women's equality and revolution were nurtured. A dashing figure, she wore men's clothes, carried a sword and boxed. In 1906 she returned to China and founded a women's journal and a branch of the Restoration Society (China's main revolutionary movement). The next year she organized an uprising of Shaoxing against the Manchu ruler, Empress Tz'u-hsi. The rebellion was discovered, and Chi'u Chin executed, yet it fed the fire of rebellions which led to the dissolution of the Manchu dynasty in 1911.

CHRISTIE, Dame Agatha
1890-1976
British writer

The creator of Hercule Poirot and Miss Marple, Agatha Christie produced internationally successful detective stories that have been outsold only by the Bible and Shakespeare. Agatha Mary Clarissa Miller was raised in Devon, England and educated privately. She married a Flying Corps officer, Archie Christie, and worked as a VAD nurse in a Red Cross hospital in the coastal village of Torquay during World War I. Christie's first published detective story *The Mysterious Affair at Styles* was an immediate success when published in 1920. She and Christie were divorced in 1928, and she married an archaeologist, Sir Max Mallowan in 1929, whom she joined on yearly excavations in Iraq and Syria, where she continued to write. She published over 70 books, including *Murder on the Orient Express* (1934) and *Death on the Nile* (1937), as well as short story collections and plays. A production of her play *The Mousetrap* was the longest running play on London's West End, lasting for over 30 years. Christie also wrote novels under the pseudonym Mary Westmacott. She has been translated into many languages and her work is often adapted for television.

Agatha Christie, celebrated author of popular detective novels, in 1946.

CHURCHILL, Caryl
1938-
British playwright

As Britain's leading female playwright, Caryl Churchill has woven historical research, pointed social commentary and biting wit into a string of box-office successes. In plays such as *Cloud Nine, Top Girls*, and *Serious Money*, Churchill dissects stereotypes with a humor and transgression that offer hope for human relationships at the same time as she caustically criticizes the status quo. She herself broke away from the limits of her role as wife and mother of three sons to write radio plays, beginning in 1962. In the 1970s she expanded to writing for the stage and television to critical and popular acclaim that grows with each new production.

CHURCHILL, Odette
1912-
French-born war worker, spy

Odette Marie Celine Bailly was born and educated in Amiens, before moving with her widowed mother to the seaside resort of Boulogne, where she met many of the English people who visited there. In 1931, she married one of them, Peter Samson, and settled in London. When the War began and her children went to boarding school, she offered her services to the British War Office. She became a member of the Women's Transport Service, attached to the First Aid Nursing Yeomanry, but this was actually a cover for her work for the Special Operations Executive (SOE). After a course in espionage techniques, she was sent to France in October 1942 to join the Marseilles-Cannes SOE circuit as a courier, under the command of Captain Peter Churchill. In spring of 1943, the network was infiltrated by the Germans, and Captain Churchill and Odette Samson were arrested. Despite heavy interrogation and torture, she refused to reveal anything. She was tried and sentenced to death, but not executed, as the Germans believed she was Captain Churchill's wife and a relation of the British Prime Minister. She was held in prison and the concentration camp at Ravensbruck until the end of the war. She was awarded the OBE and the George Cross for "courage, endurance and self-sacrifice of the highest possible order" in 1946. The following year she married Captain Churchill.

CISSE, Jeanne Martin
1926-
Guinean diplomat

In 1972 Jeanne Martin Cisse became the first woman appointed as a permanent representative to the United Nations (1972-76). She was also the first woman to preside over the UN Security Council. She entered politics in 1961, after a career in education. With the Parti Democratique de Guinee she served as the First African Secretary, Second Vice-President and First Vice-President of the National Assembly of Guinea. From 1962 to 1972 she served as Secretary of the General Conference of African Women. Throughout her career, she has striven to improve the conditions of African women's lives, so that they can be politically, socially and economically active in their countries. In 1975 she won the Lenin Peace Prize, and from 1976 to 1984 she served as the Minister of Social Affairs in Guinea.

Jeanne Martin Cisse, the first woman president of the U.N. Security Council, in 1972.

Hillary Rodham Clinton's leadership in the national health care debate has transformed the role of First Lady of the United States.

CLINE, Patsy
1932-1963
American country singer

Born Virginia Patterson Hensley in Winchester, Virginia, Patsy Cline scored her first hit with "Walking After Midnight" in 1957. Cline became a featured performer at the Grand Ole Opry and had a string of smash successes such as "I Fall to Pieces", "Crazy", "She's Got You", "Faded Love" and "Sweet Dreams". After a string of seven hit records in three years, Cline was killed in a plane crash in March 1963. Decca Records issued several albums posthumously that sold briskly, and Cline became a legend for the female country and western vocalists who followed her. A movie about her life called *Sweet Dreams* (1985) starred Jessica Lange.

CLINTON, Hillary Rodham
1947-
American lawyer, First Lady of the United States

As First Lady of the United States, Hillary Rodham Clinton has set a new precedent for the acumen and involvement of the President's wife in the nation's affairs. As a young lawyer she worked with Marian Wright EDELMAN's Washington Research Project (now Children's Defense Fund) on behalf of poor people and children's rights. In 1974 she moved to Washington, D.C., to work with the House Judiciary Committee investigation of Richard Nixon's possible impeachment. After marrying lawyer Bill Clinton in 1975, the two powerhouses combined forces, resulting in her coordinating Bill Clinton's campaigns for governor of Arkansas and occupying high-level posts in each of his four administrations. When Bill Clinton was elected president in 1993, she was praised for her intelligence and capability, while opponents criticized her for being too powerful. Appointed head of the Task Force on National Health Care Reform, she has spearheaded the development of a national health care plan.

Jacqueline Cochran became the first woman to break the sound barrier in 1953.

COCHRAN, Jacqueline
1906-80
American aviator

Jacqueline Cochran was born in Pensacola, Florida, the adopted daughter of a poor couple, and worked in a sawmill when she was just eight. She earned her pilot's license in 1920, and in 1933 she opened a beauty parlor in Chicago and a cosmetics laboratory in New York, pursuing flying as a hobby. She was the first woman to enter the Bendix Transcontinental Air Race in 1935, and she won the trophy in 1938. She was the first woman awarded the Claude B. Harmon Trophy for contributions to aviation, which she won in 1937-39, 1946, 1950 and 1953, the last time winning it after becoming the first woman to break the sound barrier, in an F-86 Sabre jet.

During World War II, Cochran joined the Air Transport Auxiliary of the Royal Air Force in England and upon her return to the United States, joined the Women's Air Force Service Pilots (WASPS), soon becoming its director of women pilots. After the war she was the first civilian awarded the Distinguished Service Medal by the United States.

Cochran served in the U.S. Air Force Reserve, retiring as a colonel in 1970. Her cosmetics business developed into a vastly successful conglomerate, twice earning her the title of Woman of the Year in Business.

COLE, Johnetta
1936-
American educator, anthropologist

On April 5, 1987, Johnetta Cole was named the first black woman president of Spelman College in Atlanta, Georgia, the oldest college for African-American women in the United States. Born in Florida, Cole received her A.B. from Oberlin College and her Ph.D. from Northwestern (1967). She first taught at Washington State University where she created the Black Studies program. She next accepted a tenure-track position at the University of Massachusetts at Amherst, where she had a critical role in the development of the Afro-American Studies program. After thirteen years she left the University of Massachusetts for Hunter College in New York. While at Hunter she wrote her ground-breaking book *All American Women* (1986), a landmark in women's studies because it discussed the intersections between gender, race, class and ethnicity. Her book *Anthropology for the Nineties* followed in 1988.

Touted for her accessibility to students in her book *Conversations – Straight Talk with America's Sister President* (1993), she honestly discussed the social problems which hinder many young African-American women.

COLE, Dame Margaret
1893-1980
British political activist, writer

A leading socialist who influenced many important Labour politicians, Margaret Cole was raised in an upper-class family. Her father, John Postgate, was a famous reformer. Her brother's imprisonment as a conscientious objector deepened her belief in socialism, and she joined the Fabian Society's Research Department, controlled by Guild Socialists who sought worker control of factories. She met her husband, socialist and scholar G.D.H. Cole, who was to become a lifelong partner in all endeavors. In 1918 they formed the Labour Research Department. A defender of egalitarian education, she organized classes for the Workers' Education Association during the 1930s. In 1935 she and her husband founded the new Fabian Research Bureau, which set the stage for later Labour reforms. Together they wrote many books about socialism and politics, and also wrote more than 30 critically acclaimed detective novels.

COLEMAN, Bessie
1893-1926
American aviator

The first woman to earn an international pilot's license, Bessie Coleman had to travel to France to learn to fly because American aviation schools would not provide her with lessons because she was black.

Coleman was the twelfth of thirteen children born to sharecropper parents in Atlanta, Texas. She learned French to accompany a Red Cross unit to France during World War I that was attached to a French flying squadron. She was taught by French pilots and acquired her license from the Federation Aeronautique Internationale in 1921.

In June 1922 Coleman flew the largest plane ever navigated, the German L.F.G. powered by a 220-horsepower engine, in Berlin. She gave lectures and flying demonstrations when she returned to the United States in August of 1922 and took part in an air show honoring the 15th Negro Infantry Regiment of the New York National Guard. Coleman died in an accident during a flying exhibition in Jacksonville, Florida, on April 30, 1926.

COLETTE, Sidonie-Gabrielle
1873-1954
French novelist

The author of over 50 volumes of lyrical prose and narrative that focus on romantic attachments, Colette was born in the small Burgundy town of Saint-Sauveur en Prisaye. In 1895 she married Henry Gauthier-Villars, a journalist known as "Willy". His company's risqué novels were ghostwritten by a stable of hack writers, of which Colette became one. Recognizing Colette's talent for the genre, he locked her in a room for four

Colette's sensuous novels were colored by her experience in Parisian music halls.

hours a day to write her memoirs, a scheme that produced the four immensely successful "Claudine" novels. Her husband published the books under his name and took all the profits.

Colette divorced Willy in 1910, and supported herself with pantomime routines and dancing in Paris music halls. The experience inspired her novel *The Vagabond* (1912). Colette also wrote a weekly column for the newspaper *Le Matin*, edited by the aristocratic Henry de Jouvenal, whom she married in 1912. In 1922 she produced *The House of Claudine* and in 1929 wrote the novel that established her reputation, *Chéri*. Colette began a long affair in the 1920s with her "Chéri," Maurice Goudeket, who was 17 years younger than her, and eventually divorced de Jouvenal and married Goudeket. Colette wrote a sequel *The Last of Chéri* in 1932. She wrote *Gigi* in 1944 when she was 71 and suffering from crippling arthritis.

Elected to the Belgian Royal Academy in 1935 and the Goncourt Academy in 1945, she was named a Grand Officer of the Legion of Honor in 1953.

COMANECI, Nadia
1961-
Romanian gymnast

One of the disciples of the demanding coach Bela Karolyi, Comaneci won her first major competition at 13 with a gold medal in the 1975 Champions All Tournament in London. A month later she won the first of three consecutive European championships defeating the five-time winner, Russian gymnast Ludmila Tourischeva. In 1976, Comaneci won the first American Cup, scoring a perfect 10 in the vault, the first gymnast to achieve this accolade.

At the 1976 Montreal Olympics she won gold medals in all-around, uneven bars, and balance beam, placed third in floor exercises, and fourth in vault. Her scores included an astonishing seven perfect scores of 10. Returning to her homeland, the 4′11″, 86-pound 14-year-old was christened a Hero of Socialist Labor.

In 1980 at the Moscow Olympics, Comaneci again won gold medals in the balance beam and floor exercises and took the silver medal in the all-around and in the team competition. Comaneci formally retired from competition in May of 1984 and later defected to the United States.

COMPTON-BURNETT, Ivy
1884-1962
British novelist

The daughter of a doctor, Ivy Compton-Burnett was born in Pinner, England, and earned a degree in classics at Royal Holloway College in London in 1902. She became the governess for the children of her father's two marriages but suffered a series of painful, emotional traumas including the death of two brothers and the joint suicide of two of her younger sisters.

In 1919 she moved into a flat with antique collector Margaret Jourdain and began writing. Not surprisingly, her novels focus on torturous family relationships, parental tyranny and internecine battles for control in Victorian and Edwardian upper-class households. Her series of 17 novels began with *Pastors and Masters* (1925) and included among its best works *Men and Wives* (1931) and *Parents and Children* (1941). Memories of her childhood and adolescence infuse her works with the power of Greek myth. The narratives rely on tightly wrought, cryptic dialogue that reveals the tension of complicated family relationships. Her later novels included *A Heritage and Its History* and *A God and His Gifts*.

CONNOLLY, Maureen
1934-1969
American tennis player

Maureen Connolly was the national juniors champion at 13, won the U.S. ladies seniors at Forest Hills in 1951, and won Wimbledon on her first attempt in 1952. She was the first woman to achieve

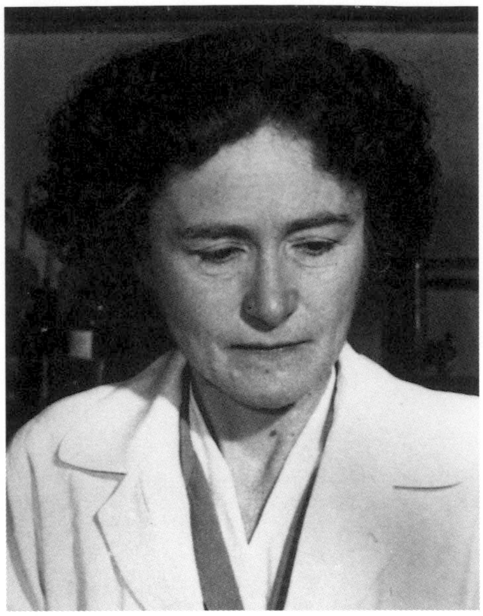

Winner of the 1947 Nobel Prize for physiology or medicine, Gerty Cori explored the structure of glycogen.

a Grand Slam by winning the Australian, French, Wimbledon and U.S. titles in 1953, a feat not equalled until 1970.

Connolly was a baseline player with strong, flat serves, penetrating accuracy and a killer instinct. She was ranked first in women's tennis from 1951 to 1953, won the U.S. clay court singles in 1953-54 and won Wimbledon three times in succession from 1952 to 1954. A skilled doubles player, she won both women's and mixed doubles at the French Open in 1954 and the U.S. women's doubles the same year.

Just after her third Wimbledon victory, Connolly injured her right leg in a riding accident and was forced to retire at 19. She married Olympic rider Norman Brinker, raised two daughters and continued as a coach and television commentator.

COONEY, Joan Ganz
1929-
American broadcasting executive

Joan Ganz Cooney was born in Phoenix, Arizona,and graduated *cum laude* from the University of Arizona in 1951. In 1954 she moved to New York and broke into the fledgling television industry as a publicity writer for NBC. From 1955 to 1962 she worked on the *US Steel Hour*, and from 1962 to 1967 was the producer of public affairs documentaries for NET. Her program, *Poverty, Anti-poverty and the Poor* won an Emmy in 1966. That same year, Cooney began to study the possibility of adapting television to preschool education. After three years of planning, including the establishment of curriculum goals, *Sesame Street*, the first program produced by the Children's Television Workshop, first aired in November 1969. The enormously popular show revolutionized children's programming, and continues to teach and entertain preschool children. Since 1970, Cooney has been the president, executive director and trustee of CTW, which still produces *Sesame Street.*

CORI, Gerty
1896-1957
Czech chemist

A native of Prague, Gerty Radnitz studied chemistry at Ferdinand University (the German University of Prague) and received an M.D. in 1920. She married fellow student Carl Cori that same year and spent two years doing medical research at the Karokinen Children's Hospital in Vienna. She and her husband emigrated to the United States in 1922 and spent nine years at the New York State Institute for the Study of Malignant Diseases in Buffalo, New York. From 1931, Cori worked at the Washington University School of Medicine in St. Louis, Missouri, becoming professor of biochemistry in 1947. There she and her husband did major research into the chemistry of glycogen and the enzymes associated with it. For effecting the first synthesis of glycogen in a test tube, they were awarded the 1947 Nobel Prize in physiology or medicine. In 1954 her solo research chemically determined the molecular structure of glycogen.

CORRIGAN MAGUIRE, Mairead
1944-
WILLIAMS PERKINS, Betty
1943-
Irish pacifists

Except through her affiliation with the lay Catholic welfare organization, The Legion of Mary, Mairead Corrigan did not participate often in public activities. However her grassroots efforts toward ending the violence in Northern Ireland would earn her, along with Betty Williams, the 1976 Nobel Peace Prize.

Mairead Corrigan was born in Belfast, Northern Ireland. Although a Catholic in the predominantly Protestant country, she had not personally suffered from the ever-growing terrorism or discrimination experienced by others in her community. This would all change dramatically on August 10, 1976, when her niece and two nephews were killed by a runaway Irish Republic Army car. Corrigan began to campaign to end the terrorism whatever its source, and publicly condemned the IRA. Strongly influenced by her religious beliefs, she felt it was her mission to foster pacifist's views.

Betty Williams, also a Belfast native, had witnessed the accident. She was so moved that she immediately went door-to-door collecting signatures on a petition, demanding an end to the violence. A week later, she and Corrigan led a march of 10,000 women, both Catholic and Protestant, to the children's graves. Joining forces, they formed the Community of Peace People.

Corrigan and Williams belatedly received the 1976 Nobel Peace Prize for their work in October 1977. Both resigned their executive positions with the Peace People in 1978.

COURT, Margaret
1942-
Australian tennis player

The winner of the most major titles in women's tennis as well as a Grand Slam in women's singles in 1970, Margaret

Margaret Court after she completed her Grand Slam in singles tennis in 1970.

Nobel Peace Prize winners Betty Williams (left) and Mairead Corrigan (right) led 10,000 women in a rally protesting violence in Northern Ireland in 1976.

Court won 11 Australian singles, five French singles, three Wimbledon finals and five United States championships from 1960 to 1973. After her seventh Australian victory she retired from the grueling tour in 1966 and married a world-class sailor, Barry Court. She returned to the tour in 1968, and en route to her 1970 Grand Slam sweep she played the longest women's singles final at Wimbledon, defeating Billie Jean KING after 46 games.

Court was a masterful doubles player as well and acheived significant victories in both women's doubles and mixed doubles play. Between 1963 and 1975 she won six Wimbledon finals, ten Australian finals, seven French championships and six United States victories. She paired with Kenneth Fletcher in 1963 for a mixed doubles Grand Slam. In her play for the Australian team in Federation Cup competition, she had an undefeated match record of 22-0. Margaret Court was named to the International Tennis Hall of Fame in 1979.

CRAWFORD, Cindy
1966-
American supermodel

Noted as much for her brains as for her beauty, Cindy Crawford is probably one of the most successful models ever. With a thriving career that includes a multi-year Revlon cosmetics contract, and a deal as a Pepsi-Cola spokesperson, it is estimated that Crawford's annual income is approximately $15 million. The Illinois native was headed toward a career as a chemical engineer when she began modeling as a teenager. Signed with the Elite Modeling Agency, she gained international attention when her face appeared on *Vogue*'s cover in 1986.

Colleagues applaud her professionalism and hard work, but she realizes she won't model forever. In recent years, she has ventured into other areas. She produced a well-received exercise videotape, and continues to appear as host on MTV's *House of Style*. She married actor Richard Gere in 1991 but shies away from pursuing acting herself.

CRAWFORD, Joan
1908-1977
American actress

She was born Lucille Le Sueur in San Antonio, Texas, and danced as Billie Cassin in the Broadway chorus of *Innocent Eyes*. This led to work as Norma Shearer's stand-in in *The Lady of the Night* (1925), but it was as Joan Crawford in *Our Dancing Daughters* (1928) that she made an impact in Hollywood. Crawford became one of the most glamorous and durable stars of the golden age of Hollywood, appearing in such classic films as *Grand Hotel* (1932), *Rain* (1932), *The Women* (1939) and *Mildred Pierce* (1945), for which she won the Academy Award as Best Actress. Her later films included *Humoresque* (1946), *Autumn Leaves* (1956) and *What Ever Happened to Baby Jane?* (1962). She was married four times, to Douglas Fairbanks Jr, Franchot Tone, Philip Terry, and Alfred Steele, the chairman of Pepsi-Cola. On Steele's death in 1959, she became a director of Pepsi, and was responsible for, and appeared in many of, their television advertisements, which were shot by Dorothy ARZNER.

CRESSON, Edith
1934-
French prime minister, politician

In 1991 French president François Mitterand appointed Edith Cresson prime minister of France, making her the first woman to hold this post. A trusted colleague of Mitterand's since 1965, in 1977 Cresson became mayor of Thure, and in 1979 won a seat in the European Parliament where she came to be known as an expert in agriculture. In 1981 she became the first woman to head the Ministry of Agriculture, then trade minister, then minister for European affairs. By the time she was appointed prime minister, she had earned a reputation as a tenacious fighter, a protectionist of French trade, and vehemently pro-business. Mitterand hoped that she would strengthen France economically for the uniting with the European Economic Community. However, following a no-confidence vote after just 10 months, she was forced to resign.

Edith Cresson was appointed prime minister of France by president François Mitterand in 1991. She resigned in 1992.

C

CRUZ, Celia
1924-
Cuban singer

The "Queen of Salsa" renowned for her exceptional improvisation within the Latin music genre, Celia Cruz was born in Havana and began singing on local radio stations during the 1940s. After studying at the Conservatory of Music, she became lead singer with Cuba's most popular orchestra, La Sonora Matancera, with whom she toured and recorded from 1950 to 1965. The group was a headliner at Havana's famous nightclub The Tropicana and Cruz had scores of hit songs, including "Bemba Colora", "del Cocoye", "Yerbero", "Moderno" and "Burundanga", the last going gold in 1957.

Cruz married Pedro Knight, her music director and manager, in 1962 and soon after defected to the United States. She joined the "King of Latin Swing", Tito Puente, in 1966 and toured America with his orchestra. She won a Grammy in 1974 for her album *Celia and Johnny*, recorded with Johnny Pacheco's Orchestra.

Other popular Cruz albums include *Celia-Ray-Adalberto-Tremendous Trio!*, *De Nuevo*, and *The Winners* with Willie Colon.

CUNNINGHAM, Imogen
1883-1976
American photographer

Imogen Cunningham was born in Portland, Oregon, and brought up in Seattle. After majoring in chemistry at the University of Washington, she travelled to Dresden, Germany, to study photographic printing and was influenced by the modern German photographer Gertrude Kasebier.

Cunningham made her debut in 1901 as an assistant to Edward S. Curtis. She later became a vanguard member of the precisionist West Coast photographers who formed the F.64 group in the 1930s. A paradigm of the precisionist style, Cunningham's crisp, clean floral studies such as *Two Callas* and stark views of industrial structures earned her a following among modern, objectivist photographers. Her 1928 photo of a female torso *Triangles* explores the geometry of the nude genre, and her studies of her second husband, the printmaker Roi Partridge, were among the first nude male photographs.

Cunningham made memorable portraits of leading figures in the arts of her day such as Gertrude STEIN, Martha GRAHAM and Upton Sinclair. She was honored with a solo retrospective of her work at the Metropolitan Museum of Art in New York in 1972 and was revered as the grandmother of modern photography when she died at 93 in 1976.

Marie Curie discovered radium in 1898. She won the 1903 Nobel Prize for physics and the 1911 Nobel Prize for chemistry.

CURIE, Marie
1867-1934
Polish-born French physicist

Born in Warsaw, Poland, the daughter of teachers, Marie Sklodowska went to Paris to study physics and chemistry and stayed to become a renowned scientist who discovered radium and was twice winner of the Nobel Prize, in 1903 for physics and in 1911 for chemistry. She was assisted in her research on radium by her husband, French scientist Pierre Curie (1859-1906). Working with Antoine Henri Becquerel's findings on radioactivity, the Curies announced their discovery of the elements polonium and radium in 1898. Subsequent studies described the properties of radium and laid the foundation for research in nuclear physics. Mme. Curie served as head of the physics laboratory at the Sorbonne and succeeded her husband as professor of physics there after his death in 1906. She published *Traité de radioactivitié* in 1910. Her daughter Irène also became a scientist and Nobel Prize winner (*see* JOLIOT-CURIE, Irène).

D

DAVID, Elizabeth
1913-1992
British cook, author

Born Elizabeth Gwynne, she married Ivor David, a career army officer, and lived in the various parts of the world to which he was posted. While doing so she collected recipes and, in 1950, published her first cookbook, *A Book of Mediterranean Food*, introducing the British public, who were still on food rationing, to recipes of a different culture which could be made with readily available ingredients. Her subsequent books, which included *French Country Cooking* (1951) and *Italian Food* (1954), were bestsellers, not only for the simplicity of the recipes, but also for the charm of their descriptions. In 1955 she published *Summer Cooking*, one of the first books to highlight good British food, using local produce, fruit, fish and game. She followed this with *English Cooking* (1970). For her work, she has received many honors including an OBE (1976), a CBE (1986) and the Order of Chevalier du Merite Agricole from France (1977).

DAVID-NEEL, Alexandra
1868-1969
French adventurer

A daring adventurer who gained entry into the forbidden city of Lhasa in Tibet by disguising herself and a young boy companion as an old woman and her son, Alexandra David-Neel began to research the Orient at the Musée Guimet in Paris. She inherited money at 20 and set off to visit India, Ceylon and North Africa, touring with the Opera Comique.

In 1904 she married a wealthy engineer, Philippe Neel, who financed her expeditions to Europe, China and India, where in 1911 she enrolled at the Calcutta College of Sanskrit. In 1912 she was the first woman to interview the Dalai Lama, who suggested she master Tibetan. She was impressed with the Tibetan anchorite nuns and spent a winter in a cave at 13,000 feet studying Buddhism, followed by three years in a Peking monastery.

In 1923 she and her young companion, Longden, entered Lhasa. She documented the experience in *My Journey to Lhasa* (1927). In 1936 she returned to France, settling in Digne. She wrote, "Travel not only stirs the blood, it also gives strength to the spirit."

Explorer Alexandra David-Neel, clad as a Tibetan nun.

DAVIES, Margaret
1861-1944
British radical, women's rights advocate

To make capital the servant of labor and abolish the wage system were two of the principles that guided Margaret Davies's lifelong work with women. Influenced by her Christian Socialist father and suffragette mother, she joined the Women's Co-operative Guild, and by 1889 was general secretary. During her 33-year tenure she fought for a minimum wage for women co-operative employees, divorce for women on the same terms as men, maternity benefits for women and improved maternity care. Among her many writings was the influential *Maternity: Letters from Working Women*, which revealed their experiences of childbirth and rearing. In favor of the Russian Revolution, she was chair of the Society for Cultural Relations with the USSR from 1924 to 1928.

DAVIS, Angela
1944-
American civil rights activist

Angela Davis, radical philosopher, has been an eloquent spokesperson and activist for the upholding of political and civil rights for American citizens. As a student, she joined the Black Panther Party, the Southern Non-violent Coordinating Committee, the Che Lumumba group and the Communist Party. When governor Ronald Reagan led a 1969 campaign to fire her from teaching at San Francisco State University because of her Communist ties, she successfully challenged the California state law forbidding Communists from teaching at state universities.

Imprisoned on charges of conspiracy following the Soledad Brothers murder trial, she began to reflect on the inferior role that women held in liberation struggles, which began a feminization of her activism. Acquitted in 1970, she went on to found the National Alliance Against Racist and Politicial Repression, and now teaches at the University of California at Santa Cruz.

DAVIS, Bette
1908-1989
American actress

Ruth Elizabeth Davis was born in Lowell, Massachusetts, studied at the John Murray Anderson Dramatic School, and worked in summer stock before making her New York acting debut in 1929. A later performance in *Solid South* brought her a Hollywood contract with Warner Brothers, and in 1934 she starred as the unsympathetic waitress, Mildred, in *Of Human Bondage*, and the following year she won her first Academy Award for *Dangerous*. Often forced by the studio into mediocre roles, over which she fought legal battles and was suspended, she never gave a bad performance. Many of her 86 feature films, such as *The Petrified Forest* (1936), *Jezebel* (1938), for which she won her second Academy Award, *The Little Foxes* (1941) and *Now, Voyager* (1942) are considered classics. Perhaps the best known of her later films is *All About Eve* (1950), although she found a new career in the 1960s appearing in *grand guignol* thrillers like *What Ever Happened to Baby Jane?* (1962). She continued to work in the theater, on television and in the movies, making her last film, *The Whales of August* (1987) two years before her death. She was the first woman to receive the Kennedy Center Honors for lifetime achievement in the performing arts in 1987 and she was honored by the Film Society of Lincoln Center in 1988.

DAY, Doris
1924-1994
American singer, actress

She was born Doris Kapelhoff in Cincinnati, Ohio, and began her career as a big band singer while she was still in her teens. Her rendition of "Sentimental Journey", recorded with Les Brown and His Band of Renown, was a great hit at the end of World War II. She was signed to a studio contract soon after, making her debut in *Romance on the High Seas* (1948), an otherwise forgettable film. She made a series of films which used her singing talent, including *Love Me or Leave Me* (1955), the film biography of singer Ruth Etting. She also sang two songs that received Academy Awards, "Secret Love" from *Calamity Jane* (1953) and "Que Sera Sera" from *The Man Who Knew Too Much* (1956). Her blonde, freckle-faced, girl-next-door appearance made her an icon of the 1950s, when she made a series of light comedies. She also appeared in a television series, *The Doris Day Show* from 1968 to 1972.

DAY, Dorothy
1897-1980
American journalist, social worker

Soft-spoken and passionate Dorothy Day, creator of the Catholic Worker movement, showed the Roman Catholic Church how to combine social justice with religious faith. A member of the Socialist Party as a girl, she spent years writing for socialist and radical journals. When her daughter was born in 1927, she joined the Roman Catholic Church to provide the child the "gift of faith." But the Church was not involved in socialist activities, so she felt cut off until she met Peter Maurin, a French Catholic who envisioned working for the needy within the Church. Joining forces, they created the *Catholic Worker*, which discussed issues from race to labor. When homeless people began coming to the newspaper's offices for help, they fed them, and provided both temporary and permanent shelter. A committed pacifist, Day helped establish the Association of Catholic Conscientious Objectors, and in later years was a vigorous opponent of the Vietnam War.

DEAN, Brenda
1943-
British trade unionist

When Brenda Dean was elected General Secretary of SOGAT (Society of Graphical and Allied Trades), she became the youngest person and the first woman to head a large trade union. She worked for the union almost all of her life, moving up from administrative secretary (1959-72) to her election as General Secretary in 1984. She received international atttention during a drawn-out labor dispute in 1986-87 triggered by owner Rupert Murdoch's relocating of the London *Times* to Wapping, costing SOGAT 6000 jobs. Since then she has worked for labor reforms that will equalize relations between labor and management.

Outspoken and intelligent actress Bette Davis often played the acid-tongued "bitch" in Hollywood movies of the 1930s and 1940s. She won two Oscars for her work.

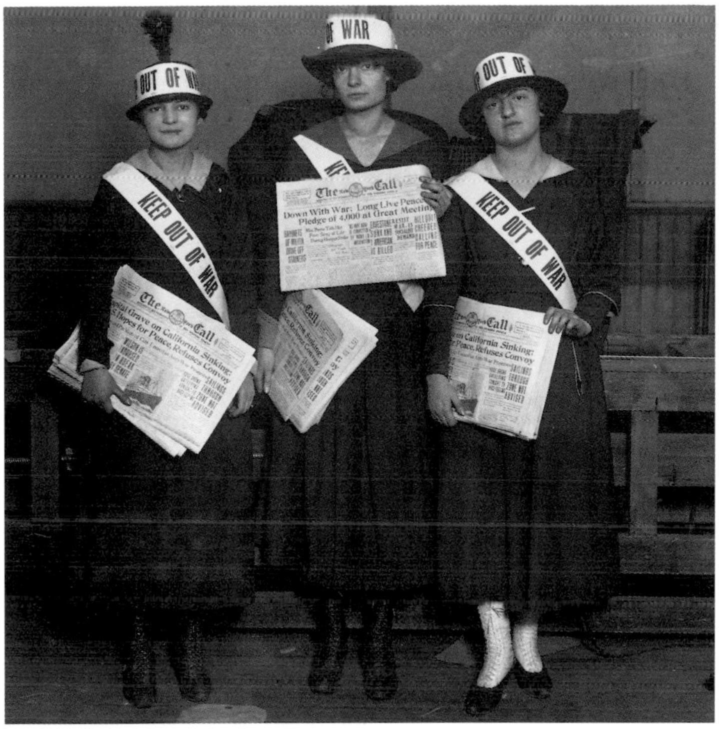

ABOVE LEFT: *Dorothy Day (center).*
ABOVE: *Bernadette Devlin.*

DELAUNAY, Sonia
1885-1979
Russian artist, designer

A founder of the art movement called Orphic Cubism in 1911, Sonia Terk was born in the Ukraine and raised in St. Petersburg. She studied art in Germany before moving to Paris in 1905 where she met her husband, Robert Delaunay, considered the first abstract French painter. Their associates were the Fauves and Cubists – Picasso, Matisse, Derain and Braque – and they distilled a unique style filled with circular themes and musical analogies whose abstract arcs had the intensity of artificial light.

Delaunay was involved with textiles, extending her designs to fabrics, theatrical costumes, book covers and tapestries. She exhibited "electric prism" paintings at the Salon des Independents in Paris in 1914 and furnished costumes for the choreographers Diaghilev and Tristan Tzara. She and her husband had a close working partnership until his death in 1941 and they synthesized elements of modern art, fashion and interior decoration in their textile studio.

DENEUVE, Catherine
1943-
French actress

She was born Catherine Dorleac in Paris, the daughter of actors. Catherine took her mother's maiden name for the stage, when she made her debut in the film *Les Collegiennes* (1956). Eight years later, she starred in the beautiful French musical film *The Umbrellas of Cherbourg* (1964) and in Roman Polanski's *Repulsion*. She has made several films with Luis Buñuel including *Belle du Jour* and *Tristana* (1970). She has also appeared in several American films, including *April Fools* (1968) and *Hustle* (1975), although her cool, sensual beauty seems almost too exotic for American tastes. She received a nomination for Best Actress for *Indochine* (1992), the film which won the Academy Award for Best Foreign Language Film. She was also, for many years, the model for Chanel No. 5.

DEVLIN, Bernadette
1947-
Irish politician, political activist

The youngest woman ever elected to Parliament, Bernadette Devlin fought all her life to gain equal rights and justice for the poor, Irish and Catholic of Northern Ireland. Born in Northern Ireland, her father filled her with stories of British dominance of the Irish. In 1966 she was awarded a scholarship to Queen's University, where she became politically active with the civil rights organization People's Democracy. When the group entered politics, she ran as an MP candidate, serving from 1969 to 1974. Refusing to stop participating in demonstrations, even as an MP, she was charged and jailed in 1969 for "riotous behavior" when a Londonderry riot turned violent. She served four months in jail. She did not win re-election, and in 1975 she co-founded the Irish Republican Socialist Party. In 1981 an assassination attempt did not stop her work, and she continues her activities in Northern Ireland.

DIANA, Princess of Wales
1961-
Princess of Great Britain

On July 29, 1981, the world gazed upon the spectacular marriage of Lady Diana Spencer and Charles, Prince of Wales, heir to the throne of England. Charles's seventh cousin, once removed, and the daughter of Earl Spencer, Diana spent much of her childhood on the royal estate of Sandringham. In fact, she was playmate to Charles's younger brothers. As a young woman, she enjoyed sports, winning many trophies for swimming. Especially fond of children, when the couple met she was teaching at a fashionable kindergarten in London. The birth of their son and heir apparent, William Arthur Philip Louis, proved a delight to the English crown, but the fairy tale soured, and in 1992, after years of rumors that the royal couple was unhappy, they separated.

Sophisticated, glamorous, and mysterious, Marlene Dietrich remained an outsider in Hollywood while fascinating audiences.

DIETRICH, Marlene
1901-1992
German-born actress, singer

Maria Magdalena von Losch was born in Berlin, and studied to be a violinist before a wrist injury changed her life. She studied with the famous German director Max Reinhardt, and appeared in several silent films and revues before she was spotted by director Josef von Sternberg, who cast her as the amoral singer Lola-Lola in *Der Blaue Engel (The Blue Angel)* (1930). When von Sternberg went to Hollywood, he took his protégé Dietrich with him. There she starred in a number of films, always as the exotic outsider. Her great fistfight with Una Merkel in *Destry Rides Again* (1939) and the song "See What the Boys in the Back Room Will Have" revealed a sense of humor that had been missing in films like *Shanghai Express* (1932) and *Garden of Allah* (1936). A virulent anti-Nazi, she refused to return to Germany, and entertained the Allied troops during World War II, frequently very close to the front lines. For this she received the U.S. Medal of Freedom and the French Legion of Honor. After the war, she continued to act, but made a second career as a nightclub singer. She was presented with a special Tony Award in 1968, and was the subject of a documentary produced by Maximilian Schell in 1984.

DINESEN, Isak (Karen Blixen)
1885-1963
Danish writer

Karen Christentze Dinesen was born in Rungstedlund, Denmark. Her father was a writer who committed suicide when she was just nine. As a child she wrote essays, poems and plays and later studied painting in Switzerland, Copenhagen and at the Royal Academy of Fine Arts. Upon returning to her country homestead, she fell in love with Hans Blixen, but when he spurned her she married his brother Bror, and the couple purchased a coffee plantation in Kenya in 1913. Dinesen met the love of her life there, Denis Finch-Hatton. Their romance as well as the beauty of the Ngong hills near Nairobi and the noble Masai and Somali tribes were the basis of *Out of Africa* (1937) which she wrote years later.

Dinesen contracted syphilis from her husband and suffered increasingly severe symptoms in her lifetime. She divorced Blixen in 1922, and after Finch-Hatton's death in a plane crash in 1931, Dinesen returned to Denmark and wrote in his language, English, to assuage her grief. She wrote *Seven Gothic Tales, Winter Tales, Shadows on the Grass*, and *Out of Africa* which was made into a popular film in 1985. *Angelic Avengers*, which she wrote under the pseudonym Pierre Andrezel, was an acclaimed gothic allegory of World War II.

Takako Doi of Japan in 1986.

DOI, Takako
1928-
Japanese political leader

In September 1986, Doi was elected the chairman of the opposition Japan Socialist Party (JSP) after having travelled the country giving rousing speeches challenging those who grew rich at the expense of others. Her victory as the first woman ever to head a major political organization in Japan inspired a record number of Japanese women to run for political office in 1989. She has been called "the conscience of Japan" because she has pushed her country to behave ethically, addressing wrongs such as the chemical weapons Japan buried in China, and admitting to the 1937 Nanking Massacre. After the JSP suffered defeat in 1991 she stepped down, continuing her term in the Lower House of the Diet (Parliament) where she became the first female speaker.

DOLE, Elizabeth
1936-
American charitable organization administrator, government official

Named one of the world's 10 most admired women in a 1988 Gallup poll, "Liddy" is one of the most powerful and successful women in Washington today. Born in Salisbury, North Carolina, Elizabeth Hanford graduated with honors from Duke University and went on to earn a law degree and a master's degree in government and education from Harvard University. She made her first mark in Washington working on Lyndon B. Johnson's Committee for Consumer Interests (1968-71), and became the deputy director of the Office of Consumer Affairs in 1971, a position she held for three years, during which time she met her future husband, Senator Robert Dole. The Secretary of Transportation under Ronald Reagan from 1983 to 1987, she campaigned for her husband's presidential bid before becoming the Secretary of Labor under George Bush in 1989. In 1991 she became the president of the American Red Cross, controlling a $1 billion budget, and immediately set about revamping the organization, which was laboring under new stresses imposed by the AIDS epidemic.

Elizabeth Dole opens the 2nd session of the Republican National Convention in 1988.

DOVE, Rita
1953-
American poet

Poet Laureate of the United States, Rita Dove has an unusual ability to capture ordinary people's speech and experience in detailed images that speak to people. In her Pulitzer Prize-winning book of poems *Thomas and Beulah* (1985), based on the lives of her grandparents, she relates the story of a generation of African-Americans drawn north by industrial jobs.

Born in Ohio, Dove graduated from Miami University (Ohio) and the University of Iowa, and currently teaches English at the University of Virginia. Through her writing, teaching, and service as the first African-American poet laureate, Dove has promoted the imagination and validity of ordinary experience. Her poems brilliantly, as she put it, "string moments as beads on a necklace."

DUBOIS, Marie
1858-1954
Dutch paleontologist

Marie Dubois traveled to the island of Java with her husband, anthropologist Eugene Dubois, in the early 1890s in search of the "missing link" in human evolution. Eugene Dubois was an evolutionist who believed, erroneously, that the apes of Indonesia, the orangutan and gibbon, were the animals most closely related to *Homo sapiens*. When the Dubois expedition returned to London in 1895 with the skull of Java Man, there was great excitement among scientists and much controversy about where a new fossil fit into the evolutionary puzzle. Eventually, it was classified as *Homo erectus*, the hominid species which, like Peking Man, most closely preceded *Homo sapiens*.

DuMAURIER, Daphne
1907-1989
British novelist, historical writer

London-born Daphne DuMaurier lived most of her life in Cornwall, which provided the backdrop to both her fiction and her historical works. The granddaughter of George DuMaurier, the writer and artist, and daughter of actor Gerald DuMaurier, she enjoyed research, especially into her family history, and filled her 17 novels and 12 volumes of stories with authentic details. Her signature is suspense, built up in a gothic atmosphere of mystery. *Rebecca* (1938), said to be based on anxieties she experienced upon finding old love letters of her husband's, was a huge success both as a novel and a Hitchcock movie. Alfred Hitchcock also filmed her story "The Birds", and her novel *Don't Look Now* was made into a film in 1974.

DUNCAN, Isadora
1878-1927
American dancer, teacher

A pioneer modern dancer who performed barefoot wearing flowing white tunics and flowers in her hair, Duncan was born in San Francisco to a poor Irish family. With her sister Elizabeth she taught dancing to wealthy patrons there and went on tour exhibiting mime routines and original choreography at engagements from Chicago to New York. Their popularity flourished and Duncan travelled to London in 1899 and on to Berlin, Budapest, Florence and Athens in 1903.

Duncan's principle was that "every emotion has its corresponding movement", and her expressive technique embraced spontaneous rhythms of the body and even found a kinship with ocean waves. Music inspired her, especially compositions by Chopin, Wagner, Schubert and Tchaikovsky that she chose to accompany her dances.

Duncan suffered great tragedies in her life. Both her children, one by the stage designer, Gordon Craig, and one by sewing machine heir Isaac Singer, were drowned in the Seine in 1931. The loss inspired her to found schools of dance for children. She established a school in Moscow in 1921 and married a Russian poet, Serge Essenin in 1922. After he committed suicide, she left Russia to open a studio in Nice, France, in 1925.

American pioneer of "free dance," Isadora Duncan often performed in a flowing tunic.

DUNHAM, Katherine
1910-
American dancer, choreographer

Katherine Dunham was a trailblazing, inspirational dancer who formed her own troupe of African-American dancers and created such captivating ballets as *Tropics and Le Jazz Hot, Primitive Rhythms*, and *The Ballet Br'er Rabbit.* She assimilated various rhythms from the African-American tradition, adapting Caribbean voodoo rituals, African drumbeat movements and "cakewalk" strutting steps into her signature style.

Born in Joliet, Illinois, Dunham financed her master's degree in anthropology from the University of Chicago by teaching dance. She choreographed several productions at the Federal Theatre in Chicago.

After founding her company in 1939, she danced in the Broadway play *Cabin in the Sky* in 1943, and went to Hollywood for its film production. She married the set designer John Pratt, and their talents met with critical acclaim. Her troupe performed for more than 25 years. She staged a ballet for the Metropolitan Opera's *Aida* and travelled in Europe with her troupe. She also choreographed a number of films in Hollywood and in Europe.

In 1992, the 82-year-old Dunham staged a well-publicized 48-day hunger strike in protest of the U.S. policy toward Haitian refugees.

Katherine Dunham (center) adopted a variety of dance styles inspired by African rhythms for her African-American dance troupe.

DuPRÉ, Jacqueline
1945-1987
British cellist

Born in Oxford, DuPré entered the London Cello School at the age of 5. She later studied at the Guildhall School of Music with William Pleeth. Considered a prodigy, she also studied with such masters of the cello as Paul Tortelier in Paris, Pablo Casals in Switzerland and Mstislav Rostropovich in Moscow. She made a number of recordings for the great cello works, including the Elgar concerto, which won her the Queen's Prize in 1960. She made her concert debut at Wigmore Hall in 1961, and her American one in 1965. DuPré married conductor Daniel Barenboim in 1967, and occasionally was the soloist at his concerts. In 1972 she was stricken with multiple sclerosis, and turned to teaching, including televised master classes. She was presented with the OBE in 1976.

DURAS, Marguerite
1914-
French writer, filmmaker

Marguerite Duras was born Marguerite Donnadieu in Giadinh, Indochina (now Vietnam). She grew up aware of the degradation of the masses which fostered a lifelong loathing for imperialism and its attendant alienation, the themes of her work. She became a member of the French Resistance and the Communist Party from 1944 to 1955, until her expulsion from its ranks.

Her early works *A Sea of Troubles* and *Moderato Contrabile* (1960) have an autobiographical framework. In 1960

Marguerite Duras has won a number of awards for her experimental novels.

Duras collaborated with Alain Resnais, a French documentary maker known for his work portraying concentration camps. Together they produced the seminal film *Hiroshima, Mon Amour*, a study that marked the turning point in Duras's career. Her fiction became more experimental, beginning with *Ten-Thirty on a Summer Night* (1962). Her brief, elusive novels presented a stream of consciousness narrative with vague settings and elliptical plots.

Duras's novel *The Lover* (1984), the story of a 15-year-old European girl and her affair with a Chinese lover, won the Prix Goncourt and catapulted to the top of international bestseller lists. Duras also published *The Malady of Death and the War* in the mid-1980s.

DWORKIN, Andrea
1946-
American radical feminist writer

Dworkin is a radical feminist who is an aggressive critic of all aspects of male sexuality and patriarchy. Her stance rests fundamentally on a subtle, but contentious understanding of the political nature of language and the function of symbolism. She is equally lauded and reviled by critics and participants of the feminist/anti-feminist debate. Dworkin is more of a sensationalist than a historian of fact, and her semi-autobiographical novel, *Ice and Fire* (1986), attracted much attention as it details violent male sexuality so realistically that some readers found it pornographic.

E

American aviator Amelia Earhart was the first woman to fly solo across the Atlantic and to fly solo nonstop across the continental U.S., in 1932.

EARHART, Amelia
1897-1937
American aviator

The first woman to receive a pilot's certificate from the U.S. National Aeronautic Association, the first woman to fly solo across the Atlantic and the first woman to receive the Distinguished Flying Cross, Earhart was a trained nurse who cared for World War I casualties before channeling her energies into flying. She took her first solo flight in 1921 and bought her first plane at 25. She founded the Ninety-nines, an organization of female flyers and flew in the first Women's Air Derby in 1929.

Flying a Lockheed Vega monoplane in May 1932, she soloed across the Atlantic in 14 hours 54 minutes, also setting a world non-stop distance record for a woman. She won a $10,000 award for a solo flight from Hawaii to the U.S. mainland in 1935 and was honored with a gold medal from the National Geographic Society.

In her round-the-world flight attempt with veteran Pan Am pilot Freddie Noonan, her Lockheed Electra ran out of fuel and was lost in the South Pacific off the coast of Australia. Neither the plane nor its passengers were ever found.

EDDY, Mary Baker
1821-1910
American religious founder, publisher

A native of Concord, New Hampshire, Mary Baker Eddy suffered from a spinal disease early in her life and read widely on questions of health. Widowed within a year of her first marriage, and separated from her only child, she sought relief and guidance in the Bible. After a near-fatal fall in 1866, she wrote that she had regained her health through reading the New Testament. For the next few years, she searched the Scriptures for laws underlying spiritual healing and formulated the principles of Christian Science, which she published as *Science and Health* in 1875. *A Key to the Scriptures* was added to the work shortly thereafter. In 1877 she married Asa G. Eddy, who helped her with the work of establishing Christian Science. She founded the Church of Christ, Scientist, in 1879 and the *Christian Science Monitor* – still one of the nation's most respected newspapers – in 1908.

EDELMAN, Marian Wright
1939-
American lawyer, civil rights activist

A passionate advocate for children's rights and dedicated to social change, Marian Wright Edelman first became an activist during the civil rights movement in the 1950s. She participated in lunch counter sit-ins in Atlanta and worked on voter registration drives throughout Mississippi. A Yale University law degree recipient, she was the first black woman admitted to the Mississippi bar. Moved to end the pervasive poverty she'd seen in Mississippi, she started the Washington Research Project. The Children's Defense Fund (CDF) evolved from this work.

Founded in 1973, the CDF's mission was to encourage awareness of issues which pertain to children. Her child advocacy was swayed by the increase in the number of children born into poverty. In her book *The Measure of Our Success: A Letter to My Children and Yours*, Edelman movingly imparts wisdom and inspirational lessons to the nation's children and their parents.

Mary Baker Eddy founded the Christian Science Monitor *in 1908.*

Dr. Joycelyn Elders is the first black woman to be appointed U.S. Surgeon General.

EDERLE, Gertrude
1906-
American distance swimmer

The first woman to swim the English Channel and who beat the fastest time by a man by two hours, Ederle accomplished this feat on August 6, 1926, swimming from Cap Griz-Nez, France, to Dover, England.

As an amateur, Ederle held freestyle records in every distance from 100 to 800 meters and in 1922 won a 3½-mile race across New York Bay to capture the J.P. Day Cup. She competed on the winning U.S. 400 meter freestyle relay team in the 1924 Olympics. She set 18 world records in 1924.

She was honored with a ticker tape parade and met by a cheering crowd of two million fans on her return to New York after the Channel swim. She joined the vaudeville circuit and earned $2000 a week giving swimming demonstrations. Unfortunately, her hearing was severely damaged by the rough waves, and she later gave swimming lessons to deaf children who shared her handicap. In 1965 she was one of 21 inductees into the International Swimming Hall of Fame.

ELDERS, Joycelyn
1933-
American physician, former U.S. Surgeon General

In 1993 Joycelyn Elders became the first black woman appointed U.S. Surgeon General. An advocate of universal health care, she grew up in a poor family where she and her family never had adequate health care. Determined to send her to college, her family picked cotton and she scrubbed floors in order to pay her way. After enlisting in the army, she went to medical school on the G.I. Bill. From 1967 to 1987 she researched and did clinical work in pediatric endocrinology, and in 1987 was appointed Director of the Arkansas Department of Health by then-governor Bill Clinton. Calling teenage pregnancy another form of slavery, as Surgeon General she was a champion of reproductive rights, contraceptives, safe sex, and the decriminalization of drugs. Her controversial views led to her removal from office in 1994.

ELION, Gertrude B.
1918-
American biochemist

Born in New York City, Gertrude Elion studied biochemistry at Hunter College and New York University, where she earned an M.S. degree in 1941. World War II offered many new job opportunities for women, and Elion took a position with pharmaceuticals manufacturer Burroughs Wellcome in Tuckahoe, New York. There she began the lifelong association with Dr. George H. Hitchings that resulted in the development of such major drugs as acyclovir, effective in treating herpes virus infections, and AZT, the drug often used to combat AIDS. With Dr. Hitchings, she was awarded the Nobel Prize for physiology or medicine in 1988. Three years later, she became the first woman inducted into the National Inventors Hall of Fame.

ELIZABETH, The Queen Mother
1900-
British royal

Mother of ELIZABETH II, the Queen Mother's grace, charm, and pragmatism has made her the most popular member of Britain's royal family. Born in 1900 into a Scottish noble family, Elizabeth Bowes-Lyon married Prince Albert, second son of George V, in 1923 and had

Biochemist Gertrude Elion won the 1988 Nobel Prize for physiology or medicine.

two daughters, Elizabeth and Margaret. When Edward VIII abdicated in 1936, Albert became the King of England. He proved an able and popular monarch, and Queen Elizabeth won universal respect and praise for her efforts during the war years and thereafter.

When her husband died in 1952, leaving the throne to her eldest daughter, Elizabeth adapted to her new role of Queen Mother with characteristic strength of character which has endeared her all the more to the British public. A keen horticulturalist and a devoted follower of horse racing, the Queen Mother continued to travel extensively and to appear at state functions well into her nineties.

ELIZABETH II, Queen
1926-
British monarch

Elizabeth Alexandra Mary, daughter of Prince Albert, Duke of York, was not originally in line for the crown. However, when her uncle, Edward VII abdicated for love of Wallis SIMPSON, her father became king, and she succeeded him in February 1952. She was crowned at Westminster in June 1953. She had married her distant cousin Prince Philip Mountbatten in 1947, and gave birth to Charles, Prince of Wales; Princess ANNE; Andrew, Duke of York; and Prince Edward. Her role is largely ceremonial but she exercises much influence through meetings with international government leaders and monitoring the business of the British government, and as the head of the Commonwealth and the Anglican Church. The second wealthiest woman in the world, she agreed to break with English tradition and pay taxes on her income.

ELLIS, Ruth
1926-1955
British murderer

In 1953 Ruth Ellis met David Blakely and began a tempestuous affair that would result in both of their deaths just two years later. The following year she also became intimately involved with Blakely's friend Desmond Cussen. When Blakely became aware of her affair with Cussen, they argued about it, often violently. This romantic triangle lasted for over a year.

On Christmas Eve 1954, Blakely caught Ellis and Cussen together and an argument ensued. In the aftermath, Ellis swore that she would break things off with Blakely. However, her obsession with him would extend the relationship for several more months. When she discovered that Blakely was seeing another woman, she said she "had a peculiar idea that I wanted to kill him."

On April 10, 1955, Ellis took a cab to an area pub, where she waited until he emerged, and shot him dead. At her trial she blatantly admitted her intent to kill him and after little deliberation the jury found her guilty. She was sentenced to death by hanging. Opponents to capital punishment valiantly fought to obtain her clemency, but on July 13, 1955 Ruth Ellis became the last woman hanged in Britain. A critically acclaimed 1985 movie *Dance With a Stranger* told her story.

ENDER, Kornelia
1958-
German swimmer

What began as an exercise for orthopedic therapy became an Olympic career when Kornelia Ender swam for the East German team in the 1972 Munich Games as a 13-year-old athlete. She won three silver medals in the 200 meter individual medley, the 4 × 100 meter freestyle relay and the 4 × 100 meter medley relay.

By 1976 in Montreal, Ender was at the top of her Olympic form, winning four gold medals (100- and 200-meter freestyle, 100 meter butterfly and 4 × 100 meter medley relay) and a silver in the 4 × 100 meter freestyle relay. She broke the world record in the 100 meter freestyle with a time of 55:65, an event in which she had already lowered the world record nine successive times.

Ender was the holder of ten East German championships and was the first woman to swim the 200 meter freestyle in less than two minutes. She was World Swimmer of the Year in 1973 and 1975 (when she won four gold medals in both World Championships) as well as in 1976. She was named to the International Swimming Hall of Fame in 1981.

Queen Elizabeth II seen on the 40th anniversary of her accession to the British throne, February 6, 1992.

ABOVE: *Edith Evans in* The Whisperers *(1967), for which she was nominated for an Oscar.*

EUSTIS, Dorothy
1886-1946
American founder of The Seeing Eye

Dorothy Eustis's interest in breeding and training German shepherds evolved from watching her pet Hans demonstrate his innate intelligence and loyalty to her. She moved to Switzerland in 1921 and established an experimental breeding kennel for dogs. There she began a research program which engendered a German shepherd with high intelligence, obedience and natural beauty. Inspired by a model of guide dogs for blind war veterans, she focused on guide dog training.

In 1929 she left Switzerland to solicit funds to establish a guide dog training school in the United States. That same year The Seeing Eye was started in Tennessee. Eustis was its first president, serving for ten years. At the time of her death, The Seeing Eye had trained over 1300 seeing-eye dogs for the blind.

EVANS, Dame Edith
1888-1976
British actress

Edith Evans was born in London, and made her first theatrical appearance as an amateur, in Cambridge in 1912. The same year she made her professional debut as Cressida in William Poel's London production of *Troilus and Cressida.* For several years she was part of Ellen Terry's company, and established a reputation for versatility. She could play Shakespeare, Restoration comedy and modern comedy with equal grace. She was best known for her performance as the Nurse in *Romeo and Juliet*, a part she played many times, and for her unforgettable Lady Bracknell in *The Importance of Being Earnest*, which she first played in 1939. During the war she entertained the troops for ENSA, and was created Dame of the British Empire in 1946. After the war, she returned to the theater and also made several films, which preserve her work. These range from *The Importance of Being Earnest* (1951) to *Look Back in Anger* (1959). She also co-starred in *Tom Jones* (1963) and *The Whisperers* (1967) and was nominated for Academy Awards for both. When she died in 1976, she had just completed her role in *The Slipper and the Rose*, the last of a career that had spanned six decades.

EVERT, Chris
1954-
American tennis player

A clay-court specialist, Christine Marie Evert appeared on the tennis scene at 16 when she won the U.S. 18-and-under girls tournament. Three years later she won her first Wimbledon final and went on to a 13-year record of winning at least one Grand Slam title each year. On clay she won 125 consecutive titles from 1973 to 1979.

Evert mastered the courts at Roland Garros Stadium in the French Open seven times, winning in 1974-75, 1979-80, 1983, and 1985-86. At Wimbledon, she won the singles in 1974 and 1981 and won both the singles and doubles (pairing with her longtime rival Martina NAVRATILOVA) in 1976. She triumphed at the U.S. Open four times, and on the grass at the Australian Open in 1982 and 1984. She played on nine Wightman Cup teams and on five victorious Federation Cup teams for the United States. She is now a perceptive television commentator at Wimbledon and the U.S. Open.

Chris Evert waves goodbye to the crowd after her last U.S. Open performance, in 1989.

F

FALLACI, Oriana
1930-
Italian journalist, writer

Fiery political journalist Oriana Fallaci is best known for her confrontational interviews with world leaders, including Henry Kissinger, Golda MEIR and the Ayatollah Khomeini.

Born in a poor family in Florence, Fallaci grew up with the inspiration of her father's participation in the Italian Resistance. She broke new ground for women reporters, covering Vietnam, the Middle East and other hot spots as international correspondent for *L'Europeo*. Passionate and irreverent social criticism punctuate her two nonfiction books, as well as her autobiography, *Interview With History* (1974). Her novels include *A Man* (1979), based on the life of her lover, Greek Resistance fighter Alexandros Panagoulis, who was assassinated in 1976. Fallaci is a two-time winner of the St. Vincent Prize for journalism in Italy, and her work is published internationally.

FARMER, Fannie
1857-1915
American cook, author

Born in Boston, Fannie Farmer suffered a paralytic stroke as a teenager that ended her formal education. She recovered well enough to help with household tasks, and developed an aptitude for cooking. Her parents enrolled her in the Boston Cooking School. After her graduation in 1889, she was hired as assistant director, and two years later became the head of the school. *The Boston Cooking School Cook Book* (now known as *Fannie Farmer*) was first published in 1896. Farmer was one of the first to stress the importance of level measurements and following directions. Her book also included menus, sections on formal entertaining and etiquette. The recipes, which were all personally tested, are still easy to follow. In 1902 Farmer opened her own school, Miss Farmer's School of Cookery, with a curriculum designed to train housewives rather than servants. In 1904 she published *Food and Cookery for the Sick and Convalescent*. Although her work predated the science of nutrition, she stressed "the knowledge of the principles of diet as an essential part of one's education."

Fannie Farmer's cookbook, first published in 1896, is still a standard nearly 100 years later.

FARRAR, Geraldine
1882-1967
American operatic soprano

Geraldine Farrar was born in Melrose, Massachusetts, and made her first public appearance at the age of 14. She made her operatic debut in Berlin as Marguerite in *Faust* in 1901, and was a member of the Monte Carlo Opera for three seasons, the first American singer to achieve a career and stardom in opera. In 1906 she made her Metropolitan Opera debut as Juliette in Gounod's *Romeo et Juliette*. She appeared in many American premieres of Puccini works, including *Madame Butterfly* with Enrico Caruso in 1907. Between 1915 and 1919, she made a series of films in Hollywood, including *Carmen* (1915) which was one of her great operatic roles, and *Joan the Woman* (1916). She had a tremendous following of young fans, known as Gerryflappers, making her one of the first stars to be so popular. She retired from the operatic stage with her final performance of *Zaza* in 1922, but continued to appear in song recitals until 1931. She was a member of the Board of the Metropolitan Opera, and served as a radio commentator for one season.

FAWCETT, Dame Millicent Garrett
1847-1929
British suffragist, writer

Her older sister, Elizabeth Garrett ANDERSON, fought for years to be granted the right to be the first practicing female physician in England. Thus inspired, Fawcett devoted her life to the struggle for women's equality.

With the encouragement of her husband, she published her first book *Political Economy for Beginners*. In 1897 she

Soprano Geraldine Farrar as Madame Butterfly at the Met.

became president of the pacifist National Union of Women Suffrage Societies (NUWSS). Dedicated to non-violence, she pressed for women's right to vote, conducted national speaking tours and lobbied Parliament.

In 1918 British women were granted civil rights. Fawcett continued to campaign for professional opportunities and legal rights for women, and wrote several books. For her service to Britain during two wars, she was created Dame of the British Empire in 1925.

FERBER, Edna
1887-1968
American novelist, short story writer, playwright

Bestselling author Edna Ferber won the Pulitzer Prize for her 1924 novel *So Big*. With her 1926 novel *Show Boat* (later turned into a classic musical) and other popular novels, short stories and plays, Ferber transformed her native Midwestern values into a template of rugged individualism.

Trained as a reporter, Ferber brought an eye for detail and dramatic framing to her stories of rural American life, its singular men and strong women. Many of her works – as seen in the subplot concerning the mulatto actress Julie in *Show Boat* – criticize racial and sexual discrimination yet her profound belief in the promise of America shines through.

FERGUSON, Ma (Miriam Amanda)
1875-1961
American politician

In 1924 Ma Ferguson ran for governor of Texas after her husband, James Ferguson, had been impeached for misuse of funds. Supported by her husband, as well as by poor and tenant farmers, she was elected the same day as Nellie Taylor Ross of Wyoming, making them the first female governors in the United States. She opposed Prohibition, and pardoned her husband (which was reversed by her successor). She lost a re-election bid in 1926, but won another term in 1932. She was able to take Texas from a budget deficit to a $7 million surplus. Making no secret of her husband's assistance in running the government, she even ran under the promise of delivering two Fergusons for the price of one.

Former Democratic vice-presidential candidate Geraldine Ferraro ran for the Senate but lost in 1992.

FERRARO, Geraldine
1935-
American politician

In 1984 Geraldine Ferraro made history when Democratic candidate Walter Mondale selected her as his running mate – the first woman to be vice-presidential candidate of a major party in the United States. Although they did not win, Ferraro inspired the nation's women to donate more than $4 million to her campaign. Ferraro has credited her work as assistant district attorney (1974-78) for Queens County, New York, with opening her eyes to domestic abuse, rape and other social problems, laying the groundwork for her progressive stands on issues such as abortion rights and economic parity for women when she served in the House of Representatives (1978-84). The 1984 Democratic presidential campaign was undercut when she faced scrutiny for her husband's business dealings. Since then, she has written her campaign memoirs, and lectures widely on issues such as drug use, for which her son was convicted.

FERRIER, Kathleen
1912-1953
British contralto

Kathleen Mary Ferrier was born in Higher Walton, Lancashire. An accomplished amateur pianist, she was encouraged to study voice after winning a prize for singing at a local music festival. After an engagement as soloist in the *Messiah* at Westminster Abbey in 1943, her professional career began in earnest. Her voice was known for its range and richness, and her technical control won her a growing reputation. In 1946 at Glyndebourne, she sang Lucretia in Britten's opera *The Rape of Lucretia*, and the title role in Gluck's *Orfeo*, a part that she made her own. Her other great success was Mahler's *Das Lied Von der Erde*, which she sang at the first Edinburgh Festival, in 1947, as her American debut in 1948, and at Salzburg in 1949. She was at the height of her career, and had been awarded a CBE in 1953, when she died of cancer.

FIELD, Jessie
1881-1971
American educator, founder of 4-H Club

A proponent of agriculture as an addition to the core curriculum in American public schools, Celestia Josephine Field spent the majority of her career fostering young people's involvement in agricultural endeavors.

While teaching in a one-room school house in Iowa, she helped her students form the Girls Home Club and the Boys Corn Club, whose missions were to teach the girls better home management skills and the boys more efficient farming techniques. In 1906, she became school superintendent for Page County and established Girls and Boys Clubs in all the schools. To publicize the clubs, she created a three-leaf-clover pin with the letter "H" (for Head, Heart and Hands) on each leaf. The fourth "H" – originally representing Home and now Health – was added in 1913. In 1914 the Clubs became a national organization, adopting the name "4-H Club."

Field resigned as Page County School Superintendent in 1912 to accept a position as national secretary for the Young Women's Christian Association (YWCA) in New York. A few years later she returned to her native Iowa.

President Vigdis Finnbogadottir of Iceland became the first woman elected head of state in a free popular election, in 1980.

Ella Fitzgerald at a 1952 rehearsal with Oscar Peterson (piano), Roy Eldridge (trumpet) and Max Roach (drummer).

FIELDS, Mrs. (Debbie)
1956-
American cookie magnate

Debra Jane Sivyer was born in East Oakland, California, and began baking cookies as a teenager. In 1976 she married Randy Fields, a financial consultant who began to serve his wife's cookies to clients. When Debbie Fields decided to sell her cookies commercially, she says she knew nothing about the business, and that her chewy cookies were not even the sort that sold. She opened her first shop in Palo Alto, Mrs. Fields Chocolate Chippery with a $50,000 loan, and advertised by offering free cookies to passers-by. By 1987, the company had opened 425 stores around the world, with sales of $87 million, and had grown from a single flavor to a variety which includes macadamia nut (the company uses approximately 10 percent of the world's macadamia nuts), coconut and oatmeal-raisin. Mrs. Fields has expanded into other areas, running a clothing store and gift shop as well as her cookie empire.

FINNBOGADOTTIR, Vigdis
1930-
President of Iceland

In 1980 Vigdis Finbogadottir became the first woman in the world to be elected in a free popular election as head of state. Daughter of a wealthy engineer, she has taught French drama at the University of Iceland, hosted a television series about theater, and from 1972 to 1980 directed a theater company in Finland's capital. Her popularity continued to grow, and in 1984 she was elected for a second term. She remains head of state, and envisions herself using the mainly ceremonial office of president to develop Icelandic culture and women's equality.

FITZGERALD, Ella
1918-
American singer

A celebrated and influential jazz vocalist, Ella Fitzgerald was born in Virginia and raised in an orphanage in New York.

Bandleader Chick Webb spotted her in an amateur competition at 16 and engaged her to sing with his group, which she took over four years later when Webb died in 1939. Her career-establishing hit record, "A-Tisket, A-Tasket" (1938), was made with Webb's band. Fitzgerald absorbed the popular "white" music of the 1930s, and her recordings of songs like "My Heart Belongs to Daddy" were best-sellers. She invented scat singing, a breathless, nonsense syllable technique for her songs "Flying Home" and "Lady Be Good". She worked with the Oscar Peterson Trio, formed a singing partnership with Louis Armstrong, toured with Dizzy Gillespie and appeared in television specials with Duke Ellington. Her popular Songbooks produced in the 1950s interpreted the music of George Gershwin, Cole Porter, Irving Berlin, Richard Rodgers, Lorenz Hart, and Duke Ellington. She sang with symphony orchestras around the world in the 1970s, and has remained an active performer in concert, television, and recordings.

FLAGSTAD, Kirstin
1895-1962
Norwegian operatic soprano

Born in Hamar, Kirstin Malfrid Flagstad came from a musical family. At the age of ten, she was given the score of *Lohengrin* and memorized the role of Elsa. She made her debut in 1913 in the role of Nuri in d'Albert's little-known opera *Tiefland*. As her voice developed she became known for her Wagnerian roles, but until the 1930s she sang only in Scandinavia. She first sang as Bayreuth in 1933, made her Metropolitan Opera debut as Sieglinde in 1935, and her debut at Covent Garden as Isolde in 1936. Flagstad was frequently cast with tenor Lauriz Melchior, and their recordings together are considered a great legacy of the golden age of opera. During World War II, she returned to Nazi-occupied Norway with her husband, who became a member of the Norwegian Nazi Party. She persuaded him to resign, and she herself was acquitted of political offense in a tribunal at the end of the war. This alienated many of her once fervent American fans, and she did not appear in America again until the 1950s. She retired from the operatic stage in 1954, but continued to record, often learning new roles. She was also the first director of the Royal Norwegian Opera, from 1958 to 1960.

Figure skater Peggy Fleming won the only gold medal for the United States at the 1968 Winter Olympics in Grenoble, France.

FLEMING, Peggy
1948-
American skater

The youngest national women's figure skater who held the United States title from 1964 to 1968, Peggy Fleming won the only U.S. gold medal at the 1968 Winter Olympics in Grenoble, France. She was the world champion from 1966 to 1968 and won the women's triple crown, earning the National, North American and World titles in 1967.

Fleming's ascendancy in the sport was especially valued following the tragic plane crash that killed all 18 members of the U.S. Skating Team in 1961. Her style was exceptionally fluid and graceful and her compulsory figures were superior. She followed her Olympic win with a flourishing professional career, appearing in the Ice Follies, Holiday on Ice and several television specials. She is a valued television commentator for amateur and professional competitions and a trustee of the Women's Sports Foundation, promoting the cause of women's athletics in America. She was named to the Women's Sports Hall of Fame in 1981.

FLEMING, Williamina (Mina)
1857-1911
Scottish-American astronomer

Born in Dundee, Scotland, Fleming was educated in public schools and taught there until her marriage and emigration to the United States in 1877. In 1881 she became an assistant to Professor Edward Pickering of the Harvard College Observatory. There she developed a new method of classifying stars based upon the study of stellar spectra – the pattern they produced when their light was refracted through a prism. In 1890 she published the *Draper Catalogue of Stellar Spectra*, classifying more than 10,000 stars according to her new system. The first woman elected to Great Britain's Royal Astronomical Society, in 1906, she published in 1910 her discovery of "white dwarfs" – hot, dense, compact stars believed to be in their final evolutionary stage.

FLYNN, Elizabeth Gurley
1890-1964
American radical, labor organizer

Elizabeth Gurley Flynn is one of the unsung founders of the American Civil Liberties Union. Inspired by the vision of the International Workers of the World, she joined them in 1906. For the next ten years she worked for the IWW, defending

their right to free speech and organizing massive strikes. In 1916 and 1917 her outspoken stand against WWI led to charges of espionage. In 1920 she co-founded the American Civil Liberties Union, which grew out of the 1919 raids of IWW organizers and allies. From 1936 to 1941 she publicized the need for women to have equal pay and protective legislation. Despite her displeasure with Soviet domination, in 1937 she joined the Communist Party, and later spent two years in jail for sedition. Elected chair of the national committee in 1961, she became the first woman to head the Communist Party in the United States.

FONDA, Jane
1937-
American actress, political activist

Jane Fonda attended Vassar College and studied acting with Lee Strasburg in New York. She made her film debut in *Tall Story* (1960), and played in several other light comedies before being transformed by her first husband Roger Vadim in *Barbarella* (1968). During the Vietnam War she became actively involved in radical politics, married Tom Hayden and became extremely unpopular with a segment of the American public. At the same time, she made one of her finest films, *Klute* (1971), for which she won the Academy Award for Best Actress. Her subsequent films, including *Julia* (1977), *Coming Home* (1978) and *China Syndrome* (1979), have all been extremely serious in nature. Even the comedy *9 to 5* (1980) could be considered a study of the treatment of women in the workplace. In 1982 she produced and co-starred with her father Henry Fonda in his last film, *On Golden Pond*. She is also well known for her series of exercise videotapes, but since her marriage to media mogul Ted Turner seems to have retired from film.

FONTEYN, Dame Margot
1919-1991
British dancer

The first ballerina of international stature born and trained in Great Britain, Margot Fonteyn was half-Irish and half-Brazilian, the daughter of a mining engineer. She joined Ninette de VALOIS's Vic-Wells Ballet in 1934 and first soloed in a 1935 performance of the *Nutcracker*. She began starring in several of de Valois's ballets, including *Odette/Odile* and *Aurora*. Over the course of the next three decades Fonteyn danced all the ballerina roles of the standard classics. Fonteyn also performed in works by young British choreographers, particularly Frederick Ashton, in his innovative ballets *Symphonic Variations* (1946), *Daphne and Chloe* (1951) and *Ondine* (1958). Fonteyn was named President of

ABOVE: *At various times in her career Jane Fonda has been a political radical, an Oscar-winning actress, and the producer of her own series of workout videos.*
BELOW LEFT: *Elizabeth Gurley Flynn addresses a meeting of the International Workers of the World in New York City in 1914.*
BELOW: *Dancer Margot Fonteyn in rehearsal for* Ondine, *1958.*

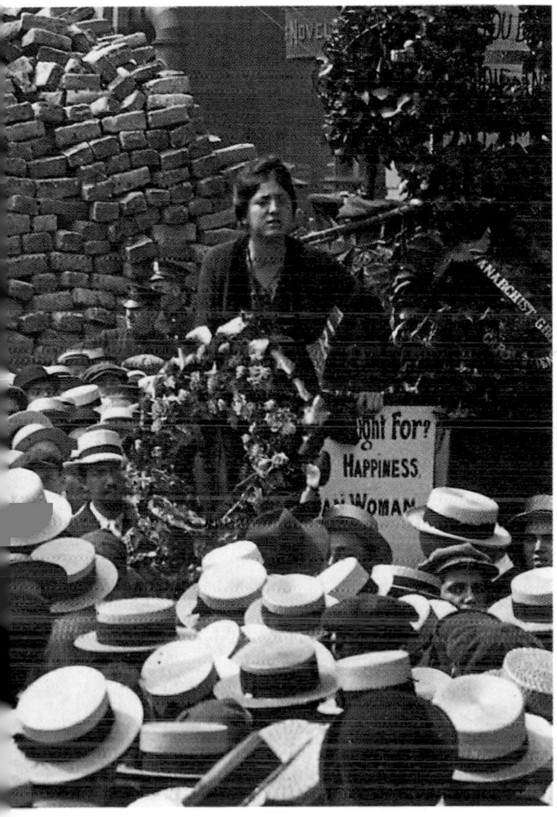

the Royal Academy of Dancing in 1954 and a guest artist to the Royal Ballet in 1959.

In 1962 Fonteyn began a sensational, decade-long partnership with the Russian star Rudolf Nureyev, with whom she would reach the pinnacle of international acclaim. Noted for her exquisite line and unassuming charm, Fonteyn was influential in popularizing ballet with the British television series "The Magic of Dance" in 1980.

FORD, Eileen
1922-
American entrepreneur

Eileen Otte was born in New York City, and grew up in Great Neck, Long Island. After school, she had a brief modeling career before she married Jerry Ford. Together they set up the Ford Model Agency in 1946. One of their advances was to put the modeling industry on a sound business basis, establishing standardized fees, and acting as agents for the models in terms of collecting fees, as well as bookings. Mrs. Ford has alway been very protective of her models, setting a strong disciplined regimen for each, and frequently giving houseroom to some of the youngest until she feels they are mature enough to cope with New York. The growth of Ford's to the most famous and successful modeling agency in the world is due in great part to Eileen Ford's flair for finding beautiful women who typify a changing and ever-fashionable look. Ford models have included Jean SHRIMPTON, Jane FONDA, Candice Bergen, Penelope Tree and Lauren HUTTON.

FOSSEY, Dian
1932-1985
American zoologist

Sponsored by anthropologist Louis Leakey, San Francisco-born Dian Fossey moved to Africa in 1967 to study the endangered mountain gorillas on the Rwanda-Zaire-Uganda border. Within three years, she had been accepted by the gorillas to an extent achieved by no other primatologist. Deeply concerned by the threat posed by loss of habitat and poaching, Fossey became an outspoken advocate for the preservation of the gorillas, whom she came to consider her family. She spent 19 years in Africa, leaving only briefly to earn a doctorate at Cambridge University and to work on her 1983 book *Gorillas in the Mist*. Her 1970 article in the *National Geographic* magazine brought the plight of the mountain gorillas to public awareness, and funding for antipoaching activities and the research of her Karisoke Center continued even after her tragic unsolved murder in 1985.

Jodie Foster wins the Best Actress Oscar for The Silence of the Lambs *(1991).*

FOSTER, Jodie
1962-
American actress, filmmaker

An Academy Award nominee at the age of 12 for her portrayal of a child prostitute in Martin Scorsese's *Taxi Driver* (1975), Jodie Foster established a career playing strong, unconventional characters in movies that raised difficult social issues. Born Alicia Christian Foster in Los Angeles, she appeared in television commercials, television series, and family films, beginning at the age of three. At 17 she enrolled at Yale University (BA 1985) and continued to receive good notices in a number of small films. Her performance in the role of a rape victim in *The Accused* (1988) won Foster her first Academy Award for best actress; *The Silence of the Lambs* (1991) won her another. That year, she also made a promising directorial debut with *Little Man Tate*, and in the following year founded her own production company, Egg Pictures.

FRAME, Janet
1924-
New Zealand novelist, poet

Award-winning author Janet Frame has published over a dozen lyrical books, remarkable works from a true survivor. A shy and insecure young woman, Frame attempted suicide in 1947. Misdiagnosed as a schizophrenic, she was subjected to shock treatments and eight years in a psychiatric hospital. Her writing saved her, literally as well as figuratively – when her first collection of stories *The Lagoon* won a literary award, the hospital decided to release her rather than proceed with the frontal lobotomy she was scheduled to undergo.

Many of her novels and three volumes of autobiography confront the contradictions of mental illness and health, and the difficulties of communication and imagination in a society obsessed with commerical values. Her novel *State of Siege* and autobiography *An Angel at My Table* have been successfully adapted as films.

FRANK, Anne
1930-1945
Dutch diarist

Anne Frank's *Diary of a Young Girl* is testimony to the spirit, grace and determination of the Jewish citizens of Europe persecuted by the Nazi regime.

Frank was born in Germany but her family fled to Amsterdam to escape the Nazis. After the German occupation of the Netherlands in 1941, the Frank family was forced to hide in the back rooms of Herr Frank's office and warehouse where they were cared for by a Dutch family that lived below. They were discovered and deported to the Belsen concentration camp, where Anne Frank contracted typhus and died.

All of Frank's family perished in confinement except her father, who was in a hospital at the time of the Auschwitz liberation. Upon his release a friend who had found Anne's diary gave it to him and he arranged for its publication.

Anne Frank confided all of her adolescent aspirations, romantic dreams and longing for freedom in lyrical passages which underscored the deep familial bonds that nurtured her hopes in a desperately dark and repressive era. Over 60 million copies of the diary translated into several languages have been sold.

FRANKENTHALER, Helen
1928-
American painter

Heir to the Abstract Expressionist movement fostered in the 1950s in New York City, Helen Frankenthaler was born there in 1925. She attended the elite private school, Dalton, where she took classes with the Mexican artist Rufino Tamayo, and later graduated from Bennington College in Vermont.

Art critic Clement Greenberg took her to Hans Hoffman's summer school where she saw Jackson Pollock paint. Frankenthaler adapted Pollock's drip style into her own staining technique, creating large-scale, cotton duck canvases poured with brilliant hues of thinned oil pigment that evoke spacious watercolor landscapes filled with light. Her *Mountains and Sea* of 1952 was an early success, and other works, *Eden, Arcadia* and *Arden* suggest pastoral harmony. Of her unusual, brushless method she claimed, "I had the landscape in my arms when I painted it . . . in my mind and shoulder and wrist." Her work was featured in articles in *Time, Life* and *Look* magazines in the early 1960s.

She married the pioneer Abstract Expressionist Robert Motherwell in 1958, joining "the young, lively, active nucleus of an art family". They divorced in 1971. Frankenthaler has had a number of solo exhibitions at major American museums.

FRANKLIN, Aretha
1942-
American singer

The "Queen of Soul," Aretha Franklin was born in Memphis, Tennessee, and went north as a child to Detroit where her father became the pastor of the New Bethel Baptist Church. She soloed there at 12, and cut a few early singles that languished before her first hit song, which she wrote in 1967, called "I Never Loved A Man (The Way I Loved You)". It sold a million records and was followed by four more gold record singles for Atlantic Records the same year, including Otis Redding's "Respect".

Franklin was given a special citation by the Southern Christian Leadership Conference and opened the 1968 Democratic Convention with her version of "The Star-Spangled Banner". A 1968 album full of hit singles such as "Think", "Since You've Been Gone" and "The House That Jack Built" was a huge success. She had been married and divorced twice and had four children by 1970, and in 1971 had more million-record sellers than any other female singer to date. She later returned to gospel music, made several television appearances and married again in 1978. She had several hit records produced by Luther Van Dross in the 1980s and 1990s, and best-selling singles "Freeway of Love" and a George Michaels duet "I Knew You Were Waiting".

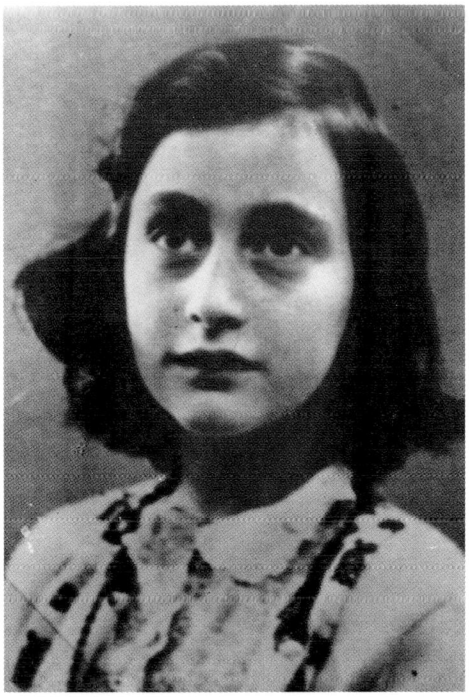

RIGHT: *Anne Frank's* Diary of a Young Girl *movingly juxtaposes the hopes and dreams of an adolescent girl with the horror of the Holocaust.*

BELOW: *Arguably the finest female soul singer, Aretha Franklin's hits include "Respect" and "(You Make Me Feel Like a) Natural Woman."*

FRANKLIN, Rosalind
1920-1958
British crystallographer

Rosalind Franklin's brief but brilliant career as an X-ray crystallographer opened the door to understanding the molecular structure of DNA – the protein building block of living cells. Her earliest research was into the molecular structure of coal, coke, and graphitic carbons. Upon receiving her doctorate from Cambridge, she went to King's College, London to study DNA with Maurice Wilkins in 1951. Within a year, she had announced her discovery that DNA existed in two forms, of which at least one was helical. This major contribution was acknowledged by American James Watson and Englishman Francis Crick when they published their paper on the model of DNA as a double helix in 1953, ushering in the science of molecular biology. However, Dr. Franklin's untimely death, of cancer, in 1958 excluded her from a share in the Nobel Prize for medicine awarded to Watson, Crick, and Wilkins in 1962.

Dawn Fraser was the first woman to swim 100 meters in under one minute.

FRASER, Antonia
1932-
British historian, novelist

An Oxford historian father and biographer mother inspired Lady Fraser's interest in a writing career. Known for her historical biographies, Lady Fraser's first major undertaking was the well-documented study, *Mary Queen of Scots*, which won the James Tait Black Memorial Prize. Other major works include *Royal Charles* and the best-selling study of women's lives in the seventeenth century, *The Weaker Vessel.* Her accounts of British history are gripping and illuminating, and she is praised for her scholarship. Married to playwright Harold Pinter, she is also the author of a series of mystery novels.

FRASER, Dawn
1937-
Australian swimmer

Dawn Fraser is the only woman swimmer to win gold medals in three successive Olympic games in the same event, the 100 meter freestyle in 1956, 1960 and 1964. Born into a large family in Sydney, Fraser was a controversial character who fought with officials and indulged in pranks which earned her a suspension from the Australian Amateur Swimming Association following the 1964 Summer Games.

In a sport that favors very young talent, Fraser did not begin to compete until she was 16 and won her last Olympic gold medal at 27. From 1956 until 1971 she held the world's record in the 100 meter freestyle, reducing her own time on nine occasions. In 1962 she was the first woman to break the one-minute barrier in the 100 meter freestyle. Her determination is proven by her last Olympic victory, which she won just six months after suffering serious injuries in an automobile accident that claimed the life of her mother.

Betty Friedan was co-founder and first president of NOW.

FRENCH, Evangeline and Francesca. *See* CABLE, Mildred

FREUD, Anna
1895-1982
British psychologist

The youngest daughter and one of six children of Sigmund Freud, Anna Freud first studied to be an elementary school teacher. In 1918 she began to attend meetings of the Vienna Psychoanalytical Society, and after analysis (by her father, which was most unusual) she began the private practice of psychoanalysis in 1923, specializing in child analysis. In 1937, before the Freud family fled to

Daughter of Sigmund Freud, Anna Freud developed a school of Freudian child psychoanalysis in London.

England to escape Nazi persecution, she published *The Ego and the Mechanisms of Defense*, the cornerstone of what became the ego psychology movement. She joined the British Psychoanalytic Society and did major humanitarian and scientific work during World War II at the Hampstead War Nursery for homeless children, which she founded with Dorothy Burlingham. Anna Freud went on to become the most honored woman psychologist of her time and the recognized authority on psychoanalytic child psychology.

FRIEDAN, Betty
1921-
American feminist, author, elderly rights advocate

Initially dissuaded from her efforts to describe honestly the pressures on American women to adhere to traditional gender roles, Betty Friedan ignored her critics and the publication of *The Feminine Mystique* in 1963 propelled her into world celebrity.

A leading spokeswoman for the burgeoning modern feminist movement, she co-founded with Gloria Steinem the National Organization of Women (NOW) and was its first president. In 1968 she co-founded the forerunner to the National Association for Repeal of the Abortion Law (NARAL).

She was named a Distinguished Visiting Professor at the Institute for the Study of Men and Women at the University of Southern California in 1988. Having devoted a majority of her writing career to gender issues, she has recently turned her attention to the plight of the elderly in her new book, *The Fountain of Age*.

FURNESS, Betty
1916-1994
American actress, broadcast journalist, consumer advisor

Elizabeth Mary Choate was born in New York City, and began modeling during summer vacations from Bennett Junior College. She was given a screen test by RKO, which led to a career in Hollywood for five years. She appeared in 35 films, but felt only two of them had been worthwhile, *Swing Time* (1936) and *Magnificent Obsession*. She returned to New York in 1948, having appeared on stage in many touring shows, and came in on the ground floor of television. Westinghouse hired her as an on-camera demonstrator in 1949, and the following year she was making $100,000 per year and had become one of the most recognized women in the world. Her work for Westinghouse during the political conventions of 1952, 1956 and 1960 led to an interest in politics and public affairs, which became part of her panel show *At Your Beck and Call* (1961) and her radio program from 1962 to 1967. In 1964 she worked for the Johnson presidential campaign, and in 1967 she became the Special Assistant to the President for Consumer Affairs. In the 1970s she joined *Today* as a consumer specialist, a position she held until the 1990s.

FURTSEVA, Ekaterina Alexeyevna
1909?-1974
Soviet government official

Ekaterina Furtseva became the only woman to rise to the Kremlin's inner circle. Born in Vyshniy Volochek to a family of textile workers, she was politicized in the Communist Youth movement. In 1937 she graduated as a chemical engineer, and began her rise in the Communist Party, assisted by Nikita Khrushchev, then-first secretary of the Moscow oblast, a position Furtseva held in 1955. In 1950, she was elected a deputy to the Supreme Soviet. In 1954 she was charged with overseeing the build-up of the city's infrastructure. By 1956 her staunch loyalty and ability to get things done had earned her tremendous respect. Khrushchev had become head of the Communist Party, and she was elected alternative member of the Praesidium, becoming the most powerful woman in the Soviet Union. In 1960 she was made Minister of Culture, a position she held until her death.

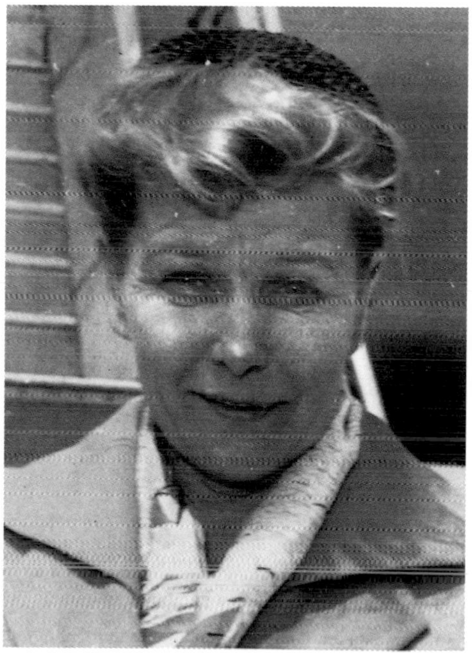

Ekaterina Furtseva was Soviet Minister of Culture from 1960 until her death in 1974.

G

GAIDINLIU, Rani
1915-
Indian freedom fighter

Daughter of poor farmers, Gaidinliu is remembered for her fierce leadership of the Naga guerrillas against the British colonial soldiers. At the age of 16, she led her forces against the British in a bitter battle that led to her arrest and life imprisonment. However, in 1947, India achieved independence and President Jawaharlal Nehru released her. She later became a social worker in Nagaland.

GANDHI, Indira
1917-1984
Indian prime minister, politician

Four-time prime minister Indira Gandhi, daughter of Jawarhalal Nehru, India's first prime minster, grew up surrounded by the men and women who led India's freedom struggle. From 1947 until 1964 she was acting First Lady. Named President of the Congress Party in 1959, she established her reputation as politically astute in her own right. In 1966 she was chosen as Prime Minister by the Congress Party. She made India a force to be reckoned with as she strived to lead the country, independent since 1946, into the modern age through economic development, nuclear and space research and socialism. Yet in 1975 she betrayed many of the democratic ideals she had espoused when she declared martial law. As a result, she was defeated in the 1977 elections, but was reinstated two years later. She was assassinated in 1984 by two of her Sikh bodyguards, just four months after responding to unrest in the Punjab by permitting an attack on a sacred shrine of the Sikhs.

ABOVE: *Indira Gandhi served as prime minister of India from 1966 to 1977 and 1979 to 1984.*
BELOW: *Actress Greta Garbo's reclusiveness added to her legend.*

GARBO, Greta
1905-1990
Swedish actress

Greta Lovisa Gustafson was born in Stockholm, and left school at the age of 13 to get work. One of her jobs put her in a publicity short which led to a part in *Peter the Tramp* (1922). The film won her a scholarship at the Swedish Royal Dramatic Theater Academy, where she met director Mauritz Stiller. Stiller cast and directed her in *The Story of Gösta Berling* (1924), the film which took them both to Hollywood. Stiller was not a successful import, but his protégé, who photographed magnificently, was. She made several silent films in the 1920s, including *Flesh and the Devil* (1927) with John Gilbert. Their love scenes and Garbo's beauty made her a star. She made the transition to talkies easily, and in the next decade she made a series of films that continue to be classics, including *Grand Hotel* (1932), *Queen Christina* (1933), *Anna Karenina* (1935), and *Ninotchka* (1939), her only comedy. The war had lost her studio, M-G-M, the profits of European distribution, and her next film which proved to be her last, *Two-Faced Woman* (1941) was not a success. Her mystique and reclusiveness ensured her lasting fame.

Judy Garland was nominated for an Academy Award for A Star is Born *(1954).*

GARLAND, Judy
1922-1969
American actress, singer

Judy Garland was born Frances Gumm in Grand Rapids, Michigan. She lived out of a trunk, trouping along with her parent's vaudeville act and singing with her two older sisters until Louis B. Mayer signed her up and christened her Judy Garland.

Her first film was a two-reeler with Deanna Durbin in 1936, *Every Sunday*, followed by a costarring role with Mickey Rooney in *Love Finds Andy Hardy* in 1938. When M-G-M could not get Shirley Temple for *The Wizard of Oz* (1939), Garland stepped into the role of Dorothy that made her a star of one of America's most popular films. She won a special Oscar for "Over the Rainbow".

The destructive cycle of pep pills and sedatives had begun, but Garland's mother pushed her to continue performing. She became M-G-M's number one box office star, teaming up with Rooney in a series of films, and scoring several blockbuster hits: *For Me and My Gal* with Gene Kelly (1942); *Meet Me in St. Louis* (1944); *Easter Parade* with Fred Astaire (1948). She earned an Oscar nomination for *A Star Is Born* in 1954 and a second nomination, for *Judgment in Nuremberg* in 1961, the same year of an historic Carnegie Hall concert. She was found dead of a barbituate overdose in her London flat in 1969.

GIBSON, Althea
1927-
American tennis player

Althea Gibson broke through the race barrier of the elite tennis world in the 1950s to become the first black U.S. champion and the first black Wimbledon champion. Born and raised in Silver, North Carolina, she was the singles champion of the black American Tennis Association for ten years from 1947 to 1957 and went on to significant victories on the international tour.

Gibson won the French and Italian championships in 1956 and the French and Wimbledon women's doubles the same year. In 1957 and 1958 she conquered the U.S. women's singles and doubles championships both years. The Women's Sports Hall of Fame elected her to membership in 1980.

GINSBURG, Ruth Bader
1933-
American lawyer, U.S. Supreme Court Justice

Ruth Bader Ginsburg's Supreme Court appointment by President Clinton in 1993 was confirmed by an almost unanimous (96-3) Senate vote, attesting both to the essentially centrist positions she took as a judge on the federal appeals court in Washington and to her work as a pioneering feminist attorney. Born in Brooklyn, New York, she graduated from Cornell (1954) and then followed her husband into law school, first at Harvard (1956-58) and then Columbia (1959), where she later became that school's first tenured female professor. Founder of the American Civil Liberties Union's Women's Rights Project, she was a liberal advocate for women's rights as an attorney in the 1970s, with strong positions on sex discrimination and the individual's right to abortion. She was distinguished for persuasive reasoning and benchmark decisions in her 13 years of service on the court of appeals prior to becoming the second woman to serve on the Supreme Court. (*See also* O'CONNOR, Sandra Day.)

GIROUD, Françoise
1916-
French journalist, government official

A high school dropout at 15, Françoise Giroud became a renowned author and social reformer within the French government. After release from a Nazi concentration camp, she conquered severe depression and became the editor of *Elle* (1945-52), co-founder and editor of the popular news weekly *L'Express* (1953-71), and director and president of *L'Express-Union* (1970-74). Highly respected for her shrewd interviews of high officials and her eloquent descriptions of the issues facing women, she became the first Secretary of State for the Condition of Women. In 1976 she was appointed Secretary of Culture. She returned to media and in 1979 became director of the *Revue du Temps Libre* (1979), and President of the Commission to Improve Cinema Ticket Sales (1989). She has written several screenplays and books, including her autobiography *I Give You My Word* (1953), and in 1993 co-authored a best-selling book on the differences between men and women in matters of the heart.

Ruth Bader Ginsburg is the second woman to serve as U.S. Supreme Court Justice.

GISH, Lillian
1893-1993
American actress

Lillian Gish began acting on stage when she was five and in 1910, through the aid of Mary Pickford, was introduced to film director D.W. Griffith. She made a number of brilliant films with him, including *The Birth of a Nation* (1915), *Broken Blossoms* (1916), *Way Down East* (1920), and *Orphans of the Storm* (1922). In the 1920s, she was signed to a contract by M-G-M who starred her in *The Scarlet Letter* (1926), *La Boheme* (1926) and *The Wind* (1928), her final silent. She made the transition to sound with no trouble, but a change in the style of movies being made sent her back to the stage. She appeared in *Uncle Vanya*, and *Camille*, and played Ophelia to John Gielgud's Hamlet. In her occasional later film roles, like *Duel in the Sun* (1946), *The Night of the Hunter* (1958) and *The Comedians* (1967), she continued to enchant moviegoers, as she did in her final film, *The Whales of August* (1987). She received a special Academy Award in 1970, and the Lifetime Achievement Award from the American Film Institute in 1984.

Lillian Gish (right) with her sister Dorothy in Orphans of the Storm *(1922).*

GOEPPERT-MAYER, Maria
1906-1972
Polish-born American physicist

Born in Katowice, Poland (then Kattowitz, Germany), Maria Goeppert earned a doctorate in physics from the University of Göttingen in 1930. A year later she married Joseph Mayer, an American physical chemist, and they moved to the United States, where they worked at Johns Hopkins University on the study of organic molecules and the separation of uranium isotopes. In 1939 the couple joined the chemistry department at Columbia University, and they moved to the University of Chicago in 1946. Goeppert-Mayer was best known for her work in quantum electrodynamics, spectroscopy, and crystal physics. She was the first American woman to win the Nobel Prize for physics (1963), which she shared with German scientist J.H.D. Jensen and Eugene Wigner of Princeton University.

GOLDMAN, Emma
1869-1940
American anarchist, women's rights advocate

Emma Goldman was a passionate campaigner for social equality. A Jew born in Russia, she emigrated to New York in 1886 where she worked in sweatshops. The hanging of the Haymarket Anarchists (who were organizing for labor rights) fed her interest in anarchy. In 1889 she met Alexander Berkman, her lover and long-time associate. As an anarchist, she believed that authority smothered people's ability to think, speak or act out of their deepest selves. During the Pittsburgh Steel Strike of 1892, she was charged with and imprisoned for attempting to kill steel magnate Henry Frick. For years she wrote, travelled and lectured about anarchism and labor rights, organizing support for labor struggles around the country. She was jailed during World War I for organizing against the conscription, and then deported to the Soviet Union in 1919. Openly critical of the Soviet Union's totalitarian government, Goldman spent the next 20 years travelling around the world, supporting anti-fascist causes.

GONCHAROVA, Natalya
1881-1962
Russian painter

Born into a distinguished family from central Russia, Goncharova joined abstract modernists such as Kandinsky, Pevsner and Chagall who fled to France during the Russian revolution in the 1920s.

Her work was based on colors and

Jane Goodall at the Gombe Stream Research Center in Nigeria, where she has been studying chimpanzee behavior for more than two decades.

shapes akin to icons found in Russian folk paintings, and she developed a theory called Rayonism in which shafts of light emanated from objects. Her canvases were noted for their bold outlines and dynamic movement. She also designed sets and costumes for Serge Diaghilev and the Ballet Russes including sets for *Le Coq D'Or, Les Noces* and *The Firebird*. She had a large retrospective in Paris in 1914 and was treated with equality among her male contemporaries.

She settled in Ouchy, France, in 1917 among her friends, Igor Stravinsky and the artist Mikhail Larionov. She married Larionov, her lifelong partner, on her 74th birthday.

GONNE MACBRIDE, Maud
1865-1953
Irish revolutionary

Tired of being told that only men could fight for Irish independence, Maud Gonne founded the revolutionary Inghindidhe na hEireann (Daughters of Erin) on Easter Sunday 1900. They organized massive demonstrations, one of which was the largest Dublin had ever seen. She first became involved in the nationalist cause when she saw Irish tenants carelessly evicted by landlords who wanted their land for cattle raising, and led protests against these evictions in Donegal. In the 1890s she traveled to Europe and the United States speaking out on the Irish cause and raising funds. An inspiration to many of her countrymen, including poet W. B. Yeats who wrote many of his love poems with her in mind, she told her story in *A Servant of the Queen* (1938).

GOODALL, Jane
1934-
British zoologist

Jane Goodall has been described as the founding mother of ethology – the scientific study of the behavior of animals in the wild. She was an ardent naturalist from childhood and fulfilled her ambition of going to Africa at the age of 23. In Kenya, she became secretary to anthropologist Louis Leakey, who encouraged her to study chimpanzees. Her projected three-month study at Tanzania's Gombe Stream Reserve became a six-year stay, interrupted only by six terms at Cambridge University working toward a doctorate (although she had no undergraduate degree). In 1964 Goodall married Dutch photographer Baron Hugo van Lawick, who shared her passion for animals. Together, the couple established the Gombe Stream Research Centre, in which Goodall is still active at this writing.

South African novelist Nadine Gordimer won the 1991 Nobel Prize for literature for her anti-apartheid fiction.

GOOLAGONG CAWLEY, Evonne
1951-
Australian tennis player

A lanky and graceful athlete, Goolagong was born of Aborigine heritage. Goolagong took Wimbledon by storm when she won the 1971 women's singles title. She was already a star in Australia, having garnered 42 regional and national age-group titles. In 1971 Goolagong also won the French Open and the Australian Open women's doubles with Margaret COURT. She won the Italian Open in 1973 and the Australian Open singles from 1974 to 1977 as well as the Virginia Slims Championship in 1974 and 1976.

She married, retired from the circuit and had her first child in 1976, but she returned to win Wimbledon again in 1980. This victory matched Bill Tilden's record for the longest gap between Wimbledon singles championships.

GORDIMER, Nadine
1923-
South African writer

The 1991 winner of the Nobel Prize for literature whose fiction is fueled by anti-apartheid sentiment, Nadine Gordimer's books were banned for several years in her native South Africa. Gordimer's writing examines the customs, rituals and superstitions that separate blacks and whites in an imperialist society, and she is particularly sympathetic to the special burdens borne by black women. Her novels include *The Lying Days* (1953), *The Conservationist* (1975), *Burger's Daughter* (1979), *July's People* (1981), and *None to Accompany Me* (1994). The publication of her critically acclaimed short story collection *Jump and Other Stories* coincided with the announcement of her receipt of the Nobel Prize. A white South African, Gordimer has been politically active, speaking out against press censorship, helping found the Congress of South African Writers (98 percent of its members are black) and supporting the Department of Arts and Culture of the African National Congress (ANC).

Steffi Graf stands second only to Martina Navratilova in career earnings.

GRAF, Steffi
1969-
German tennis player

In 1988 Steffi Graf became the third woman to win the Grand Slam. She also collected an Olympic gold medal at Seoul and began a streak of victories that would keep her number one ranking for a record 160 consecutive weeks. In 1989 Graf lost only the French Open of the Grand Slam and was named the Associated Press Female Athlete of the Year and the Women's Sports Foundation Professional Sportswoman of the Year. In 1991 she won her third Wimbledon victory and became the youngest player, at 22, to win more than 500 tour victories. Graf won her fourth Wimbledon victory in 1992. She won the French Open, Wimbledon, and the U.S. Open in 1993 and the Australian Open in 1994. She stands second to Martina NAVRATILOVA in career earnings, listed at over $13 million, and in 1994 was the number one-ranked player on the tour.

GRAHAM, Katherine
1917-
American newspaper proprietor

Katherine Meyer was born in New York and educated at Vassar College and the University of Chicago. In 1938 she began her career in journalism as a reporter on the *San Francisco News*. The following year she joined the editorial staff of the *Washington Post*, the small paper her father bought in 1933. He sold her all his voting stock in 1948, when she married. Graham was president and publisher of the Washington Post Company, whose holdings eventually included *Newsweek*, *Art News*, the *International Herald-Tribune*, and several television and radio stations, until 1978. This time included the Watergate era, during which two young *Post* reporters, Carl Bernstein and Bob Woodward, followed up a seemingly innocuous story about a break-in at the Democratic headquarters. Mrs. Graham supported their investigation, even while being pressured by government officials. Today she is still the chairman and CEO of the company, and is considered one of the most influential women in the United States.

GRAHAM, Martha
1894-1991
American dancer, choreographer, teacher

Martha Graham was born in Pittsburgh and later moved to California where she pursued a dance career despite strong parental opposition. She appeared with The Greenwich Village Follies in 1926 and founded her own company, the Martha Graham School of Contemporary Dance.

Graham was a challenging, dramatic personality whose methods were described as "stark, gymnastic and intellectual" as she stripped away all but the essentials of stage production and movement. She emphasized percussive and angular techniques, performing to musical scores by Aaron Copland such as "Appalachian Spring" with strikingly simplified decor by the sculptor, Isamu Noguchi. Graham embraced Greek mythology, American heroism and exotic, oriental influences. She continued to dance until well into her late sixties. Several significant dances she choreographed were *Clytemnestra, Frontier, Night Journey, Judith* (which premiered in Israel in 1962), *Seraphic Dialogue* and *Acrobats of God*, a work based on the trials of the dance studio.

GRASSO, Ella
1919-1981
American politician

In 1978 Ella Tambussi Grasso became governor of Connecticut, the first woman to be elected governor without following on her husband's heels. She began her political career during World War II as assistant director of research for the Federal War Manpower Commission, became Connecticut's Secretary of State (1959-70), and in 1975 won election as governor in a landslide victory. As a politician, she earned a reputation as an old-time politician who knew how to listen carefully to people's pressing concerns. As governor, she faced Connecticut's huge deficit, and by enforcing strict austerity measures she managed to get the state into the black without instating an income tax. She was forced to resign because of debilitating cancer, of which she died.

LEFT: *Katherine Graham.*

The grande dame of modern dance, Martha Graham was principal dancer of her school for decades, and trained many eminent dancers and choreographers.

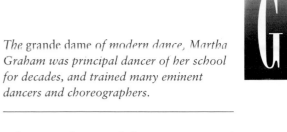

GRAVES, Nancy
1940-
American sculptor

Life-size Bactrian camels made up of wood and steel armatures, covered with skins and tinted with oil paint, were the highlight of Nancy Graves's first solo show at the Whitney Museum in 1969 and they created a sensation in the art world. Graves's fascination with the fields of anatomy, biology and archaeology was derived from her childhood in Pittsfield, Massachusetts, where her father was a director of the local art and natural science museum.

Graves graduated from Vassar College, received her MFA at Yale and went to Paris as a Fulbright Scholar. After extensive travels to Italy, North Africa and the Near East, she returned to New York and began constructing sculptures with bones, found objects and abstract totems akin to the fetishes of tribal societies. In the 1980s Graves began to employ all manner of organic and mechanical pieces in her bright-colored, bronze assemblages: flowers, ferns, dead frogs, potato chips, corrugated paper and twisted metal flanges appear in her lyrical airborne configurations. Her *Tarot* of 1984 suggests magic and rituals with its fanciful array of oriental fans, sleek white branches, coiling wire tubing and jellyfish forms. Graves has had solo exhibitions at major American museums, and her work is represented in several important international collections.

GRAY, Eileen
1879-1976
Irish furniture designer, architect

Eileen Gray was born in Wexford, Ireland, and studied at the Slade School of Art in London before moving to Paris in 1902. She practiced lacquer techniques in Soho, London, and later apprenticed with the designer Sugawara in Paris. In 1913 she exhibited her own furniture at the Salon des Artistes Decorateurs patronized by the preeminent collectors Jacques Doucet and Madame Mathieu Levy. Her style was a departure from the Art Deco flourishes then in favor to a more streamlined, architectural form.

In 1922 Gray opened "Jean Desert", a furniture showroom in Paris to market her lacquered screens, lamps, carpets, wall hangings and original furnishings. Her work was not popular with French critics but was admired by the DeStijl architect Jacobus Ord as well as the preeminent modern architect Le Corbusier, whose designs influenced her. Encouraged to practice architecture, she planned a house at Roquebourne with Jean Badorici as well as his studio in Paris in 1931 and Tempe A Pailla near Menton. Her models for a vacation center appeared with Le Corbusier's projects in his pavillion at the Paris exhibition in 1937. Her final effort was a masterplan for a cultural and social center in Paris. She died there in 1976.

GRAY, Hanna Holborn
1930-
American educator

Ambitious, self-confident and goal-directed, Hanna Gray rose through the ranks of leading American universities to achieve prominence in academic administration. She broke precedent when she became the first non-Yale graduate to hold its Provostship. She successfully maneuvered the university through a major fiscal deficit and was a leading candidate for its presidency in 1977.

In 1978 she became the first female president of the University of Chicago and the first female president of a major co-educational university. Her primary concern was maintaining academic excellence. During her 15-year tenure, she sought increased teaching and administrative opportunities for women. A Presidential Medal of Freedom recipient in 1991, she resigned from her position at Chicago in 1993, and returned to teaching in the History Department.

G

GREER, Germaine
1939-
Australian feminist, writer

Germaine Greer was thrust into the public eye in 1970 with the publication of her book *The Female Eunuch*. This landmark feminist work analyzed female sexual stereotyping and surveyed the various forms of female subordination.

After earning her Ph.D. at Cambridge in 1981, she spent several months in India researching a book on the politics of human fertility. This work led to *Sex and Destiny: The Politics of Human Fertility*. Familiar on the British talk show circuit, she is deemed a witty and combative adversary. She has also worked as a columnist with the *Sunday Times*. In 1991 she published *The Change: Women, Aging and the Menopause* in which she criticized society for its emphasis on youth and beauty.

GREGORY, Lady Augusta
1859-1932
Irish playwright

Lady Augusta Gregory left her imprint on the Irish stage as a gifted playwright, theatre manager and patron of the arts.

A widow, she befriended W.B. Yeats in 1895, and her home at Coole Park became the center of the Irish Renaissance. Gregory, Yeats and J.M. Synge founded the Abbey Theatre in 1904, whch she managed with great success from 1909 until the end of her life. In more than 40 plays, including *Spreading the News*, *Kincora*, and *The Workhouse Ward*, Lady Gregory charmed audiences with her knack for comic storytelling, at the same time as the Irish folklore and country customs she preserved fed the nationalist pride of her beleaguered homeland.

GUGGENHEIM, Peggy
1898-1979
American philanthropist, art collector

Born in New York and privately educated, Peggy Guggenheim went to Europe and to its many art galleries with her family every year as a child. She returned to Europe on her own after World War I, and stayed for 21 years. In 1938 she opened a gallery, Guggenheim Jeune, in London. The first exhibition was of works by Jean Cocteau, and she later sponsored one-man shows for Yves Tanguy and Vasily Kandinsky. She made a habit of buying one work from each show, which became the basis of her collection. The gallery was not a financial success, so she planned to start a museum. The day World War II was declared, she went to France determined to buy at least one work each day, which she did until she was sent back to the United States in 1941. In 1942 she opened Art of This Century, her New York gallery, and gave one-man shows to a number of avant-garde and Abstract Expressionist painters such as Robert Motherwell and Jackson Pollock. In the 1950s she returned to Europe, finally opening her museum in Venice. She continued to collect and sponsor artists, and was one of the first to show an interest in collecting Pre-Columbian art.

GUTHRIE, Janet
1938-
American auto racer

Janet Guthrie was born in Iowa City, Iowa, the daughter of an Eastern Airlines pilot. She got her pilot's license at 17. After receiving a degree in physics from the University of Michigan in 1960 she became an aerospace engineer on Long Island. She began rebuilding Jaguar racing cars and entered driving school. In 1968 she won the Governor of Florida's Award in the Sebring race there. In the early 1970s she began rebuilding and racing Toyotas, entering the 1972 Toyota 2.5 Challenge Series and winning the North Atlantic Road Racing Championship in 1973. She did not race again until a patron offered her a car for the Indy 500 in 1976. She withdrew before the event because of mechanical difficulties but made history the following year by becoming the first woman to qualify for the race. In 1978, racing with a broken wrist, she was sponsored by Texaco in the Indy 500 and finished ninth overall.

Feminist Germaine Greer's The Female Eunuch *(1970) was one of the landmarks of the "sexual revolution."*

HALE, Clara (Mother)
1906-1993
American child care worker

Mother Hale, the founder of Hale House in Harlem, New York, dedicated almost 25 years to nurturing 1,000 babies born drug-addicted or with HIV. Born in Elizabeth City, North Carolina, she married Thomas Hale and lived in New York City, where she did domestic work. Widowed at 27, she began caring for children for two dollars a week. She became a licensed foster parent in 1940, and raised 40 children over the course of four decades. She was 64 when her daughter encouraged a drug-addicted young woman to bring her baby to Mother Hale. She nursed the baby through withdrawal, asking for no money from the mother. Within six months Mother Hale had 22 drug-addicted babies in her care, and Hale House was born. In 1985 President Ronald Reagan hailed her as an American hero; she saw herself simply as a person who loved children.

HALL, Radclyffe
1883?-1943
British novelist, poet

Radclyffe Hall's literary achievements have been overshadowed by the controversy her life itself generated. From the age of 21 when she inherited her grandfather's wealth and therefore gained her independence, Hall immersed herself in the literary world, producing her first volume of poetry in 1907. Three more books of poems followed, a volume of short stories, and several novels, including the award-winning *Adam's Breed* in 1926. She is best remembered for her 1928 novel *The Well of Loneliness*, an explicit portrayal of lesbian life in Paris in the 1920s. Rather than garnering public sympathy, as she had hoped, Hall was condemned for obscenity in a public trial, and the book was banned in her native England and in America. In her personal life as in her writing, Hall challenged the conventions of her time.

Radclyffe Hall in 1927, the year before her controversial book The Well of Loneliness *was banned following charges of obscenity.*

HAMER, Fannie Lou
1917-1977
American civil rights activist

Discerning a link between the poverty of Mississippi blacks and their lack of access to the political process, Fannie Lou Hamer spent her life fighting for democracy for black people.

The youngest of 20 children of Mississippi sharecroppers, she worked as a girl and young woman as a cotton sharecropper and had no formal education. An active member in the Student Nonviolent Coordinating Committee, she became their field secretary in 1963. From then on, she worked on voter registration drives and on programs to aid the deprived blacks in Mississippi.

In 1964 she co-founded the Mississippi Freedom Democratic Party (MFDP), a predominantly black independent political party. As member of the MFDP's delegation at the Democratic National Convention in New Jersey, she stirringly challenged Mississippi's Democratic Party's all-white delegation for not representing the state's 50 percent black population. She returned to the Democratic Convention as a delegate in 1968, and in 1969 she founded the Freedom Farms Corporation, designed to help poor families grow crops and raise livestock.

She opposed the American military policy in Vietnam and was elected to the Central Committee of the National Women's Political Caucus in 1971.

HAMILTON, Edith
1865-1963
American classicist

Best known for her popular compendium of Greek tales entitled *Mythology*, Hamilton was born in Dresden, Germany, and raised in Fort Wayne, Indiana. After completing her undergraduate and graduate degrees at Bryn Mawr College, she had a distinguished teaching career. She was the first woman admitted to the University of Munich in 1895.

In 1930, at the age of 62, she wrote *The Greek Way*, a text that established her as a prominent classical scholar. *The Roman Way* followed in 1933. *Mythology* was published in 1940. King Paul of Greece bestowed upon her the Golden Cross of the Order of Benefaction and made her an honorary citizen of Athens in 1957.

Fannie Lou Hamer addresses delegates at the 1968 Democratic Convention.

Jean Harlow capitalized on her sexy image in 1930s Hollywood.

HAMNETT, Katherine
1952-
British fashion designer

Born in Gravesend, Kent, the daughter of a diplomat, Katherine Hamnett attended Cheltenham Ladies College, and studied fashion at St. Martin's School of Art in London. She worked as a freelance designer, setting up a short-lived company, Tuttabanken, before starting her own company in 1979. She draws inspiration for her designs from workclothes, and from the various movements that she supports, including the peace movement, and the women's anti-nuclear movement, which inspired her oversize T-shirts, printed with statements such as "Stop Acid Rain." She has recently moved into the area of menswear as well.

HANSBERRY, Lorraine
1930-1965
American playwright

The only black dramatist to be awarded Best Play of the Year by the New York Drama Critics, which she won at 29 for her 1959 play *A Raisin in the Sun*, Lorraine Hansberry was born on the south side of Chicago. When she and her family moved into the affluent neighborhood of Hyde Park, they were taunted and physically threatened and later evicted. Her father, a real estate broker, hired NAACP lawyers to plead their case and the Supreme Court voted a landmark decision in their favor.

Elements of this experience were portrayed in *A Raisin in the Sun*. The Broadway production, starring Sidney Poitier, Ruby Dee and Diana Sands, was a critical and financial success, but it was staged only after Hansberry raised money herself to put the play in theaters in New Haven, Philadelphia and Chicago. It became a popular Hollywood film in 1961. Hansberry died of cancer at 34 when her second play, *The Sign in Sidney Brustein's Window*, was in production on Broadway. Her autobiographical *To Be Young, Gifted and Black* was produced off-Broadway in 1969, and the Broadway production of *Les Blancs* was voted Best American Play in 1970.

HARLOW, Jean
1911-1937
American actress

She was born Harlean Carpenter in Kansas City, Missouri, and moved to California when she was ten. In 1928, and recently married, she was persuaded to register with Central Casting. She soon began to appear in small parts in many Hal Roach comedies, but made her first real impact as the love interest in Howard Hughes's World War I flying epic, *Hell's Angels* (1930). This was the first film to exploit her particular sensuality and striking beauty. She also appeared in such films as *Platinum Blonde* (1931), *Public Enemy* (1931), *Red Dust* (1932) and *Dinner at Eight* (1933). By the age of 22, she was a top box-office star, whose bias-cut wardrobe, platinum blonde hair and narrow eyebrows were widely copied by her fans. In *Bombshell* (1933) she even mocked her own image. She died suddenly of uremic poisoning at the age of 26 while shooting *Saratoga* (1937). The film was completed with a double.

HARRIS, Emmylou
1947-
American singer

Born in Birmingham, Alabama, Harris chose a medley of folk music for her early Greenwich Village club performances. Reprise Records offered her a contract, and she produced a mix of original rock and roll songs with a country flavor on *Pieces of the Sky* (1975). *Elite Hotel* (1976) won a Grammy for best performance by a country singer and had two hit singles, "Sweet Dreams" and "One of These Days".

Harris's work from the late 1970s into the 1990s included successful collaborations with other country music singers and songwriters. She recorded a version of Loretta LYNN's "Blue Kentucky Girl"; "To Daddy", a Dolly PARTON composition; "Together Again" with Buck Owens; "That Loving You Feeling Again" with Roy Orbison; "If I Needed You" with Don Williams; and "Mister Sandman" with Dolly Parton and Linda Ronstadt. Her albums include *Roses in the Snow, Light of the Stable, Cimarron, Last Date*, and *Cowgirl's Prayer*. Her mellifluous vocal style suits a varied repertoire from country ballads to honky-tonk to rock and roll.

HARRIS, Patricia Roberts
1924-1985
American lawyer, government official

Patricia Roberts Harris was the first woman to hold two U.S. Cabinet positions. Always confident of her abilities despite economic hardships and blatant racism in the neighborhood in which she was raised, she excelled in all her activities. After a career in human resources, she studied law, graduating first in her class in 1960. In 1961, she was named associate dean of students and law lecturer at Howard University, and by 1969 had become the dean of the Howard University Law School, the first woman to head a law school in the United States. From 1977 to 1979 she served as the Secretary of Housing and Urban Development, followed by service as the Secretary of the Department of Health, Education and Welfare (1979-81). In 1982 she ran for mayor of Washington, D.C., but lost to Marion S. Barry, Jr.

HAYES, Helen
1900-1993
American actress

Helen Hayes Brown was born in Washington, D.C., and made her professional debut at 5, her Broadway debut in *Old Dutch* at 9, and her first film, *Jean and the Calico Doll*, at the age of 10. She continued to work in both mediums into the 1970s, appearing on stage in plays

Helen Hayes as the Queen in the 1935-36 Broadway production of Victoria Regina.

that ranged from Barrie's *Dear Brutus* (1918) and Anderson's *Mary of Scotland* (1933-34) to Anita Loos' *Happy Birthday* (1946), for which she won one of her Tony awards. Her best known stage role was as the Queen in *Victoria Regina* (1935-36). She could play comedy in *What Every Woman Knows* (which she performed in three different decades) and drama in *The Glass Menagerie* (which she also performed in three different decades). She won the Academy Award for her first film as an adult, *The Sin of Madelon Claudet* (1931), and for her last, *Airport* (1970). In the 1970s and 1980s she also appeared on television. She even won a Grammy in 1976 for her recording of The Bill of Rights. Honored by a Lifetime Achievement Tony in 1980, she was also the recipient of the Presidential Medal of Freedom and the Kennedy Center Honors. She even had two Broadway theaters named after her. She was, in short, the First Lady of the American Theater.

HEAD, Bessie
1937-1986
South African novelist, short story writer

One of Africa's most famous writers, Bessie Head offers a persistent message of hope, even as she plumbs the depths of personal pain and ambiguity. Her novels, stories and historical chronicles speak out against apartheid and all forms of discrimination, just as they resist madness and loss of identity.

Born in a mental hospital, where her wealthy white mother was confined for the "madness" of becoming pregnant by a Zulu worker, Head was raised by a colored foster family. A teacher and journalist, she fled South Africa for Botswana in 1964. For the rest of her life she taught, wrote and worked with other political refugees at Bamangwato Development Farm. From her first novel, *When Rain Clouds Gather*, in 1969, to her last work *A Bewitched Crossroad: An African Saga* in 1984, each of her six books added to her vision.

HEAD, Edith
1907-1981
American costume designer

Edith Head received 32 Academy Award nominations for her costume designs for films and won eight Oscars. She was raised in mining camps in Arizona and Nevada where her father was an engineer. Her career was launched when she took her fashion sketches to the studio designer at Paramount. She became the chief costume designer there in 1938, the first woman to achieve this position. In her heyday, her clothes appeared in as many as 35 pictures a year. She dressed Barbara Stanwyck in *A Lady Eve*, Ginger ROGERS in *Lady in the Park* and Ingrid BERGMAN in *For Whom the Bell Tolls*. Her range of styles varied from Spanish ponchos to full-length mink dresses to denim blue jeans and overalls.

Her first Oscar was for Olivia de Havilland's period attire in *The Heiress* in 1949. Her Oscars for costume design were for *Samson and Delilah* (1950), *All About Eve* (1950), *A Place in the Sun* (1951), *Roman Holiday* (1953), *Sabrina* (1954), *The Facts of Life* (1960), and *The Sting* (1974).

Edith Head with costumes for The Sting.

HEALY, Bernadine P.
1944-
American health administrator, cardiologist

In 1991 Bernadine P. Healy became the first female director of the National Institutes of Health (NIH). The directorship had been open for a year and a half and the organization was bogged down in conflict. With her long career in science policy as well as experience in medicine and research, it was hoped that she could solve the problems of one of the world's premier biomedical-research facilities. Healy was born in New York City, graduated from Vassar College and Harvard Medical School (MD 1970), and became a professor at Johns Hopkins School of Medicine (1976-84). After a brief stint at the White House Office of Science and Technology Policy, Healy headed the research efforts of the Cleveland Clinic Foundation (1985-91) and also served as president of the American Heart Association (1988-89). Ousted in the first weeks of the Clinton administration, she could count among her accomplishments the $625 million Women's Health Initiative project and a new strategic plan for NIH.

HEARST, Patricia
1954-
American kidnap victim, convicted bank robber

An heiress to the Hearst family's media fortune, Patty became notorious in 1974 when she was kidnapped from her California apartment and indoctrinated into the revolutionary Symbionese Liberation Army (SLA). For several months the nation was fascinated by her situation – was she a victim or a willing accomplice?

While held captive, Hearst emerged as "Tania", denounced her family and pledged allegiance to SLA. She participated in the armed robbery of a San Francisco bank. After several months underground, she was arrested. Despite the efforts of renowned attorney F. Lee Bailey, she was convicted of armed robbery and sentenced to seven years in federal prison.

In 1979, under clemency order by President Jimmy Carter, she was released from prison. Two months later, she married her former bodyguard, Bernard Shaw. In her book *Every Secret Thing*, she recounts her ordeal.

HEBERT, Anne
1916-
French-Canadian poet, novelist

Anne Hebert's novels and poems are simultaneously rooted in her native Quebec – the historical events, the details of the land itself – and reaching into the supernatural provinces of vampires, fairy tale creatures and ambiguous deaths.

Born into a literary family, her powerful stark writing has drawn good reviews since the publication of her first book of poetry in 1942. She gained fame with her passionate 1970 novel *Kamouraska* (later filmed), which unearthed a 1839 scandal of murder and adultery, and helped to establish a *quebecois* genre of novels. In 1982 she won the Prix Femina in France for her volume of poetry, *In the Shadow of the Wind*.

HELLMAN, Lillian
1906?-1984
American playwright, memoirist

New Orleans-born playwright Lillian Hellman's gripping dramas set a new standard for Broadway, engaging the intellect and the conscience as well as the heart. Her powerful debut *The Children's Hour* (1934) shocked audiences by broaching a lesbian theme in a disturbing tale of slander. Four more long-running plays ensued. Later, her tumultous life itself provided material for four volumes of memoirs. In *An Unfinished Woman* (1969) Hellman examines how art, love and politics shaped her life and her 30-year relationship with Dashiell Hammett, the detective story writer. *Pentimento* (1977) became the award-winning film *Julia*, the true story of a childhood friend who convinced Hellman to carry $50,000 into Nazi Berlin to ransom political prisoners. In *Scoundrel Time*, Hellman painfully recounts the political persecution of the McCarthy era, her lasting message a defiant vote for personal integrity.

HENIE, Sonia
1912-1969
Norwegian figure skater

A child prodigy who was the Norwegian figure skating champion at 9 and made her Olympic debut at 11 in Chamonix, France, in 1924, Henie was born in Oslo, the daughter of a cycling champion. She won gold medals in three Olympics (1928, 1932 and 1936) and won an unequalled streak of ten world championship titles. She also designed the short, swingy skating skirt and wore white boots, breaking away from the somber and restrictive traditional costumes worn by women skaters.

Henie left amateur competition in 1936 and devised her own skating show, the Hollywood Ice Revue. She made ten movies for 20th Century Fox during the 1930s that popularized figure skating when she teamed up with leading men like Clark Gable, Don Ameche and Tyrone Power. These productions helped her accrue the largest female sporting fortune in history, estimated at $37.5 million at her death in 1969. With her third husband, Norwegian shipping magnate Niels Oustad, she amassed a valuable collection of abstract art and with it founded a modern art museum in Oslo, Norway.

Lillian Hellman with director William Wyler on the set of Dead End *(1937).*

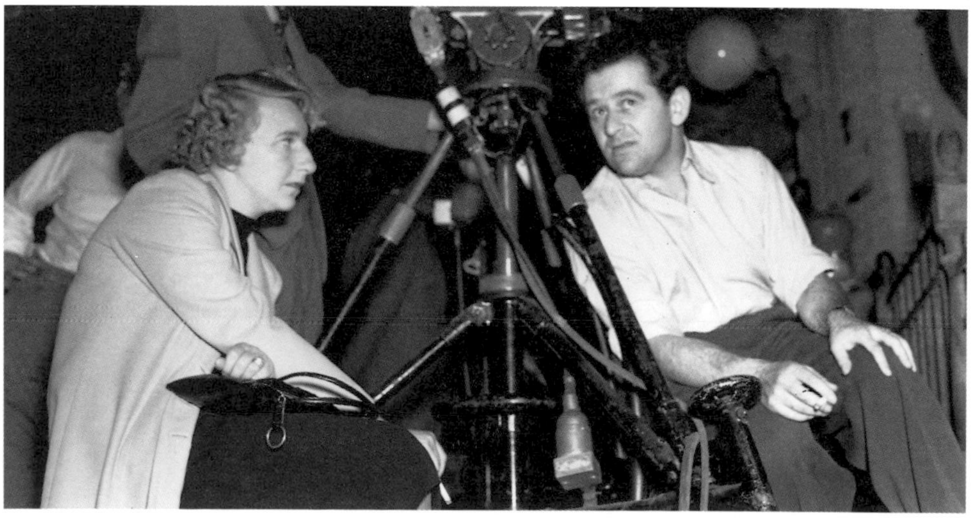

HENSON, Lisa
1961-
American business executive

In 1994 Lisa Henson became the youngest person, and second woman (after Sherry Lansing at Paramount Pictures), to head a major Hollywood film studio (Columbia Pictures). The oldest child of puppeteer Jim Henson, she was reared in Connecticut and New York with the Muppet characters and *Sesame Street*. A student of mythology and folklore at Harvard, she was the first woman head of the *Harvard Lampoon*. After graduation, Henson joined Warner Bros., quickly rising to executive vice president of production. Her father's death in 1990 involved her and her four siblings in a difficult but successful fight to preserve Henson Productions. After completion of her contract at Warners, where she was known as open, direct, and well-informed, with a preference for comedies and action adventures, she went to Columbia Pictures as production president in August 1993. The next year, she was named studio president.

HEPBURN, Audrey
1929-1993
Belgian-born American actress

Edda Hepburn-Ruston was born in Brussels, the daughter of a Dutch baroness and a Scottish bank director. Her parents separated, and Edda spent the war with her mother in Holland, taking ballet, and later working for the Resistance. After the war she resumed dancing, appearing in her first film, and changing her name to Audrey, becoming a chorus girl in London. While making a forgettable film in Monte Carlo, she was spotted by COLETTE, whose novel *Gigi* had just been adapted for the New York stage. The play opened in 1951 and Hepburn received rave reviews. Her performance as Gigi took her to Hollywood to make *Roman Holiday* (1953), for which she won the Academy Award as Best Actress. Her career as a leading lady lasted for the next 15 years as she starred in *Funny Face* (1957), *The Nun's Story* (1959), *Breakfast at Tiffany's* (1961), *Charade* (1963), *My Fair Lady* (1964) and *Wait Until Dark* (1967). In 1988 she became a roving ambassador for UNICEF, traveling to Ethiopia, Latin America and Somalia in 1992. She was presented with the Presidential Medal of Freedom for her work in 1992, and also was given the Jean Hersholt Humanitarian Award posthumously at the Oscars in 1993, two months after her death.

Katharine Hepburn never allowed her movie-star image to interfere with her individualism. She is known for her strong character as much as for her acting talent.

Actress Audrey Hepburn, goodwill ambassador for UNICEF, visits with children in a remote village in northern Vietnam in 1990.

HEPBURN, Katharine
1909?-
American actress

Hepburn was born in Hartford, Connecticut, and went to Bryn Mawr College. She played in summer stock before making her Broadway debut in 1928. Her first film, *A Bill of Divorcement* (1932), starred John Barrymore, but Hepburn's angular beauty and personality almost stole the film. She won the Academy Award for Best Actress for *Morning Glory* (1933), and also starred in *Stage Door* (1937) and a series of screwball comedies with Cary Grant, *Bringing Up Baby* and *Holiday* (1938). In 1940 she returned to Broadway to star in *The Philadelphia Story*, a play she liked so much she bought the film rights. In 1942 she

Barbara Hepworth attends the unveiling of her 21-foot-high granite sculpture Single Form *at the United Nations in New York.*

made *Woman of the Year*, the first of the seven films she made with Spencer Tracy. She also starred in *The African Queen* (1951) with Humphrey Bogart, and in *A Long Day's Journey into Night* (1962) for which she won Best Actress at Cannes. She won her second Academy Award for her last film with Tracy, *Guess Who's Coming To Dinner* (1967), her third for *The Lion in Winter* (1968) and her fourth for *On Golden Pond* (1982). She also appeared on Broadway in the title role in *Coco* (1969). She has always been an individualist, with a strength which came across on the screen, and a unique aura of confidence.

HEPWORTH, Dame Barbara
1903-1975
British sculptor

An abstract sculptor best known for her 1964 monumental memorial to Dag Hammerskjold, *Single Form*, on view at the United Nations in New York, Hepworth was born in Yorkshire, England. She attended the Leeds School of Art on a scholarship where she met Henry Moore, whose massive, simplified figures influenced her style. She later graduated from the Royal College of Art in London and received a grant to study in Italy for two years.

Hepworth was an advocate of direct carving rather than modelling, and fashioned pure, organic shapes in wood, stone and bronze, working on large-scale pieces. She was created Dame of the British Empire in 1965 and died ten years later in a fire in her studio.

HESS, Dame Myra
1890-1965
British concert pianist

Myra Hess was born in London, and studied piano at the Royal Academy of Music under Tobias Matthay. She was an immediate success on her first appearance, playing Beethoven's G Major Concerto. She became a well-known recitalist and chamber music player, her playing marked by classical precision and poetic imagination. She was a renowned interpreter of Bach and Schumann, and her performances were instrumental in broadening the general public's interest in live performances of classical music. During World War II, when all London concert halls were closed, she organized lunchtime concerts in the emptied National Gallery, and was a popular and frequent performer. For this in particular she was created Dame Commander of the British Empire in 1941. After the war, she continued to travel and perform. She made numerous piano transcriptions for two and four hands of many works, notably Bach's Cantata 147, "Jesu, Joy of Man's Desiring," which she made popular.

HILL, Octavia
1838-1912
British housing reformer, leader of open-space movement

In 1864 Octavia Hill undertook a revitalization project of a poor neighborhood in London. Her efforts were supported and financed by art historian John Ruskin. Beginning with three houses, she carefully invested the money Ruskin loaned her and renovated them. She later directed mass housing projects throughout London. Her program disallowed overdue rent and was imitated throughout Britain and the United States.

She co-founded the Charity Organisation Society, which investigated living conditions in poor areas. Concerned by the crowded living conditions in London's slums, she sought to preserve the city's parks and open spaces. Her efforts led to the foundation of what would become in 1909 the National Trust for the Preservation of Places of Historic Interest and National Beauty.

HILLMAN, Bessie
1889-1970
Russian-born American labor leader

After fleeing her Russian town in 1905 during the pogroms, Bessie Abramowitz settled in Chicago, where she was employed as a garment worker and protested the paltry wages and unsafe conditions. A persuasive speaker, she led 16 women on a walkout at one prominent men's clothing plant, catalyzing the 1910 garment workers' strike. Out of this strike was born a union – the Amalgamated Clothing Workers of America (ACWA).

In 1916 she married Sydney Hillman, co-founder and the union's first president. They moved the ACWA's headquarters to New York, where she worked as an organizer and headed several educational programs. For nearly a quarter-century she served as the ACWA's vice president. An advocate of equal rights for women, Hillman was also active in the civil rights, peace and child welfare movements.

HINDLEY, Myra
1942(?)-
British serial murderer

A participant in England's Moors Murders, Hindley (along with her boyfriend Ian Brady) was convicted in 1966 of murdering two children and one young man.

She met Brady in 1961 where she worked as a typist and became instantly infatuated with him. They became lovers and he persuaded her to help him procure children for pornographic pictures. They had already murdered at least two young girls and buried them in shallow graves on the Saddleworth Moor when Hindley's brother-in-law David Smith witnessed their killing of Edward Evans. Smith immediately informed the police and Brady and Hindley were apprehended. On May 6, 1966, Hindley was found guilty for her part in the three murders, and was sentenced to life in prison.

In the mid-1980s Hindley told the authorites where they could find another body – a missing 20 year old. A Hindley biography, *Inside the Mind of a Murderess*, attempts to offer insight into what motivated her.

HODGKIN, Dorothy
1910-1994
British crystallographer

Born in Egypt, the daughter of Dr. J.W. Crowfoot of the Egyptian Ministry of Education and his wife Grace, an expert on Coptic textiles, Dorothy Hodgkin grew up in Norfolk and the Middle East. She studied chemistry at Somerville College, Oxford, and married Thomas Hodgkin, a historian of Africa, in 1937. Early in her career, she became the first scientist to determine the chemical structure of any substance solely by X-ray analysis. Her analysis of penicillin made her a Fellow of the Royal Society in 1947, and she won the Nobel Prize for chemistry in 1964 for analyzing the structure of vitamin B12, a substance vital to the treatment of pernicious anaemia.

HODGKINS, Frances
1869-1947
New Zealand painter

Frances Hodgkins was born in Dunedin, New Zealand, and was taught watercolor painting by her father and trained in oils by the Italian painter G.P. Berti. She attended the Dunedin Art School and gave piano lessons to finance a trip to Europe. From 1901 to 1904 she toured Italy, France, Holland and Morocco, finally returning to Wellington. Finding no success in New Zealand, she settled in Paris in 1907 and taught at the Colarossi Art School before opening her own watercolor academy whose enrollment was primarily women.

In 1912 and 1913 she gave several noteworthy exhibits in New Zealand and Australia and then moved to St. Ives, Cornwall, in England at the outbreak of World War I. In the mid-1920s she worked as a designer in Manchester for the Calico Printers Association and joined the Manchester Society of Painters. She received major critical acclaim for her work shown at London's Claridges Gallery in 1928, and in 1929, at 58, was invited to join the Seven and Five Society, a group of progressive painters whose members included Winifred and Ben Nicholson, David Jones and Cedric Morris. Her later work contrasted with her early, soft, post-Impressionist watercolors – it was strong and stylized with robust color and poetic nuances.

HOFFMAN, Claire Giannini
1904-
American business executive

Born in the year that her father, Amadeo Peter Giannini, founded the Bank of Italy (later the Bank of America) in San Francisco, Claire Giannini was reared in an atmosphere of business and finance. She was her father's confidante and, at his death in 1949, his successor as a director of the bank, the first woman to hold such office. A supporter of equal opportunity for women in business, she was also a director of the American International Investment Corporation and a trustee of the Center for International Economic Growth. In 1963, she became the first woman to serve as a director of Sears, Roebuck & Co., then the largest general merchandise company in the United States.

HOLIDAY, Billie
1915-1959
American singer

This celebrated jazz singer was born Eleanora Fagan to poor teenage parents in Baltimore, Maryland, and was soon abandoned by her father when he left home to follow his own musical career. After she and her mother moved to Manhattan in 1928 and her mother became ill, she turned to prostitution, but soon got work singing in clubs in Harlem. Discovered by producer John Hammond, the series of recordings she made with small groups between 1933 and 1942, featuring some of the finest players of the day, including Lester Young and Teddy Wilson, established the preeminence of her unique resonant voice. She sang with Count Basie's orchestra for a year (1937) but suffered racial mistreatment with Artie Shaw's white band and quit to lead her own units.

Her best love songs had a bittersweet tinge and many songs are linked with her:

"God Bless the Child", "Strange Fruit", "Porgy", "My Man", "More Than You Know", "Good Morning Heartache" and "The Man I Love". At her peak she was New York's highest-paid club performer. A European tour in 1954 was a career highlight, but her heroin addiction brought arrests, hospitalizations, uneven performances and eventually, her death. Her biography *Lady Sings the Blues* was made into a 1972 film starring Diana Ross.

HOLM, Eleanor
1913-
American swimmer

An Olympic gold medalist who converted her victory into a show business career, Eleanor Holm was born in New York City and first swam in the 1928 Olympics when she was 14, placing fifth in the 100 meter backstroke. In 1932, she captured the gold in the same event in Los Angeles with a time of 1:19.4 and set a world record in 1935. En route to the 1936 Berlin Games, she broke training rules by sharing a bottle of champagne with celebrants on the ship to Europe and was dropped from the U.S. team.

She married the musician Art Jarrett and sang on tour with his band. After a divorce from Jarrett, Holm married the show business entrepreneur Billy Rose and performed with his Aquacade at the 1940 New York World's Fair.

HOLTZMAN, Elizabeth
1941-
American politician

When she upset Representative Emmanuel Celler's 50-year tenure in the Congress in 1972, Elizabeth Holtzman became the youngest woman ever elected to Congress. One of her actions in Congress was to sue the U.S. District Court for waging war without Congressional approval. Although the U.S. District Court ruled in her favor in a precedent-setting decision, it was later overturned. As she fought for passage of the Equal Rights Amendment, low-income housing, and the welfare of people rather than businesses, she became known for her no-compromising integrity. In 1990 she became Comptroller of New York City, yet left in 1994 following charges that she had chosen a contractor based on campaign contributions.

Celebrated jazz singer Billie Holiday combined an impeccable sense of timing with great emotion.

HOLZER, Jenny
1950-
American artist

An avant-garde contemporary artist who explores the values of language in her large-scale, publicly displayed signs, Jenny Holzer was born in Gallipolis, Ohio, and graduated from Ohio University and the Rhode Island School of Design. While a member of the Whitney Museum's Independent Study Program from 1976 to 1977, she began using language separated from image as her medium.

Holzer's "Truism" series of 1977 was a collection of flat-worded, politicized one-liners like "Abuse of power comes as no surprise" and "Sex differences are here to stay" which she pasted on posters and distributed throughout downtown New York. These became more brash as she employed moving, electric signs mounted on museum walls. Holzer expanded her repertoire using T-shirts and hats to carry her slogans, and she set up a huge Spectacolor board in Times Square as well as displays at Caesar's Palace in Las Vegas. In the 1980s she devised a particularly strident series of threatening text called "Inflammatory Essays", whose statements encapsulated universal issues of poverty, freedom and torture.

Holzer's solo shows have been held at major American museums, and she was the first American female artist to have her work displayed at the Venice Biennale, in 1990.

HOPPER, Rear Admiral Grace
1906-1992
American mathematician, computer pioneer

A native of New York City, Grace Hopper earned a Ph.D. in mathematics from Yale University in 1934 and taught at Vassar College until she enlisted in WAVES (Women Accepted for Voluntary Emergency Service) in 1944. This branch of the Navy assigned her to work on programming an early version of the electronic computer called the Mark I. After the war ended, Hopper retained her naval reserve status while teaching at Harvard's applied physics computation laboratory. In 1966 the navy recalled her to develop the concept of automatic programming that led to the Common Business Oriented Language (COBOL). Known to her colleagues as "Amazing Grace", Hopper was appointed rear admiral in 1983 and received the U.S. Medal of Technology in 1991.

HORNE, Lena
1917-
American actress, singer

A native of Brooklyn, New York, Lena Horne started out as a dancer at Harlem's legendary Cotton Club when she was 16. She went on tour accompanying the dance bands of Noble Sissle and Charlie Barnet and sang in the Broadway musical *Blackbirds* in 1939. She became the first black performer to sign a major studio contract when she joined M-G-M, and was well received in a number of film roles, including *Panama Hattie* (1942), *Cabin in the Sky* (1943), *Broadway Rhythm* (1944), *Ziegfeld Follies* (1946), *Meet Me in Las Vegas* (1956), and *Death of a Gunfighter* (1956).

From the 1950s onward, Horne shone most brightly as a nightclub entertainer. Her throaty, mellow voice is distinctive and expressive, matched by a sensuous style. Horne published two autobiographies, *In Person: Lena Horne* (1950) and *Lena* (1965). She was a recipient of a Kennedy Center Honor in 1984 and a New York Governor's Award in 1985.

ABOVE: *German-born psychoanalyst Karen Horney was a strident critic of Sigmund Freud's views on feminine psychology, rejecting the notion that "anatomy is destiny."*

BELOW: *Rear Admiral Grace Hopper salutes crew members as she boards the* U.S.S. Constitution *at her retirement in 1986. Her computer work led to the development of COBOL.*

HORNEY, Karen
1885-1952
German-American psychoanalyst

A native of Germany, Karen Horney studied medicine at Freiburg University and underwent analysis with Karl Abraham, a close associate of Sigmund Freud. She taught at the Berlin Psychoanalytic Institute until 1932, when she emigrated to the United States to become assistant director of the Chicago Institute of Psychoanalysis. Horney became well known for her criticisms of Freud's view of feminine psychology, which was grounded in his dictum that "anatomy is destiny". She emphasized the cultural factors in human psychology and risked her livelihood in the process. Expelled from the New York Psychoanalytic Institute in 1941, she promptly founded the Association for the Advancement of Psychoanalysis. Her best-known works are *The Neurotic Personality of Our Time* (1937), *New Ways in Psychoanalysis* (1939), and *Our Inner Conflicts* (1945).

Julia Ward Howe became the first woman member of the American Academy of Arts and Letters in 1908.

HOUSTON, Whitney
1963-
American singer, actress

A mellifluous singer whose poise and finely-honed voice have been matched by careful management and promotion, Whitney Houston has accrued many of the music industry's major awards at a relatively young age.

Houston's mother, Cissy, was a well-respected gospel singer and her cousin is Dionne Warwick. Clive Davis signed Houston with Arista Records in 1983, and her debut album *Whitney Houston* (1985) was a phenomenal success. Her songs were a mix of up-tempo rhythm and blues, disco dance medleys and romantic ballads. Three songs made it to the top of the Billboard charts: "Greatest Love of All", "How Will I Know", and "Saving All My Love for You" which won the 1986 Grammy for Best Popular Song.

Houston's second album *Whitney* (1987) earned her a 1988 Grammy for Best Female Popular Vocal Performance. She costarred with Kevin Costner in the 1993 film *The Bodyguard*, and won the 1994 Grammy for Best Female Vocal Performance for her rendition of Dolly PARTON's song "I Will Always Love You".

HOWARD, Mabel
1893-1972
New Zealand politician

Never afraid to speak her mind, the witty Mabel Howard once shocked fellow Members of Parliament when she held up a pair of women's bloomers to make the point that women's clothes should be sized in inches. Always an advocate for women's rights, the underprivileged and animals, she made history when she became national secretary of the New Zealand Federated Laborers Union. She was the first woman to hold such a position in the all-male trade union organization. She served in Parliament from 1947 to 1969, and as minister of Health and Child Welfare she was the first female Cabinet minister. New Zealand's first animal protection act came about because of her efforts.

HOWE, Julia Ward
1819-1910
American social reformer, editor, poet, songwriter

An activist for women's rights, abolition, and world peace, Howe is best remembered for writing the words to "The Battle Hymn of the Republic." She was paid only $4.00 for the lyrics, first published in *Atlantic Monthly* in 1862. Her election to the American Academy of Arts and Letters in 1908, making her the first woman so recognized, inaugurated a new phase for women in American literature. She was the editor of *Women's Journal*, and co-editor of the abolitionist newspaper *Commonwealth*. Author of two volumes of poetry and three other

Journalist Charlayne Hunter-Gault.

books, Howe was most famous as a charismatic lecturer and organizer. The many women's groups she founded had a lasting impact on turn-of-the-century politics.

HUERTA, Dolores
1930-
Mexican-American labor leader, social activist

This intelligent and intense woman originally worked with the Community Service Organization in Stockton, California, promoting voter registration and organizing within the Mexican-American community. It was through this organization that she met Cesar Chavez. Together they established in 1962 a union to benefit California's migrant workers, the Farm Workers Association, precursor to the United Farm Workers union (UFW).

Huerta was the first woman organizer for the UFW and had an integral role in initiating the lettuce and grape boycotts which garnered the union national attention in the 1970s. She successfully lobbied state and federal legislators for migrant worker benefits and served as the UFW's vice president in the early 1970s.

In 1988 in San Francisco, she was clubbed by police during a peaceful demonstration at a presidential rally. Seriously injured, Huerta required emergency surgery. Undaunted, she is praised for bringing forth an ideal of non-violence to boycotting and social change.

HUNTER-GAULT, Charlayne
1942-
American journalist

Born in Due West, South Carolina, Charlayne Hunter wanted to be a journalist from the time she was 12. The only college in Georgia with a journalism school in the late 1950s was the University of Georgia which was segregated. She attended Wayne State University in Detroit while civil rights activists filed for an integration order. She transferred as soon as it was passed, becoming the first black woman to attend the University of Georgia. Upon graduation in 1963, she went to New York and became a secretary at *The New Yorker*, on the condition that she be considered for writing assignments. She was a contributor to "Talk of the Town" from 1964 to 1967, when she

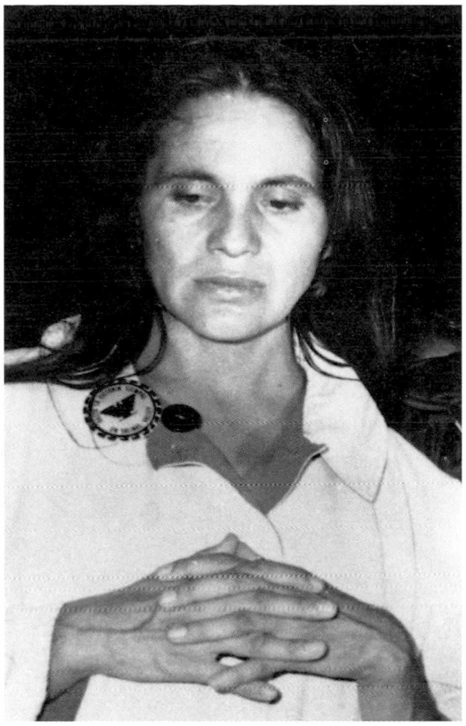

Dolores Huerta, seen here in 1970, founded the precursor to the United Farm Workers union with Cesar Chavez in the 1960s.

moved to Washington to join the staff of WRC as an investigative reporter and anchorwoman for the local evening news. In 1968 she returned to New York, to the *New York Times*, where she specialized in stories on Harlem and won three Publishers Awards. Since 1978 she has been a correspondent and field reporter with WNET's *McNeill-Lehrer News Hour*. She won a Peabody Award in 1986 for her segment, "Apartheid's People". She was also a correspondent in the Gulf War, concentrating on the women in the military.

HURST, Margery
1914-
British entrepreneur

Margery Hurst attended the Royal Academy of Dramatic Arts for two years before working as a typist and eventually returning home to run the clerical side of her father's building business. She eventually became office manager of the firm, which employed about 50 people. After World War II she opened an office, with herself as the only employee, to furnish secretarial skills on a temporary basis. Finding that she had more work than she could handle, she hired others. This was the beginning of the Brook Street Bureau. By means of original advertising, rigid testing of the skills of the temporary staff and interviews with prospective employees, she brought the caliber of the temporary office worker up to a high level. Within 25 years the company had grown to over 210 branches all over the world. Margery Hurst has also founded a college for adminstrative and secretarial studies.

HURSTON, Zora Neale
1901?-1960
American novelist, anthropologist, folklorist

"No, I do not weep at the world – I am too busy sharpening my oyster knife." With cutting humor and zest, Zora Neale Hurston left her controversial imprint on the Harlem Renaissance.

Educated at Howard, Barnard and Columbia universities, she returned to her home town of Eatonville, Florida, the first incorporated all-black town in America, to examine black folk culture through the lens of anthropology, preserved in her book *Mules and Men* (1935). Her masterpiece is the novel *Their Eyes Were Watching God* (1937), whose heroine Janie finds love and self-realization within a vibrant black community. Hurston's focus on women's status and the African roots of black America was ahead of its time, and often criticized. Hurston died poor and her works out of print, but her works have enjoyed a revival in the last 15 years.

HUTTON, Lauren
1943-
American fashion model, actress

Stranded in New York after the demise of an ill-planned trip to Africa, Lauren Hutton found a job as a Christian Dior house model. Encouraged by a dynamic companion, she sent her portfolio to the city's top modeling agencies.

Her unusual face graced numerous covers of *Vogue* during the 1970s. She honestly admits to modeling for the money, and her contract with Revlon cosmetics put her at the top. In the early 1980s she acted in several films including *American Gigolo*. As a model approaching 50, she experienced a renaissance when she appeared in advertisements, challenging the modern notion that youth and beauty are inextricably linked.

I

IBARRURI, Dolores
1895-1989
Spanish political leader and revolutionary

Called "La Pasionaria," Ibarruri is remembered for her resistance to General Franco during the Spanish Civil War. Born near Bilbaõ, her rise within the Communist Party began in 1920. A spellbinding orator, she travelled through Spain organizing strikes and protests to repressive rule from 1923 to 1930. She also edited the Communist paper *Worker's World*. In 1934 she helped organize the National Committee of Women Against War and Fascism as part of the Popular Front which joined leftist and liberal parties. When the Front won elections in 1935, Ibarruri was elected to the Cortes (Parliament). In opposition to General Francisco Franco, Ibarruri travelled throughout the country organizing thousands of women in anti-fascist committees, her battle cry *¡No Pasaran!* (They shall not pass) resonating throughout the country. She fled Spain after Franco came to power in 1937, and while in exile became president of the Spanish Communist Party. In May 1977 she returned to Spain after Franco's death, and was reelected to the Cortes.

ICHIKAWA, Fusaye
1893-1981
Japanese politician and feminist

In 1952 Fusaye Ichikawa became the first woman member of the Japanese Diet, the legislative branch of the Japanese government. Formerly a schoolteacher, Ichikawa became the first female reporter for the newspaper *Nagoya Shimbun*. She founded the New Women's Association between 1918 and 1920. This group fought for women's right to make political speeches, at a time when women were not even permitted to attend political meetings. During the 1920s she directed the Women's Committee for the International Labour Organization, and in 1924 co-founded the Women's Suffrage

The founder of Japan's League of Women Voters, Fusaye Ichikawa.

League. In 1945 she founded the League of Women Voters. Always on the cutting edge of the fight for women's political rights, she was elected to the Upper House of Councillor in the Diet in 1952, where she served until 1970.

INGLIS, Elsie
1864-1917
British physician

Inspired to become a doctor by Sophia Jex-Blake (1840-1912), Elsie Inglis was born in India, studied medicine in Edinburgh, where she founded a free hospice for women and children of the city's slums. When World War I broke out, she raised £25,000 in a single month to set up the Scottish Field Hospital, staffed entirely by women, from surgeons to orderlies. When the British War Office refused to send any female doctors to the front, Dr. Inglis worked with the Scottish Federation of Women's Suffrage Societies to organize hospitals sent out under the auspices of the French and Belgian Red Cross. She herself, with Dr. Kathleen MacPhail, set up a series of field hospitals in Serbia to combat the typhoid epidemic that had broken out there. Dr. Inglis's hospital was captured by the Austrians, and she and her patients were imprisoned. By 1916 the War Office was actively recruiting female doctors for service abroad.

INGRAHAM, Mary Shotwell
1887-1981
American founder of the United Service Organizations (USO)

Ingraham's career began with the Young Women's Christian Association (YWCA). She served as president for the Brooklyn YWCA from 1922 to 1939, then served five years as national board president.

In 1941 she founded the United Service Organizations (USO), which provided social, welfare and recreational services to the armed services during World War II. For her service to the United States, President Harry Truman awarded her the United States Medal for Merit in 1946, making her the first woman to achieve such an honor. The USO continued to benefit troops during both the Korean and Vietnam wars.

IRELAND, Patricia
1945-
American lawyer, social activist

In December 1991, Patricia Ireland was named ninth president of the National Organization for Women (NOW), succeeding septuagenarian Molly Yard. Reelected in 1993, she emphasized her goal of attracting a new generation of women to the organization. Born in Oak Park, Illinois, and reared in Indiana, she entered De Pauw University at the age of 16. After a short-lived marriage, Ireland graduated from the University of Tennessee, briefly attended graduate school, then moved with her second husband to Miami, where she worked as a flight attendant. Her success in challenging the airline's discriminatory health insurance plan encouraged her to earn a law degree at the University of Miami (1975). While working in corporate law for 12 years, she also did pro bono work for NOW, becoming increasingly engaged in working for women's rights. In 1985 she managed Eleanor Smeal's campaign for the NOW presidency, and two years later was herself elected executive vice president on the ticket with Molly Yard.

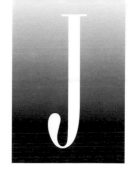

JACKSON, Dame Barbara Ward
1914-1981
British economist, ecologist

A native of York, Barbara Ward was educated in Paris and at Oxford. She published her first book, *The International Share Out*, in 1938 and subsequently wrote for the *Economist* magazine. During the 1940s she became very well known for her participation in the popular radio program "The Brains Trust." She married an Australian diplomat, Sir Robert Jackson, in 1950. Her interest in economics generated a deep commitment to ecology, as seen in *The Rich Nations and the Poor Nations*, written while she was a visiting professor at Harvard and Columbia. This was closely followed by *Spaceship Earth* (1966) and *The Lopsided World* (1968). In 1972 the United Nations asked her to write *Only One Earth: The Care and Maintenance of a Small Planet*. In 1976 she was made one of Britain's few female life peers.

JACKSON, Glenda
1937-
British actress, politician

Glenda Jackson was born in Hoylake, near Liverpool, and attended the Royal Academy of Dramatic Arts. She worked in rep for six years, making her stage debut in *Separate Tables* at Worthing in 1957. She made her London debut the same year in *All Kinds of Men*. She made her film debut in 1963 in *This Sporting Life*. In 1964 she joined the Royal Shakespeare Company, and appeared as Charlotte Corday in Peter Brooks's production of *Marat/Sade* (1965). She also played the part in the film in 1967, but the public became aware of her in *Women in Love* (1970), the role that earned Jackson her first Academy Award for Best Actress. The following year she made two films, *Sunday, Bloody Sunday*, and *Mary Queen of Scots* in which she played Queen Elizabeth I, a role she had also played in the BBC drama *Elizabeth R*. She won another Academy Award for Best Actress in 1973 for her performance in *A Touch of Class*. She has continued to work in the theater, appearing in such classics as *Hedda Gabler* and *Strange Interlude*, and in films, giving extraordinary performances in *Stevie* (1978), *Return of the Soldier* (1982) and *Turtle Diary* (1986). Always politically minded, she stood for prospective parliamentary candidate for the Labour Party for Hampstead and Highgate in 1990, and was elected in 1992.

JACKSON, Mahalia
1911-1972
American gospel singer

A church choir singer from the age of five, Mahalia Jackson was born in New Orleans and raised with the sounds of Ma Rainey, Bessie SMITH, ragtime and jazz. During the Depression era, she became exclusively a gospel singer. Jackson moved to Chicago at 16, where she joined the Great Salem Baptist Church and sang with the Johnson Gospel Singers. She began her solo gospel recordings in 1935.

In 1947 she recorded "Move On Up A Little Higher", which sold over two million copies. Her popularity soared through appearances on the Ed Sullivan show, at the National Baptist Convention and on her own radio and TV programs syndicated out of Chicago.

Jackson was active in the civil rights movement in the 1960s. She sang "I Been 'Buked and I Been Scorned" before Martin Luther King delivered his "I Have a Dream" speech on the steps of the Lincoln Memorial in Washington, D.C. "The Queen of Gospel Singers", as Jackson is known, had a cameo role in the film *Jazz on a Summer's Day* in 1960 singing The Lord's Prayer.

JACOBS, Aletta
1854-1929
Dutch physician

The daughter of a doctor, Aletta Jacobs faced a long struggle before she succeeded in becoming Holland's first female physician. She was first an apprentice pharmacist, awarded a diploma in 1870. She then persuaded her father to write to the prime minister for permission to study medicine at the university level. Despite hostility from male students and the press, she graduated in 1878 and joined her father's practice. Subsequently, she became active in many causes involving women's and children's rights and opened the world's first birth control clinic in Amsterdam (1882). By 1903 she had become president of the Dutch Women's Suffrage Association and lectured widely in this capacity until 1919, when women won the right to vote.

JAMES, Dame Naomi
1949-
New Zealand sailor

James was the first woman to sail solo around the world, and she broke the record in 1978 for the fastest journey by completing her trip in 272 days. She was created a Dame of the British Empire for her feat.

New Zealander Naomi James was the first woman to sail solo around the world.

The wife of the director of a yacht charter company owned by Chay Blyth, she sailed the 53-foot *Express Crusader* on her solo voyage.

Naomi Power spent her early life on a New Zealand farm before moving to Great Britain in 1970, where she taught before joining the crew of a yacht charter. She has published several volumes of autobiography.

JANSEN, Elly
1929-
Dutch-born social worker

Jansen is the founder and International Director of The Richmond Fellowship for community mental health. She promotes re-integration of mental health patients into the larger society and was a forerunner in advocating therapeutic communities (halfway houses). The Richmond Fellowship has some 30 houses in Britain, and others in the U.S., Australia, New Zealand and Austria.

Born in Holland, Jansen studied psychology, trained as a nurse, and went to England in 1955 to study to become a missionary. She began doing social work, and in 1959 rented a house near Richmond which became the first halfway house. Its success led to the Richmond Fellowship. She was made Officer of the Order of the British Empire (OBE) in 1980. Her publications include *The Therapeutic Community Outside the Hospital* and *Towards a Whole Society*.

JANSSON, Tove
1914-
Finnish writer, illustrator

Tove Jansson is a rare example of an author who has successfully made the transition from writing and illustrating outstanding books for children to composing equally outstanding adult fiction. Even in her early works, adult concerns about art and community permeate the tales of trolls and elves in her immensely successful Moomin books, just as a childlike sense of dream is preserved in her short stories and novels.

Brought up in the creative clutter of her father's sculpture studio, Jansson studied art in Helsinki, Stockholm and Paris. She published the first of the Moomin books in 1946, and the series has been translated into 27 languages. Her autobiography *Sculptor's Daughter* (1968) and short story collection *The Doll's House* (1978) represent her finest adult literature, with piercing insights into the mind and relationships of an artist.

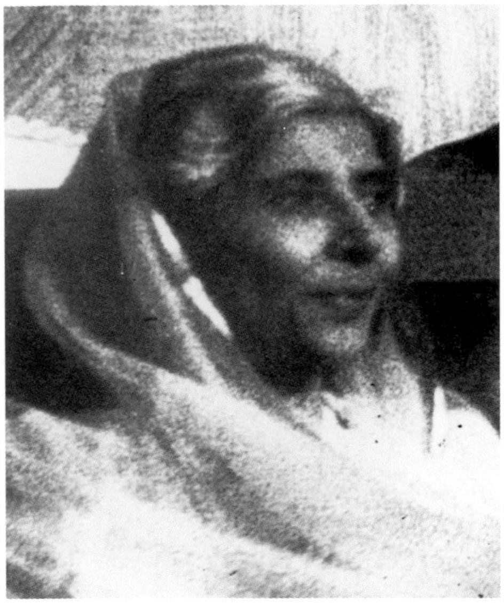

Fatima Jinnah worked with her brother Mohammed Ali Jinnah for the independence of Pakistan, which was realized in 1947.

JEKYLL, Gertrude
1843-1932
British landscape architect

An English horticulturalist who brought the ebullient colors of the French Impressionists to the English garden, Gertrude Jekyll was born in London into a wealthy family and studied painting, silverwork and wood carving as a young woman. She travelled widely among the circles of high society and provided decorative gardens for its notables such as the Duke of Westminster. A close friend of the renowned architect Edward Lutyens, she also designed gardens for many of his clients.

Her innovative schemes replaced the traditional stiff, formal patterns of English gardens with floral arrangements freely organized to produce masses of color and variegated harmonies. She used many native plants – scented but not flamboyant species such as honeysuckle, pinks and mignonette. She particularly enjoyed the beauties of the flowering cottage gardens that dotted the English countryside and sought to translate their freshness and charm in her larger designs. Her personal taste and style can be seen in the gardens of many of the finest English estates of the modern era.

JESENSKÁ, Milena
1890-1944
Czech journalist, humanist

Brilliant and rebellious, Milena Jesenská always defied expectations. Her father had her confined to a mental hospital as a teenager for insubordination. Upon her release, she married Jewish writer Ernst Polak, and moved with him to Vienna. As a correspondent for Czech newspapers, she discovered Franz Kafka's writings, and wrote to ask him if she might translate them. This correspondence blossomed into love, despite their few opportunities to meet, and in 1921 Kafka entrusted his diaries to her as he became seriously ill with tuberculosis. First known as an outstanding journalist and translator, Jesenská's outspoken stand against Nazism forged her reputation as a humanist. Though not a Jew herself, she put on a Yellow Star. She was sent to Ravensbruck in 1942 for her outspoken opposition to the Nazis, and died there in 1944.

JHABVALA, Ruth Prawer
1927-
Polish-Indian novelist, screenplay writer

Born in Germany to Polish parents and educated in England, Ruth Prawer married Cyrus Jhabvala, an Indian architect and moved to Delhi in 1951, where her adopted country and new family deeply colored her development as a writer. She wrote "to present India to myself, in the hope of giving myself some kind of foothold." She explores the clash of cultures in her novels, such as *Heat and Dust*, and in *Out of India: Selected Stories*.

In the early 1960s, Jhabvala began her highly successful partnership with producer Ismail Merchant and director James Ivory. Together they have produced a score of richly detailed films for cinema and television, including the award-winning *A Room With a View* (1986), *Howard's End* (1992) and *Remains of the Day* (1993).

JINNAH, Fatima
1893-1967
Pakistani politician

Sister of Mohammed Ali Jinnah, the creator and first Governor-General of Pakistan, Fatima Jinnah worked side by side with her brother for Pakistan's independence, which came in 1947. In 1934 she began opposing conservative Muslim orthodox views of women, and sought the social emancipation of women. She led the All-India Muslim Women's Committee which was formed in 1938, and founded Fatima Jinnah Women's Medical College.

After her brother's death, she went into seclusion until she became so angered by the totalitarian regime of General Mohammed Ayub Khan that she consented to run against him in 1965. Although she lost, perhaps because of fraud, she helped focus the tremendous amount of opposition to him.

JOHN, Gwen
1876-1939
British artist

Gwen John was born in Wales, the younger sister of portrait painter Augustus John. Gwen attended the Slade School of Art in London where she was trained in the Impressionist style. She was apprentice to the American expatriate, James McNeill Whistler, in Paris where she settled in 1903 and remained for her lifetime. She had a love affair with Auguste Rodin, for whom she modelled, and kept up a correspondence with his secretary, the German poet Rainer Maria Rilke.

John was shy and reflective, reluctant to display her canvases and fortunate that a wealthy patron, John Quinn, provided her with a stipend and became her chief collector. A devout Catholic, many of her portraits were residents of the convent near her Paris flat. Her favorite images were quiet, contemplative venues of Paris and still-lifes of her garret studio, described with subtle gradations of color, delicate light patterns and haunting detail.

JOHNSON, Lady Bird
1912-
American environmentalist, former First Lady of the United States

Nicknamed Lady Bird for her sweetness as a child, Claudia Alta Taylor was born in Karnack, Texas, and grew up to be a very shy woman. Her 1934 marriage to Lyndon B. Johnson saw her become a spokesperson for a variety of causes. She financed his first Congressional campaign, and during his military service from 1941 to 1942, managed his Congressional office. The next year she bought a failing radio station, and gradually turned it in to a multi-million-dollar business. During Johnson's vice-presidential and presidential campaigns, she travelled around the country with him, addressing women's organizations and giving press conferences.

Lady Bird Johnson's conservation work led to the Highway Beautification Act of 1965 and the creation of the National Wildflower Research Center.

While First Lady, Lady Bird became a passionate advocate of the conservation of nature and believed that beauty should be part of everyday life. Her influence led to the creation of many park reserves around the country and passage of the Highway Beautification Act of 1965, which initiated controls on billboards and junkyards. She later founded the National Wildflower Research Center to help protect nature.

JOHNSON, Sonia
1936-
American feminist

As a Mormon housewife and mother, Johnson had little knowledge of the women's rights movement until a friend introduced her to popular feminist writings. In 1978 her church opposed the Equal Rights Amendment (ERA), but failed to provide concrete doctrines supporting their position. Johnson became a dedicated proponent of the ERA, co-founded Mormons for ERA and marched on Washington. Her public crusade for passage of the ERA led to her excommunication in 1979.

She eventually adopted a more radical view of feminism. In 1984 she was the Citizen's Party presidential candidate and during the campaign co-founded Feminists International for Peace.

Her writings include *From Housewife to Heretic* (1981), *Going Out of Our Minds: The Metaphysics of Liberation* (1987), and *Wildfire: Igniting the She/volution* (1989).

J

JOHNSON, Virginia
1925-
American sociologist

Aspiring to study sociology, Virginia Johnson applied for a job as research associate to William Masters, a professor of obstetrics and gynecology at the Washington University School of Medicine in St. Louis, in 1957. Their research into the physiology and psychology of sex at the Reproductive Biology Research Foundation in St. Louis, where major – and controversial – studies resulted in new forms of treatment for sexual dysfunction, produced several important publications. The best known are *Human Sexual Response* (1966), *Human Sexual Inadequacy* (1970), and *The Pleasure Bond* (1975). In 1988 they published *Crisis: Heterosexual Behavior in the Age of AIDS*, with Robert Kolodny. Johnson and Masters were married in 1971, and divorced in 1992. Although she has no academic credentials, Johnson has become one of the most influential women in modern psychology.

JOLIOT-CURIE, Irène
1897-1956
French physicist

The daughter of scientists Pierre and Marie CURIE, 17-year-old Irène Curie accompanied her mother to the battlefront with a mobile radiographic unit during World War I and served as a nurse there. Afterward, she worked as a laboratory assistant to Marie Curie at the Radium Institute that she had founded in Paris. There she met and married Frédéric Joliot (1900-1958), a recent graduate of the Paris Institute for Industrial Physics and Chemistry. Both took the surname Joliot-Curie. In 1935 they won the Nobel Prize for chemistry for their work in producing radioactive isotopes artificially by bombarding elements with alpha particles. This method was later developed by Enrico Fermi to achieve nuclear fission. Both Joliot-Curies achieved high posts in atomic energy research in Paris during the 1940s, but their commitment to communism after World War II put them out of favor with the French government during the 1950s.

JONES, Mary Harris (Mother)
1830-1930
Irish-born American labor activist

Mother Jones travelled throughout the United States to help low-paid and mistreated workers learn their rights and fight injustice. Born Mary Harris in Cork, Ireland, Jones studied in Canada before going to the United States and working as a dressmaker, then a teacher. During a fierce yellow fever epidemic in 1867 she lost her entire family, and then worked as a nurse until its end. After that she began her life as an itinerant organizer, working with railroad laborers, mine workers, and even Mexican revolutionaries jailed in the United States. A brilliant strategist, in 1903 she led striking children of textile workers to President Theodore Roosevelt's home in Oyster Bay, New York. In 1911 she resumed organizing with mine workers, and in 1912 was convicted of conspiracy to commit murder. The public outcry contributed to her release, and she continued organizing for workers' rights until she died.

Irène Joliot-Curie won the 1935 Nobel Prize for chemistry with her husband for work that led to nuclear fission.

Labor organizer Mother Jones worked with textile workers, mine workers, and railroad laborers until her death at age 100.

JOPLIN, Janis
1943-1970
American singer

A female superstar of 1960s rock whose lusty, raw-nerved performances at the Monterey Pop Festival and Newport Folk Festival earned her a cult following, Janis Joplin was born in Port Arthur, Texas. Her mother was an amateur singer and Janis sang with the church choir and the high school glee club. A rock promoter, Chet Helms, landed her a job as lead singer for Big Brother and the Holding Company in San Francisco.

She sang "Love Is Like a Ball and Chain" at the 1967 Monterey Pop Festival and signed a contract with Bob Dylan's manager. Her album *Cheap Thrills* sold over a million copies. She formed the Full Tilt Boogie Band in 1970 but had already slid into drug and alcohol abuse, with a bottle of Southern Comfort as her trademark prop. In October 1970 Joplin was found dead in a Los Angeles motel of a drug overdose.

JORDAN, Barbara
1936-
American lawyer, politician, educator

Barbara Jordan became famous in 1974

when she served on the House Judiciary Committee that reviewed the possible impeachment of Richard Nixon. Her powerful national address argued for Nixon's impeachment, noting that she would uphold the U.S. Constitution which represented all American citizens, regardless of race or gender.

Born to a poor family in Houston, Texas, she credits her maternal grandfather for training her to think for herself, a gift that she passes on to her students at the University of Texas at Austin. In 1965 she won election to the Texas House of Representatives, becoming the first black person elected since 1883, and the first woman ever. She fought for minimum-wage laws and anti-discrimination clauses. She was the keynote speaker at the 1976 Democratic National Convention. In 1972 she was elected to Congress as a Democrat, and as of 1994, she is chair of the Commission on Immigration Reform. She was awarded the Presidential Medal of Freedom by President Clinton that year.

Barbara Jordan speaks at the 1992 Democratic Convention in New York.

JOYNER-KERSEE, Jackie
1962-
American track and field athlete

Winner of the Olympic gold medal in the long jump in 1988 and the heptathalon in 1992 and in 1988, in which she set a world record of 7219 points, outdistanced her nearest rival by 500 points and surpassed the old record by almost 1000 points, Jackie Joyner-Kersee was raised in the ghetto in East St. Louis, Illinois. Encouraged by her brother Al (who won the 1988 gold medal in the triple jump and is married to the 100 meter dash record holder Florence Joyner), Jackie began practicing the long jump as a teenager and entered her first pentathalon at 14. At UCLA she began training with track coach Bob Kersee (whom she married in 1986), who steered her to the heptathalon, which includes the 200 meter dash, 100 meter hurdles, high jump, long jump, javelin throw, 800 meter run, and shot-put. In 1983 she won the Broderick Award as the nation's top female collegiate athlete, and in 1984 took the silver medal in the heptathlon at the Los Angeles Olympics. In addition to her Olympic medals, Joyner-Kersee has won several national awards as best female and best amateur athlete.

JUHACZ, Marie
1880-1956
German socialist and feminist

Juhacz was born near Brandenburg and worked in a factory as a seamstress. Active in the suffrage movement, she joined the Social Democratic Party and founded the Workers' Welfare Organization. She was a member of the National Assembly in 1919. Later a member of the Reichstag from 1923 to 1933, she fled Germany because of the Nazis, and did not return until several years after war's end in 1949, when she resumed her work in social welfare.

JUNG CHANG
1952-
Chinese biographer, historian, commentator

In her groundbreaking book *Wild Swans: Three Daughters of China*, Jung Chang not only captured the broad sweep of twentieth century Chinese history but also mesmerized readers with tales of her own remarkable family. From her grandmother, sold as a concubine, to her parents, loyal Communist Party officials who were imprisoned and tortured during the Cultural Revolution, Jung Chang frames her life between the horrors of dictatorship and the tenacious strength of survivors.

Jung Chang worked as a "barefoot doctor", a laborer and an English teacher before receiving a scholarship to study in England. In 1982 she was the first Chinese student to earn a doctorate from a British university. A 1988 visit from her mother and subsequent research inspired her to write *Wild Swans*. Jung Chang currently teaches at London University and is a commentator on China for the BBC.

Jackie Joyner-Kersee wins the gold medal in the heptathlon at the 1988 Olympics.

K

KAHLO, Frida
1907-1954
Mexican painter

Kahlo was born in Coyoacan, a suburb of Mexico City. She lived a difficult life, marred by a near-fatal bus accident at 15 that crushed her spine, requiring her to wear heavy braces that often appear in her self-portraits. These images, marked by her arresting gaze, long, dark hair and bright-colored, embroidered clothing, are popular paintings among her collectors. One sold for over $1 million in 1990, the first Latin American painting to achieve this figure. References to pain – eyes brimming with tears, drops of blood from thorny branches – abound in her portraits. She has become a symbol of strength in adversity to many female artists.

Kahlo was married twice to Diego Rivera, a well-known Mexican muralist who worked in New York during the 1930s. Their relationship was stormy and she rued her inability to bear children, another subject of her paintings. She also formed alliances with diverse political figures such as Leon Trotsky and the modern art patron, Nelson Rockefeller. Her work is internationally renowned, and her birthplace, Casa Azul, is now a museum.

KANG KEQING
1912-
Chinese revolutionary and women's leader

Since 1986 Kang Keqing has been part of the ruling Presidium of the Sixth National People's Congress. As a teenager she joined the Chinese Communist Party, and ran away from her foster parents to escape an arranged marriage. She married General Zhu De, co-founder of the Red Army, and began organizing armed Communist guerrillas for the army. One of the few women to make the Long March, the 800-mile trek across the country from 1934 to 1936, she did organizational and propaganda work. Throughout her rise to leadership she has organized women, and in 1949 after the establishment of the People's Republic of China she became one of the senior leaders of the Chinese Women's Movement. In 1973 she was made President of the All-China Women's Federation.

Mexican painter Frida Kahlo.

KARAN, Donna
1948-
American fashion designer

Born in Forest Hills, New York, Donna Karan attended Parsons School of Design. After her second year, she went to work for Anne Klein in 1964, and never went back. Anne Klein was beginning to design clothes for working women, a market that was suited to Karan's simple, yet sophisticated clothes. In 1971 she became the associate designer, and in 1984 was given her own company by Takihyo Corporation, who owned Anne Klein. The same year she won her third Coty Award (she had previously won them in 1977 and 1981). Karan's clothes are known for their wearability. She designs classic sportswear with a stylish edge.

KEELER, Christine
1942-
British mistress

Keeler's simultaneous affairs with Captain Yevgeni Ivanov, a Soviet naval attaché, and John Profumo, British state secretary for war, led to a major scandal in 1963.

Keeler met Dr. Stephen Ward when she was 19 years old, and he introduced her to a number of rich, influential men. In 1961, she met John Profumo. When his connection with Keeler was made public, Profumo denied any impropriety and insisted they were just friends. However, rumors persisted. In addition, Profumo was accused of compromising state security because Keeler was involved with Ivanov at the same time. Ivanov had allegedly asked Keeler to obtain atomic secrets from Profumo. All this erupted during the 1962 Cuban Missile crisis.

Eventually, John Profumo resigned his seat in the House of Commons, Ward was brought up on morals charges and Keeler faded into obscurity. A 1989 film, *Scandal*, retold the story.

KELLER, Helen
1880-1968
American educator, author
SULLIVAN MACY, Anne
1866-1936
American educator

Challenged by two physical handicaps, Helen Keller overcame tremendous odds to excel in her quest for knowledge and championship of the blind.

Afflicted with scarlet fever which left her deaf and blind, she was an almost feral child deemed ineducable by the local Tuscumbia, Alabama, teachers. In a last attempt, her parents hired teacher Anne Sullivan, a native of Feeding Hills, Massachusetts, trained at the Perkins Institute of the Blind.

Sullivan painstakingly taught Keller the manual alphabet and finger spelling. Noting Helen's intelligence, Sullivan pushed more and more challenges upon

ABOVE: *Helen Keller (right) seen with her teacher Anne Sullivan Macy in a photograph taken in 1920.*

Helen. Keller made rapid progress and learned Braille and speech through touching Sullivan's throat while she spoke.

An outstanding scholar, Keller attended Radcliffe College where she studied Classics and philosophy. She spoke fluent French and German. She published her first book, *The Story of My Life*, in 1903.

Along with Sullivan who was her constant companion, Keller traveled extensively, lecturing and demonstrating through example the capabilities of the handicapped. She campaigned on behalf of the American Foundation for the Blind. She resented all forms of condescension to the disabled and wished to be judged on equal achievement.

KELLY, Grace
1929-1982
American actress, princess of Monaco

Grace Patricia Kelly was born in Philadelphia, where she attended private schools. She studied at the American Academy of Dramatic Arts in New York, modeling to cover her tuition. She made her Broadway debut in a production of Strindberg's *The Father* in 1949. She was spotted by a talent scout and signed to a seven-year contract by M-G-M. Her first film, *Fourteen Hours* (1951) was forgotten, but in her next film, *High Noon* (1952) with Gary Cooper, she was extremely believable as the sheriff's Quaker bride. Her blonde, aristocratic beauty and her talent were used perfectly in films like *Dial "M" for Murder* (1954) and Alfred Hitchcock's *Rear Window* (1954). In 1954 she won the Academy Award for Best Actress for *The Country Girl.*

In 1955, during the making of *To Catch a Thief* in Monaco, she met Prince Rainier, whom she married the following year. Her marriage marked her retirement from films, and she became much loved for her charity work. Her death in an automobile accident in 1982 led to the foundation of the Princess Grace Foundation, which continues her charitable work.

Glamorous and elegant, Grace Kelly was best known for her roles in thrillers by Alfred Hitchcock, and as "Princess Grace" after marrying Prince Rainier of Monaco.

KELLY, Petra
1947-1992
German politician

In 1979 Petra Kelly co-founded the radical Green Party which sprang out of an environmental and political movement that joined anti-nuclear protests, women's rights, human rights, economic justice, and care of the environment. She was born Petra Karin Lehmann in Günzberg, Bavaria, and was a frail child. During the 1960s, while studying at American University in the United States, she volunteered on the electoral campaigns of Hubert Humphrey and Robert Kennedy and participated in protests against the Vietnam War and the U.S. nuclear defense policy. Returning to Europe in 1970, she became a member of the German Social Democratic Party, but left to create the Green Party, and in 1983 became a member of the West German Parliament. In 1992 she and her longtime companion Gert Bastian were found dead. Neither the motive nor the cause – murder or suicide – was discovered.

KENYON, Dame Kathleen
1906-1978
British archaeologist

The daughter of Sir Frederic Kenyon, director and principal librarian of the British Museum, Kathleen Kenyon studied history at Oxford. Her first archaeological dig was Dr. Gertrude Caton-Thompson's expedition to Zimbabwe, Africa, the legendary site of King Solomon's mines. Subsequently, she learned advanced techniques with Sir Mortimer Wheeler, with whom she worked to uncover the Roman amphitheatre at Verulamium (St. Albans), near London, and dug in Samaria, Libya, Jericho, and Jerusalem. Her discoveries at the latter two sites threw new light on the prehistory of the Middle East. She helped found London's Institute of Archaeology during the 1930s and became its acting director during World War II. From 1951 to 1966 she was director of the British School of Archaeology in Jerusalem, after which she served as Principal of St. Hugh's College, Oxford, until 1973.

Petra Kelly, co-founder and leader of the Green Party and Bundestag member.

KING, Billie Jean
1943-
American tennis player

One of the most competitive and aggressive female tennis players, Billie Jean Moffitt was born in Long Beach, California. She won a remarkable 20 Wimbledon titles, breaking Elizabeth Ryan's longstanding record of 19 titles. She also won 13 U.S. Open titles between 1964 and 1980, and the Australian Open (1968), the French Open (1972) and the German Open (1971). Known for her serve-and-volley game, her physical talents were matched by fierce determination.

A spokeswoman for pay parity in women's sports, King founded two athletic leagues: World Team Tennis and the Women's Professional Softball League. In 1973 King won the single largest purse for a tennis match at that time, earning $100,000 by defeating Bobby Riggs (a former Wimbledon and U.S. Open winner) in a highly publicized event called "The Battle of the Sexes".

Arthur Ashe wrote of her in his memoirs *Days of Grace*, "Billie Jean King is rare in combining unquestionable brilliance and success as a tennis player with the passion of a crusader for justice. Using – sometimes sacrificing – her tennis fame, Billie Jean advanced the cause of women and gay people on a number of fronts".

KING, Carole
1942-
American songwriter, singer

A prodigious songwriting talent whose 1971 hit album *Tapestry* was on the Billboard record charts for over five years, Carole King was born Carole Klein in Brooklyn, New York. With lyricist Gerry Goffin, whom she married, she formed an extraordinary songwriting partnership which produced many hits, including "Just Once in My Life" for the Righteous Brothers in 1965, "A Natural Woman" in 1967 for Aretha FRANKLIN and "Hi-De-Ho" for Blood, Sweat and Tears in 1970, among a score of others. When King and Goffin divorced, she went solo, producing *Tapestry*, which had three hit singles, "It's Too Late", "I Feel the Earth Move", and "You've Got a Friend" which also became a hit for her friend James Taylor. In 1971, King went on tour with James Taylor and the album sold 13½ million copies, the most by any LP to that date. King scored successive hit albums with *Rhymes and Reasons*, *Fantasy*, *Simple Things*, *Touch the Sky*, and *Speeding Time*. She lives on the Robinson Bar Ranch near Stanley, Idaho.

KING, Coretta Scott
1927-
American civil rights activist

Born in Marion, Alabama, Coretta Scott attended northern universities and trained in voice at the New England Conservatory of Music. There she met Martin Luther King, Jr., whom she married in 1953. When her husband became swept up in the civil rights movement, she maintained a strong home base, raising their four children and organizing movement activities from their home. She preceded her husband in the peace movement, having joined the Women's International League of Peace and Freedom in 1961. When he was assassinated, she created the Martin Luther King, Jr. Center for Social Change, and expanded her social activism to include women's empowerment, economic justice and the fight against apartheid.

KINGSTON, Maxine Hong
1940-
American writer

Maxine Hong Kingston's powerful book *The Woman Warrior: Memoirs of a Childhood Among Ghosts*, a creative blend of myth, history and autobiography, won the National Book Critics Circle Award in 1976, and was adapted for the stage in 1994. In it, she combines traditional Chinese legends with elements of her own childhood in Stockton, California, where her parents ran a laundry, and stories of her mother's and other female relatives' lives in China. Together with *China Men* (1980), Kingston portrays a generation between two cultures. Kingston currently teaches at her alma mater, the University of California at Berkeley. Her comic novel *Tripmaster Monkey: His Fake Book* was published in 1988. The manuscript of a new novel was destroyed by fire in 1991.

KIRKPATRICK, Jeane
1926-
American diplomat

Political science scholar and professor Jeane Kirkpatrick caught then-President Ronald Reagan's attention with her hard-line stance against the Soviet Union, and her conviction that "moderately repressive regimes" could be tolerated if they supported U.S. policy. When Reagan appointed her U.S. Permanent Representative to the United Nations (1981-85), she became the first woman to hold that post. Kirkpatrick became politically active in response to the anti-war movement which she saw as a shift away from traditional values. In 1972 she was a co-founder of the Coalition for Democratic Majority which sought to promote conservative values in the Democratic Party. In addition to her service to the UN, she was a member of the Cabinet and the National Security Council.

KITZINGER, Sheila
1929-
British childbirth educator

A pioneer in childbirth education, Kitzinger developed a method which reduced the pain and fear associated with childbirth through relaxation and knowledge.

She was born in Somerset, studied to be a drama teacher and eventually acquired a degree in social anthropology. During the early 1950s she researched race relations in the United Kingdom. In 1958 she became a member of the Advisory Board of National Childbirth Trust. Through this affiliation she became a National Childbirth Trust teacher.

Among the several books she has written are *The Experience of Childbirth* (1962), *Pregnancy and Childbirth* (1980), and *Breastfeeding Your Baby* (1989).

ABOVE: *Jeane Kirkpatrick, the first woman U.S. ambassador to the U.N. (1981-85).*

BELOW: *Alexandra Kollontai (center) with members of the banned Workers' Opposition in Russia in 1921.*

KLEIN, Melanie
1882-1960
Austrian psychoanalyst

Born in Vienna, Melanie Reizes was attracted to a career in medicine but decided against it when she became engaged at the age of seventeen. However, when she became a patient of Sandor Ferenczi, one of Sigmund Freud's associates, she became interested in the application of psychoanalysis to young children and published her first paper in 1919. Two years later, she joined Karl Abraham's Psychoanalytic Institute in Berlin. Her major contribution to psychology was the technique of analyzing children's play for insight into their emotional development. Her research led her to conclude that aggressive feelings toward the mother were more important than Freud had thought. Her publications include *The Psychoanalysis of Children* (1932), *Envy and Gratitude* (1957), and the case study *Narrative of a Child Analysis* (1961). Klein's work has affected contemporary views on infant care and upbringing as well as developmental psychology.

KNIGHT, Dame Laura
1877-1970
British artist

One of the most successful twentieth century English artists and only the second woman elected to the Royal Academy, Laura Johnson was born in Long Eaton, Derbyshire, and studied at the Nottingham School of Art. Her style, based on old masters' techniques, was characterized by vigorous draftsmanship and ebullient color. She painted popular images of circus scenes, music halls, ballets, sports arenas and theaters. Her pleasure in recording the activities of public venues is reflected in her autobiography *Oil Paint and Grease Paint* (1936). She worked closely with her artist husband, Harold Knight, with whom she shared an exhibit at the Carnegie Institute in Pittsburgh in 1914. She often used the pseudonym "Orovida".

During World War II, Knight was appointed one of Great Britain's war artists and she was commissioned to sketch the Nuremberg War Crimes Trial. Her work is in the permanent collections of a number of major museums.

KOLLONTAI, Alexandra
1872-1952
Russian revolutionary, feminist and politician

Alexandra Mikhaylovna Kollontai abandoned the comfortable circumstances of her birth and marriage to become one of the most important figures in the Russian Revolution. She joined the workers' movement and left her husband to study economics in Zurich (1898). As a member of the Bolshevik Party she spoke out on the importance of women's rights. Although forced into exile in 1908, she continued traveling in Europe, working for international socialism and women's rights. After the fall of the monarchy, she returned to Russia and was made Commissar for Public Welfare. She campaigned for reforms in domestic life which included free love, group childcare and the simplification of divorce. She became disillusioned with the government, and in 1920 joined the Workers' Opposition, which was banned in 1921. Her opposition and her relationships with men who had been purged led to her virtual exile; appointed an ambassador, she spent the rest of her life outside her country.

KOLLWITZ, Käthe
1867-1945
German artist, sculptor

A socialist whose prints convey a profound compassion for the oppressed, Käthe Schmidt was born in East Prussia and went to Berlin to study, where she met her husband, Dr. Karl Kollwitz, who had a practice in Berlin's working-class section. A master draftsman, she often sketched impoverished patients as they sat in the doctor's waiting room. The first woman elected to the Prussian Academy in 1919, she was forced out by the Nazis for her political beliefs. The Gestapo closed her husband's practice because of his leftist views and in 1943 her home and studio was destroyed by a bomb.

Her figural etchings focus on tragic aspects of human life and were protests against poor working conditions and the vagaries of war. A memorable series included *Weaver's Revolt*, *Peasant's War* and *Death Greeted as a Friend*. She suffered losses in both World Wars – her son in World War I and her grandson in World War II. She sculpted an impressive 10-foot-tall bronze relief called *Mourning* in 1938 and wrote a play called *The Awakening of Spring*. She continued to work until the last year of her life, but the Nazis prevented her from exhibiting her work.

KOLSTAD, Eva
1918-
Norwegian politician

Formerly a teacher of bookkeeping, Kolstad's political career has been founded on her support for women's rights. Born in Halder, Norway, Eva Lundegaard qualified as an independent chartered accountant in 1944. She worked for the International Alliance of Women and served on the board from 1949 to 1958, 1961 to 1968 and in 1973. From 1956 to 1968 she was president of the Norwegian Association for the Rights of Women and a member of the UN Committee on the Status of Women (1969-75). From 1960 to 1975 she served on the Oslo City Council. Meanwhile, from 1958 to 1961 and 1966 to 1969, she served as a Member of Parliament, eventually becoming a leader of the Government Council on the Equal Status of Men and Women, followed by her appointment from 1979 to 1988 as Ombudsman.

KORBUT, Olga
1955-
Russian gymnast

Olga Korbut began serious training in gymnastics at 11 under the guidance of Soviet coach Renald Knysh, who encouraged her daring moves such as a backward somersault on the balance beam and a similar dismount from the uneven bars. In 1970 she won a gold medal in the World Championships.

Scheduled as an alternate on the 1972 Soviet Olympic squad, she replaced an injured teammate and won three gold medals, in balance beam, floor exercises and team overall ranking as well as a silver medal on the uneven parallel bars. The Associated Press named her Female Athlete of the Year. Korbut toured the United States with the Russian team and her popularity stimulated vast interest in the sport of gymnastics for thousands of young girls. She took part in the 1976 Montreal Olympics and earned another gold in the balance beam and one in the team competition. Soon after, she retired to become a coach.

Käthe Kollwitz, the first woman member of the Prussian Academy of Arts, was considered "revolutionary" for her honest portrayal of the oppressed.

Olga Korbut performs on the balance beam at the 1972 Munich Olympics. She won three gold medals there for the USSR in women's gymnastics competition.

KREPS, Juanita
1921-
American economist, government official

Juanita Morris was born in Lynch, Kentucky, a small town in Harlan County. She attended Berea College, graduated in 1942, and received both her M.A. and Ph.D. from Duke University. During World War II, she was a junior economist for the National War Labor Board, before she began her teaching career. Returning to Duke in 1955, she was made a full professor in 1968, and was given the James B. Duke Chair in 1972. The same year she joined the Board of Directors of the New York Stock Exchange. She left that position in 1977 when she was appointed Secretary of Commerce by President Jimmy Carter. She became the first woman and the first professional economist to hold that cabinet post. She resigned in 1979 to return to Duke, where she specializes in labor demographics, with particular attention to the employment of women and older workers.

KRONE, Julie
1963-
American jockey

The leading money-winner among women jockeys, the winner of the most races by a woman jockey and the first woman jockey to win a Triple Crown race, Krone was born in Benton Harbor, Michigan. Her first recognized race was at Tampa Bay race track in 1981. In 1982, she took the jockey title at Atlantic City race track and won more than $1 million in purses. By 1988, she was the leading jockey at Monmouth Park and the Meadowlands in New Jersey, and was fourth in the nation's jockey standings. That year she became the first woman to ride in a Breeder's Cup race.

In 1991, Krone was the first woman jockey to ride in the Belmont, the third and most grueling leg of the Triple Crown, and in 1993 she won the Belmont, another first for a woman jockey. She was badly hurt in a fall at Saratoga in 1993 but was back racing in the summer of 1994. Her gritty determination seems boundless: "I don't want to be the best female jockey, I want to be the best jockey."

KUHN, Maggie
1905-
American social activist

"Sheer luck" is Maggie Kuhn's explanation of how she has lived a life of independence, romance and activism. She is best known as the founder and chief spokesperson of the Grey Panthers, which has worked to end the Vietnam War, make health care available for all, and end the stereotypical portrayal of the elderly in the media. Born in Buffalo, New York, and educated at Case Western Reserve in Ohio, Kuhn spent many years working for the YWCA, helping working women to gain tools to fight for social and political change. She has broken racial, age and class taboos in her love life and caused a furore when she suggested that "older women who cannot find male lovers . . . should look to each other for love."

KULTHUM, Umm
1908-1975
Egyptian singer

A phenomenally popular Egyptian vocalist, Umm Kulthum was born in a small village in the Nile delta and began singing in religious celebrations. Guided by the famous singer Shykh Abu aj-'lla, Kulthum went to Cairo in 1922. She was strongly influenced by the Egyptian poet Ahmad Rami, whose works provided the lyrics for many of her songs.

Kulthum was noted for her mastery of traditional intervals. Her four-hour-long concerts consisted mostly of traditional religious chants and her rich, resonant voice had a hypnotic effect upon her audience. Her performances were given in open air arenas before huge crowds. Called the "Mother of Middle Eastern Music", at her death Cairo Radio broadcast the chanting of the Koran, an honor usually provided only for heads of state. World dignitaries joined thousands of mourners at her funeral service.

L

LA FRESSANGE, Ines de
1955-
French fashion model, designer, boutique owner

Ines de La Fressange epitomizes French chic, sophisticated and intelligent. Karl Lagerfeld's leading model during the 1980s, de La Fressange was the face of Chanel, with one of the best contracts ever offered a French model. After a rift with her mentor, she decided to retire and open her own designer boutique in Paris which demonstrated her unique sense of style. It was a success, and she opened another salon in New York. Influenced by bohemian parents, her strength of character led her to educate herself, and develop talents which would transform her into a successful business-woman.

LAGERLÖF, Selma
1858-1940
Swedish writer

The first woman to win the Nobel Prize for literature, Lagerlöf had an idyllic childhood, and the fairy tales and legends of Swedish country life she learned in her youth would be the constant subject matter of her narratives. After attending the Royal Women's Superior Training School, she taught secondary school for several years, writing fiction as a sideline for magazines. Her first full-length book, *The Gösta Berling Saga*, was adapted into a feature film with Greta GARBO in her first starring role. The setting of the two-volume *The Wonderful Adventures of Nils*, for which she won the 1909 Nobel Prize, was derived from her childhood homestead, Marbacka, and the prize money enabled Lagerlöf to purchase the property. The popular books were translated into 34 languages.

In 1914 Lagerlöf was named the first female director of the Swedish Academy. Her later works include *Jerusalem*, *Lillicrone's Home* (a sequel to *The Gösta Berling Saga*), and *The Outcasts*, a fervent protest against war. In the last year of Lagerlöf's life, she arranged for a visa to Sweden for the German-Jewish poet, Nelly SACHS, who would win the Nobel Prize in 1966.

Selma Lagerlöf was the first woman to win the Nobel Prize for literature, in 1909.

LAINE, Cleo
1927-
British singer

A native of Southall, Middlesex, popular singer Clementine Dinah Laine joined the Dankworth Orchestra in 1953. Her special gifts of phrasing versatility and a range over four octaves could adapt to both scat singing and the blues ballads of Billie HOLIDAY. She is acclaimed for reaching the highest recorded singing note by a human voice on her recording of Stephen Sondheim's song "Being Alive" from her album *Cleo's Greatest Show Hits*.

Laine's recording popularity was promoted by television concert specials. She also acted in the 1958 play *Flesh to a Tiger*, for which she won a Moscow Art Theatre Award. During the 1960s her renditions of the works of modern composers were performed in London and at the Edinburgh Festival, notably in the Brecht/Weill collaboration *The Seven Deadly Sins* in 1961.

Her first marriage was dissolved but her second marriage to the musician John Dankworth in 1958 enhanced her career as he composed and arranged many of her finest songs.

LANDERS, Ann (Esther Pauline Friedman Phillips)
1918-
VAN BUREN, Abigail (Pauline Esther Friedman Phillips)
1918-
American syndicated columnists

Under their pen names Abigail Van Buren and Ann Landers, these twins from Iowa became household names, synonymous with advice for the troubled and the

One of Dorothea Lange's best-known photographs, Migrant Mother, Nipomo, California *(1936).*

RIGHT: *Polish harpsichordist Wanda Landowska revived interest in baroque music and in the use of early keyboard instruments.*

love-lorn.

Esther Phillips was a housewife who decided on a whim to apply for the "Ann Landers" position at the *Chicago Sun-Times* in 1955. She got it, and by 1979 had acquired a readership of 60 million. Her columns, now syndicated, are filled with no-nonsense advice, and went beyond giving personal advice when she came out against the Vietnam War and supported gun control.

Pauline became her sister's rival in 1956 when she started her "Dear Abby" column with the *San Franciscio Chronicle*. Pauline advises readers of her syndicated column not to smoke, drink, or engage in premarital sex in a column that is much more traditional than her sister's.

LANDOWSKA, Wanda
1879-1959
Polish harpsichordist, pianist, teacher

Born in Warsaw, Wanda Alexandra Landowska studied piano there and in Berlin, where she was a professor at the Hochschule from 1913 to 1919. She subsequently moved to Paris where she founded a school of early music interpretation in 1925. She researched centuries-old music and early keyboard instruments at a time when recordings were making it possible for a wider audience to enjoy this music. Landowska influenced the modern revival of interest in the harpsichord in part by requesting modern composers, including De Falla and Poulenc, to write for the instrument. She became known especially for her recording of Bach's "Well-Tempered Clavier", and is acknowledged as one of the greatest performers on the harpsichord. Her research was visible in her performance where she seemed to reproduce effortlessly the "graces" of earlier players, and also in the books she wrote on the subject, including *La musique ancienne.*

LANGE, Dorothea
1895-1965
American photographer

One of America's first documentary photographers whose work was noted for its intense, gritty images of the dispossessed of the Depression era, Dorothea Lange was born in Hoboken, New Jersey. She trained with Clarence White, a member of the Linked Ring, an international group of photographers that included Alfred Stieglitz and Edward Steichen among its international membership.

Lange started out as a society photographer in San Francisco before being recruited by Roy Stryker to join a government-sponsored photography project for the Federal Resettlement Administration. Lange's photographs of Depression victims reveal a compelling compassion for the downtrodden and rallied popular support for Roosevelt's plan to aid the rural poor. Lange worked alongside Walker Evans and Ben Shahn and she published a book in 1939 *An American Exodus: A Record of Human Erosion.*

During World War II, Lange continued as a courageous and crusading photographer, recording the Japanese-Americans interned at prison camps in the U.S. Her portraits also included international dignitaries and studies of the Shakers.

LATYNINA, Larissa
1934-
Russian gymnast

Latynina elevated the standards of gymnastics, devising intricate, technical moves that changed the performance and look of the sport. In a 12-year career between 1954 and 1966, during which she had two children, Latynina won 18 Olympic medals in three consecutive Games and in world competition earned 10 individual and five team titles. Her nine Olympic gold medals set a new record, and she is the only gymnast, male or female, to have won medals in every event in two Olympics (1956 and 1960) and to have been overall champion in both. She was a member of the victorious Soviet gymnastics team in 1956, 1960 and 1964 and was the highest scorer for them in all three Olympiads.

Latynina's best event was the floor exercises, which emphasized her supple grace and technical proficiency at transitions in a complex arrangement of floor moves. She retired in 1966 and coached the Soviet gymnastics team. She was a pivotal figure in the career of Olga KORBUT, pressuring officials to allow her to compete as an adult at a very young age.

Estée Lauder in a 1989 photograph.

LAUDER, Estée
1908?-
American cosmetics entrepreneur

Josephine Esther Mentzer was born in

L

Corona, Queens, and started working as a saleswoman, persuading beauty salons and then department stores to carry skin creams invented by her uncle, a chemist. In 1953 she introduced her first successful product, Youth Dew bath oil. She built the single product into an empire of four distinct product lines, each directed at a particular age group. These include Clinique for young girls and women in their 20s, Prescriptives for those in the 30- and 40-year age range, and Estée Lauder for older women. She also produces Aramis for men. It was Lauder who first had the marketing idea of giving away introductory samples, and most other cosmetics companies also now do this. She remained CEO from 1946 until 1982, and is still the chairman of the board of Estée Lauder Inc., a company that generates nearly $26 billion per year. In 1989 she presided over the opening of an Estée Lauder shop on Gorky Street in Moscow – the first western perfumery in the country to offer cosmetics to ordinary Soviet citizens who could pay for them in rubles.

LAURENÇIN, Marie
1886-1956
French painter, designer, poet

A member of the avant-garde artistic circle of Braque and Picasso in Paris, Marie Laurençin was born there in 1886 and attended the Lycée Lamartine and studied art at the Academie Humbert. Her paintings were displayed in the Salon des Independents in 1907 and later at the Galerie Barbazouges. Between 1907 and 1913 Laurençin had a difficult relationship with the poet Guillaume Apollinaire. She married the German artist Otto van Waerjen in 1914, and they settled in Barcelona, Spain. She contributed poems to a Dadaist journal called "391" and had a volume of her poems, *Petit bestiare*, published in 1926. She returned to Paris after her divorce in 1920 and achieved increasing recognition for her oil paintings, lithographs and decorative designs. She fashioned dresses for the Art Deco designer Paul Poiret, and furnished wallpaper patterns for André Groult. She also provided sets and costumes for Diaghilev's ballet *Les biches* which was performed by the Ballet Russes in 1924. Laurençin also was commissioned for a variety of society portraits which were painted in her signature style with elongated limbs and an air of hauteur.

LAWRENCE, Gertrude
1898-1952
British actress

Gertrude Alexander Dagmar Lawrence-Klasen was born in London and made her first appearance on stage at the age of 12. She studied dance and acting at the Italia Conti school where she met her life-long friend Noel Coward. Her first real success was in *Charlot's Revue of 1924*, in which she introduced the song "Limehouse Blues". Two years later she had another great success in the Gershwins' *Oh, Kay*. In 1930, she starred in the original London production of *Private Lives*, the play that Noel Coward had written for her. They also both played it in New York the following year. She also appeared in his series of one-act plays, *Tonight at 8:30* in 1936. Her other famous performances include *Susan and God* (1936), which she repeated for television years later, and Kurt Weill's *Lady in the Dark* (1941). During World War II she toured for ENSA and the USO, and was a favorite of troops in both armies. She starred in a revival of *Pygmalion* after the war, and also appeared in the film version of *The Glass Menagerie* (1950). In 1951, she starred in *The King and I*, another part which had been written for her, but died of cancer during the run.

Gertrude Lawrence in the film version of The Glass Menagerie *(1950).*

LEAKEY, Mary D.
1913-
British archaeologist

Working closely with her husband, archaeologist Louis S. Leakey (1903-1972), Dr. Mary Leakey discovered the remains of some of modern man's earliest known ancestors. In Tanganyika, East Africa, the couple discovered fossil remains of a primitive hominid (*Zinjanthropus*) that lived some 1,500,000 years ago. In 1961 they found fossils of a creature they named *Kenyapithecus*; although it was more than 14 million years old, it appeared more manlike than apelike. From these findings, the Leakeys

Mary Leakey studies skull fragments with her husband at the Olduvai Gorge, 1959.

concluded that human life began in Africa and that several human species developed side by side, of which only *Homo sapiens* has survived.

LEAVITT, Henrietta
1868-1921
American astronomer

Working independently some years before the installation of the 100-inch reflector telescope at Mt. Wilson, California, Henrietta Leavitt made a discovery that helped astronomers measure the distance to faraway galaxies. In 1912 she was studying variations in brightness of a class of stars known as the Cepheids, whose brightness varies regularly within short time periods. When she discovered that the absolute brightness of these stars could be determined by the time periods involved, it became possible to measure the distance to galaxies which contained such stars. Prior to this discovery, the newly discovered galaxies had been too far from Earth to measure their distance by the method used to find the distance to nearer stars.

LEE, Gypsy Rose
1914-1970
American entertainer, writer

An unusual combination of burlesque queen and mystery writer whose narratives drew upon her experiences as an entertainer, she was born Rose Louise Hovick and was raised in Seattle, where she began a singing and dancing act with her sister (who became the actress June Havoc). Her speciality was a song "Hard-Boiled Rose" and at 15, she soloed as a stripper at burlesque houses. Calling herself Gypsy Rose Lee, she became a star at Minsky's and debuted with the Ziegfeld Follies in 1936.

Her first mystery *The G-String Murders* was a bestseller in 1941, followed by *Mother Finds a Body* and *The Naked Genius*. She supplied articles with a witty, offbeat style to the *New Yorker* and *Collier*'s magazines.

Her 1957 autobiography *Gypsy* became a Broadway musical comedy in 1959 and a film in 1965. She acted in the movies *Stage Door Canteen*, *Belle of the Yukon* and *Doll Face* (based on *The Naked Genius*). Her paintings appeared in Peggy GUGGENHEIM's notable exhibit *Art of This Century*.

LEE, Peggy
1920-
American singer, songwriter, actress

A platinum-blonde songwriter and chanteuse whose club performances of popular songs were consistent sellouts for over three decades, she was born Norma Doloris Egstrom in Jamestown, North Dakota. Benny Goodman first spotted her in a Chicago nightclub in 1941 and she made her first records with Goodman's jazz group. Her first big hit was a 1948 album *Mañana*, with singles such as "Black Coffee".

A song stylist noted for her interpretative, rhythmic versatility, Lee's repertoire embraced songs from Bessie SMITH to popular ballads among Top 40 Billboard hits. She has written over 500 songs. In the mid-1950s she produced a successful album, *Call It a Day*, and her signature song "Is That All There Is" (1969) was derived from a Bertolt Brecht poem.

Lee appeared in two Hollywood films: *The Jazz Singer* with Danny Thomas (1953) and *Pete Kelly's Blues* (1955), for which she received an Academy Award nomination.

LeGUIN, Ursula K.
1929-
American writer

The daughter of a renowned anthropologist and a folklorist, Ursula Kroeber was born and raised in Berkeley, California, attended Radcliffe College and Columbia University and went to Paris as a Fulbright scholar in 1953. There she met and married an historian, Charles LeGuin, with whom she settled in Portland, Oregon.

LeGuin's fantasy worlds are sometimes inhabited by mixed gender species as in *The Left Hand of Darkness* (1969). LeGuin devises imaginative social relationships and personalities for her science fiction characters with a parallel discourse of commentary on real world problems. Her novels include *Rocannon's World* (1966) and *The Dispossessed* (1974), and her short story collections include *The Wind's Twelve Quarters* (1975) and *The Compass Rose*. In addition, she wrote the prize-winning children's science fiction trilogy about a world called Earthsea whose volumes include *The Wizard of Earthsea*, *The Tombs of Atuan* and *The Farthest Shore*.

LEHMANN, Lotte
1888-1976
German operatic soprano

Lotte Lehmann was born in Perleberg in eastern Germany and studied in Berlin. She made her debut in 1910, as the second boy in *The Magic Flute* in Hamburg, and her first London appearance as Sophie in *Der Rosenkavalier* at Drury Lane in 1914. Strauss selected her to sing the Composer at the premiere of *Ariadne auf Naxos* in 1916. She later sang both Octavian and the Marschallin in *Der Rosenkavalier*, and made her Covent Garden debut in the latter role in 1924. She didn't appear in the United States until 1930, when she sang Sieglinde in *Der Walkure* at the Lyric in Chicago. It was the same role she sang for her Metropolitan Opera debut in 1934. She continued at the Met until 1945, and gave her final farewell concert in 1951. She taught thereafter, at Northwestern and several other universities, and was famous for master classes that attracted students like Grace BUMBRY. Considered one of the greatest singers of the century, she specialized in Mozart, Strauss and Wagner.

Soprano Lotte Lehmann as The Marschallin in Der Rosenkavalier.

Suzanne Lenglen, French lawn tennis star of the 1920s.

LEIBOVITZ, Annie
1950-
American photojournalist

Best known for her portraits of actors, writers and celebrities, Annie Leibovitz attended the San Francisco Art Institute. In 1970 she took a portfolio of photographs to the art director of the avant-garde *Rolling Stone* magazine in San Francisco, who hired her on the spot. Within a month, her portrait of John Lennon appeared on the front cover of *Rolling Stone*, where she became the chief photographer in 1973.

She combines both photojournalism and formal portraiture of unusual characters in a manner akin to that of Diane Arbus and Robert Adelman. She contributes to *Vanity Fair*, *Vogue*, *Esquire* and *Rolling Stone*, among other publications, and has published two volumes of her celebrity photographs (1983 and 1991) and *Sarajevo the Besieged* (1993).

LENGLEN, Suzanne
1899-1938
French tennis player

The first star of lawn tennis, Suzanne Lenglen was the world's singles and world's doubles champion before her fifteenth birthday in 1914. She went on to win six Wimbledon singles titles (1919-23 and 1925). She was also a six-time women's doubles champion at Wimbledon, partnering with Elizabeth Ryan (1919-23 and 25), and she also won the mixed doubles three times (1920, 1922 and 1925). She won the Olympic gold medal in women's singles and mixed doubles in 1920.

Lenglen retired into professional tennis in 1926. Known for her glamor and temperament as well as for her legendary accuracy, Leglen set the practical style of short skirts and bare arms for female tennis players. She was posthumously awarded the French Cross of the Legion of Honor.

LENYA, Lotte
1898-1981
Austrian singer, actress

Karoline Wilhelmine Blamaur was born in Vienna, and began her career as a dancer in Zurich during World War I. She moved to Berlin in 1920, working in the various cabarets that sprang up in Weimar Germany. In 1926 she met composer Kurt Weill, whom she married. She made her debut as a singer in the first version of Weill's opera *The Rise and Fall of the City of Mahagonny* in Baden-Baden in 1927. In 1928 she created the role of Jenny in Weill's *The Three-Penny Opera*. Lenya also appeared in the film version directed by G.W. Pabst in 1931. She and Weill moved to the United States in 1935,

Lotte Lenya in her role as procuress in Roman Spring of Mrs. Stone *(1962).*

where Lenya appeared with Helen Hayes in *Candle in the Wind*, and several other productions including a revival of *The Three-Penny Opera* in 1951, the year after Weill's death. She devoted much of her life to the preservation and production of Weill's works, even instructing certain singers like Teresa Stratas in their performance. She also appeared in several films, including *From Russia With Love* (1964).

LESSING, Doris
1919-
British novelist

Doris Tayler was born to British parents in Persia and was raised on a 3000-acre farm in Zimbabwe. Her first marriage at 20 to Frank Wisdom produced two children; she had another child by her second husband, Gottfried Lessing, whom she divorced in 1949. Thereafter, she settled in London, joined the Communist Party and made her living as a professional writer. Her first novel *The Grass Is Singing* (1950) was a success. She followed it with a series of four novels whose heroine was Martha Quest, a woman confronting racism as well as a variety of personal issues. In *The Golden Notebook* (1962), she analyzed the socialization processes women undergo, and *Summer Before the Dark* (1973) probes the relationship between identity and aging. Lessing's "space fiction" journeys were *Shikasta* (1973) and *The Marriages Between Zones Three, Four and Five* (1980). She published *The Good Terrorist* in 1985; *The Fifth Child* in 1988; and *The Real Thing* and *African Laughter* in 1992.

LEVI-MONTALCINI, Rita
1909-
Italian biochemist

The daughter of an educated Jewish family in Turin, Rita Levi-Montalcini surmounted many obstacles to enroll at Turin University's school of medicine in 1929 with the goal of becoming a medical researcher. Guided by Professor Giuseppe Levi (no relation), she studied nerve cells grown *in vitro* and earned an M.D. in neurology. She continued her research despite Fascist opposition during World War II and emigrated to the United States in 1950 to work with Dr. Stanley Cohen at Washington University's Viking Hamburger Laboratory.

Maya Lin holds a miniature of her design for the Vietnam Veterans Memorial in Washington, D.C., in 1981.

There they discovered "nerve growth factor", or NGF, for which they earned the Nobel Prize in medicine or physiology in 1986. From 1961 she divided her time between St. Louis and Rome, where she founded the Institute of Cell Biology. Her autobiography, *In Praise of Imperfection: My Life and Work*, was published in 1988.

LIN, Maya
1960-
American architect, sculptor

Maya Lin is best known for her design of the Vietnam Veteran's Memorial in Washington, D.C., a public commission she completed at just 22. Dedicated in 1982, the sculpture consists of a sleek, polished black granite V-shaped wall inscribed with the names of more than 58,000 war dead.

Born in Athens, Ohio, Lin graduated from the Yale School of Architecture in 1986 and has finished six public site commissions, with two more planned as of 1994. Lin designed the Civil Rights Memorial at the Southern Poverty Law Center in Montgomery, Alabama, and a sculpture to commemorate women at Yale. For the Wexner Center for the Arts at Ohio University, she created *Groundswell*, her version of a Japanese Zen garden made up of 40 tons of crushed, recycled glass from the Ford Motor Company, placed in an undulating pattern of mounds. Her work is primarily abstract, employing natural and recycled materials that bring attention to the earth's resources and beauty.

LINDBERGH, Anne Morrow
1906-
American novelist, essayist

Anne Lindbergh is as well-remembered for the improbable life she led as for her insightful novels, travel accounts and essays. From a wealthy family, she married aviator Charles Lindbergh in 1929, and the couple became the darlings of the press. When their son was kidnapped and killed in 1932, the case riveted the nation. Following the tragedy, the family moved to Europe, and Lindbergh turned to writing to heal her grief. A new scandal hit when they returned to the United States in 1939, and their isolationist stance drew accusations of Nazi sympathies. Scorned by the public, Lindbergh concentrated on raising her five children and writing. Her beautiful essays in *A Gift From the Sea* (1955) distill the fragile balance she found between public and private worlds, renewing her popularity with a broad readership.

LITTLEWOOD, Joan
1914-
British theatrical impresario, producer, director

Born in London and trained at the Royal Academy of Dramatic Arts, Joan Littlewood founded the Theatre Union, an experimental company, in 1935. It was reformed in 1945 as the Theatre Workshop. Its left-wing ideology brought a fresh approach to the staging of established plays, and it looked to working-class playwrights for new material. The Theatre Workshop opened at the Theatre Royal, Stratford East in 1953 with Littlewood's production of *Twelfth Night*. They were also invited to represent Britain at the Theatre des Nations in Paris in 1955 and 1956. In 1955, Littlewood directed the first British production of Brecht's *Mother Courage*, and played the title role. She was also responsible for

Joan Littlewood, director of the Theatre Workshop, in 1974.

early stagings of Brendan Behan's *The Quare Fellow* in 1956 and Shelagh Delany's *A Taste of Honey* in 1958. In 1963 she created the anti-war revue *Oh, What a Lovely War*. Since 1975 she has worked outside Britain much of the time, running an international summer school in Tunisia and Calcutta. In 1994 she published her autobiography, *Joan's Book*.

LONG, Marguerite
1874-1966
French pianist, teacher

Marguerite Marie Charlotte Long was born in Nîmes, and began piano lessons as a child. She studied with Mermontel at the Paris Conservatory, and was appointed an instructor in 1906, a position she held until 1940. In 1920 she founded her own school, promoting contemporary French music. She was noted for her performances of works by her friends Fauré, Ravel and Debussy. She wrote several books on the performing of the works of those three composers. In 1932 she was the soloist at a performance of Ravel's Piano Concerto in G, with Ravel conducting. The piece had been dedicated to her. In 1940 violinist Jacques Thibaud joined her at her music school, and on the concert stage. Together they established the Long-Thibaud music competitions in 1943.

LONSDALE, Dame Kathleen
1903-1971
Irish physicist

Born Kathleen Yardley into a Baptist family in Newbridge, Ireland, she became a Quaker and an ardent pacifist upon her marriage to Dr. Thomas Lonsdale. Her work in X-ray crystallography made her the first woman to be elected to the Royal Society, in 1945. Fifteen years later, she became its vice-president. From 1949 to 1968, she was Professor of Chemistry at London University, and she served as the British Association's first woman president in 1967-8. Throughout this period, she was active in the cause of peace. During World War II, she spent a month in prison for refusing to register for civil defense duties, apart from firewatching. In 1951 she accompanied a peace mission to the Soviet Union and wrote the influential book *Is Peace Possible?* When asked her race for an entry visa, she replied, "Human."

The most accomplished X-ray crystallographer of her generation, Kathleen Lonsdale also worked for peace.

LOOS, Anita
1893?-1981
American writer

Most famous for her 1925 novel *Gentlemen Prefer Blondes: The Illuminating Diary of a Professional Lady*, Anita Loos's satire shaped a generation of American comedy.

Starting with *The New York Hat* (1912), her first silent film scenario penned when she was a teenager, Loos wrote over 150 sparkling scenarios and screenplays. Her dozens of collaborative scripts with husband John Emerson were mostly written by her. Lorelei Lee, the naive young flapper of *Gentlemen Prefer Blondes* won such wide appeal with her inane observations and gold-digging charms that the work was adapted as a play, two musicals and two movies, and translated into 14 languages. Despite her phenomenal success, California-born Loos didn't take herself or Hollywood glamour very seriously, commenting on her writing, "I did it for the money, and it was the easiest money I ever made."

LOPEZ, Nancy
1956-
American golfer

When Nancy Lopez won nine LPGA tournaments in 1978 including the LPGA championship, she became the only golfer, male or female, to win the Rookie of the Year and Player of the Year titles in the same year.

Raised in Roswell, New Mexico, she won her first golf tournament at 9 and by 12 was the New Mexico State Women's Amateur Champion. By 16 she was the top-ranked amateur player in the nation and as a high school senior, placed second in the U.S. Women's Open. After attending the University of Tulsa on an athletic scholarship, she joined the professional tour in 1977. She dominated the LPGA in 1978, 1979 and 1985, receiving Player of the Year honors each year. The Associated Press named her Female Athlete of the Year in 1978 and 1985. By 1991 she had won more than $3.2 million. Heading into the 1994 Dinah Shore Classic, having curtailed her touring to 15 major events a year, she had 47 tour victories in her extraordinary career.

LOPOKOVA, Lydia
1892-1981
Russian dancer, actress

A Russian ballerina who made her first stage appearance at 9, Lopokova was born in St. Petersburg and graduated from the Imperial Ballet School. She joined its corps ballet at the Mariinsky Theatre in 1909. Diaghilev selected her for his Ballets Russes in 1910 where she created the role of Columbine in *Carnival* and replaced Tamara Karsavina in *The Firebird* in 1911. That year she left to dance and act in the United States, but she returned to Diaghilev's group in 1916.

She performed the lead in *Les Femmes de Bonne Humeur* (1916), the can-can dancer in *La Boutique Fantastique* (1919) and the lilac fairy in *The Sleeping Princess* (1921). In 1921 Lopokova married the renowned British economist John Maynard Keynes and together they founded the Arts Theatre in Cambridge. Lopokova danced in Frederick Ashton's *Facade* at the Camargo Club in 1931 and in *Coppelia* for the Vic-Wells Ballet in 1933. From 1933 to 1937 she performed in a variety of roles at the Old Vic: as Olivia in *Twelfth Night*, Nora in *A Doll's House*, Hilda in *The Master Builder* and Celimine in *Le Misanthrope*. From 1946 to 1949 Lopokova was a member of the Arts Council of Great Britain.

LOS ANGELES, Victoria de
1923-
Spanish lyric soprano

Victoria Gómez Cima was born in Barcelona, and studied at the Conservatory there before she gave her first public concert in 1944. She made her operatic debut at the Liceo in Barcelona the following year, and won first prize at the International Contest of Music and Singing in in Geneva in 1947. The natural beauty of her voice gave her a new name, and was perfect for many roles in the standard repertoire, including Violetta in *La Traviata*, and Marguerite in *Faust*, the role she sang at both her Paris and Metropolitan Opera debuts. She remained on the Met's roster from 1951 to 1961, the first year she sang at Bayreuth, as Elisabeth in *Tannhäuser*. Although she retired from opera in 1969, she continued to grace the concert stage for many years, excelling in renditions of French art songs and Spanish folk songs, frequently accompanying herself on the guitar.

LOW, Juliette Gordon
1860-1927
American founder of the Girl Scouts of America

Juliette Magill Kinzie Gordon was born in Savannah, Georgia, and educated in private schools. She married William Mackay Low in 1886, and after her husband's death, while traveling in England in 1911, she met Robert Baden-Powell, founder of the British Scouts, and later of the Boy Scouts of America. With his encouragement, she organized several Girl Guide troops in Britain.

Upon her return to the United States, she organized the first American Girl Guides in her native Savannah, Georgia. These young girls were trained in citizenship, good conduct and outdoor activities. As more troops were formed, the national organization Girl Guides was created. In 1915, three years after their formation, the Girl Guides officially became the Girl Scouts of America. Low served as the Girl Scouts' first president until 1920.

LOWELL, Amy
1874-1925
American poet

A descendant of a wealthy and well-known Boston family, Amory Lowell was born in Brookline, Massachusetts. Her Imagist poetry is noted for its spare, pictorial phrasing. Two collections of her poems were published, *A Dome of Many-Colored Glass* in 1912 and *What's O'Clock* in 1925, for which she was awarded the Pulitzer Prize posthumously. The latter included "The Sisters", an ode to women's rights. Lowell also translated the work of six French poets who had influenced the Imagist movement, and wrote a biography of John Keats as well as literary criticism.

Amy Lowell was an influential Imagist poet and a memorable personality.

Her substantial physical size, financial heft (she tried unsuccessfully to buy two poetry magazines whose editors resisted her control) and her passion for cigars helped make her a memorable personality. She was also a generous patron of such writers as D.H. Lawrence.

LUCE, Clare Boothe
1903-1987
American journalist, playwright, diplomat

The witty, sharp-tongued Clare Booth Luce has been called one of the world's most admired women. Born in New York and educated at private schools, she began her many-careered life as a journalist, editing for *Vogue* (1930) and *Vanity Fair* (1931-34). She married millionaire Henry Luce in 1935, founder and owner of Time Inc., and became a *Life* correspondent during World War II. She had remarkable success with her comic plays *The Women* (1936), *Kiss the Boys Goodbye* (1938) and *Margin for Error* (1940), and when appointed ambassador to Italy (1953-57), the first American woman head of a mission to a major post, she remarked that casting characters for a play was excellent preparation for diplomacy, for she was expert at noting people's inflections, gestures and manners of speaking. From 1982 until her death, she was a member of President Reagan's foreign intelligence advisory board.

Clare Booth Luce's multifaceted life included a term as U.S. ambassador to Italy (1953-57).

LUGARD, Dame Flora Shaw
1852-1929
Irish journalist

The first female correspondent for a British newspaper, Flora Shaw was the daughter of a major general in the British army. After her education at home in Ireland, she lived in Woolwich, London, where she implemented a cooperative venture for buying staples in bulk and taught the local poor.

Shaw became the first woman to head a department of *The Times* when she was placed in charge of Overseas News just months after becoming the first woman on staff there. She covered the slave trade and labor conditions in South Africa, New Zealand and Australia, and was also sent to the Klondike in the Yukon territory to cover the gold rush.

In 1902 she married Sir Frederick Lugard, the High Commissioner of Nigeria who later was governor of Hong Kong. The couple was active on behalf of refugees during World War I and Shaw was an ardent feminist who believed women should serve in the armed forces.

Loretta Lynn is one of the most popular and successful women in country music.

LUTYENS, Elizabeth
1906-1983
British composer

Agnes Elizabeth Lutyens was born in London. Her father was Sir Edwin Lutyens, the architect of New Delhi. She studied at the École Normale de Musique in the early 1920s, and at the Royal College of Music from 1926 to 1930. While still at college her setting of Keats's poem "To Sleep" was performed. She was one of the first British composers to adopt the 12-tone atonal technique in her *Chamber Concerto No. 1*, in 1939. Though a prolific composer, many of her compositions were not immediately accepted. Two of her works written in the 1950s, the chamber opera *Infidelio* and the cantata *De Amore*, were not performed until 1973. She was awarded a CBE in 1969, and composed her last work, the *Triolet II for Cello, Marimba and Harp*, the year before her death.

LUXEMBURG, Rosa
1870-1919
Polish revolutionary, feminist, pacifist

Born in Russian-ruled Poland to Jewish parents, Rosa Luxemburg, co-founder of both the German Communist Party and the precursor to Poland's Communist Party, strongly influenced European and Russian revolutionary thought. In 1893 she founded the Social Democratic Party with her lover Leo Jogiches. She organized workers' revolts in Poland, opposed nationalism and organized the Spartacus League for the pacifist extreme left. She spent much of World War I in prison, where she continued to write supporting revolution. She was beaten to death by German troops sent to put down an uprising she led in Berlin.

LYNN, Loretta
1935-
American country singer, songwriter

The first woman in country music to become a millionaire, Loretta Webb was born and raised in the coal mining Appalachian region of eastern Kentucky. She was married to "Moonie Lynn" at 14. A talent scout for Zero Records who saw her perform in Washington State in the late 1950s signed her up to record "I'm a Honky Tonk Girl". Soon after, she and her band were touring major cities including Nashville, Tennessee. In the 1960s she moved there, signed with Decca Records and produced a string of hits that included "Success", "Before I'm Over You", "Blue Kentucky Girl", "Dear Uncle Sam" and "You Ain't Woman Enough". Her albums, such as *Loretta Lynn* and *I Like 'Em Country* were critically well-received and popular bestsellers. She joined the cast of the Grand Ole Opry in Nashville in the late 1960s, and she was Billboard's Top Country Female Artist in 1967 and 1968. Sissy Spacek earned an Oscar for her portrayal of Loretta Lynn in the 1980 movie *Coal Miner's Daughter*.

LYNN, Dame Vera
1917-
British singer

A trouper from early childhood, Vera Lynn was raised in East Ham, London and first sang in public at 7. By 1935 she was recording with Loe Loss and became a member of the Charlie Kruz band. She sang for several years with the Ambrose Orchestra before going solo. During World War II, Lynn's appealing blonde looks and sweet, soft voice earned her the moniker of "Forces Sweetheart", and she sang to the armed troops on remote fronts such as Burma. Her radio show, "Sincerely Yours", ran from 1941 to 1947. Such tunes as "There'll Be Bluebirds Over the White Cliffs of Dover" and "We'll Meet Again" brought a tear to many an eye during the war years. The first British performer to reach the top of America's hit parade, her most famous song in the States, "Auf Wiedersehen", sold over 12 million copies. Lynn was created a Dame of the British Empire in 1975 and was awarded Freedom of the City of London in 1978.

LYONS, Dame Enid
1897-1981
Australian politician and newspaper columnist

While husband Joseph Lyons, Australian prime minister from 1932 to 1939, helped Lyons make her entry into politics, she soon carved her own niche. Brought up in Tasmania and a schoolteacher as a young woman, she married Lyons when she was 17, raised their 11 children, and assisted her husband in his career. After her husband's death in 1939, she entered politics and became the first female member of the House of Representatives for Darwin, Tasmania (1943-51). A newspaper columnist, she worked from 1951 to 1962 as a member of the Australian Broadcasting Commission. She wrote two autobiographies: *So We Take Comfort* (1960) and *Among the Carrion Crows* (1973).

Mary McCarthy, author of The Group *(1963), in a 1964 photograph.*

McAULIFFE, Sharon Christa
1948-1986
American passenger on space mission

A citizen passenger on the tragically fated Challenger space shuttle that exploded on January 28, 1986, Christa McAuliffe was born and raised in Boston, Massachusetts. A teacher at Concord High School in New Hampshire McAuliffe was chosen from 11,000 applicants for the role as the first citizen passenger on a space mission. One of McAuliffe's goals in flight was to have provided science lessons to school groups by satellite television.

McCARDELL, Claire
1905-1958
American fashion designer

A fashion designer whose styles embodied the functional, comfortable American look of ready-to-wear clothes that first appeared in the late 1930s, Claire McCardell was born into a prosperous family in Frederick, Maryland.

She attended the New York School of Fine and Applied Arts (now Parsons) and went to Paris to see *haute couture* showings in 1927. Returning to New York in 1930, she met her mentor, Robert Turk, the head of the sportswear firm Townley Frocks, who hired her as its chief stylist. She developed a separates line in 1934 and during World War II, employed denim in many of her outfits. Her "Popover" was a popular denim wraparound dress, and she also created a bodysuit leotard in wool jersey as well as harem pajamas. McCardell won all the major awards offered by the fashion industry in the 1940s and published *What Shall I Wear* in 1956. She later taught at Parsons School of Design and was named an advisor to the Costume Institute at the Metropolitan Museum of Art in New York.

McCARTHY, Mary
1912-
American writer

A journalist noted for her biting critical essays and liberal political sympathies, McCarthy was born in Minneapolis and raised by relatives after her parents died in the flu epidemic. Following her graduation from Vassar College in 1933 she wrote for the *Partisan Review*. After her first husband died, she married literary critic Edmund Wilson, who encouraged her fiction writing. She published short stories (*The Company She Keeps*, 1942), a novel (*The Groves of Academe*, 1952) and an account of their relationship (*A Charmed Life*, 1955). She is best known for *The Group*, a 1963 novel that chronicled the lives of eight women after college and the repression and lack of opportunity confronting well-educated women. Her *Cannibals and Missionaries* of 1979 explored modern liberalism.

After divorcing Wilson, McCarthy wed Bowden Broadwater in 1946, whom she later left for an American intelligence officer in Poland, James West. She was known for her searing articles opposing U.S. involvement in Vietnam. She is also highly respected for her writings on art, theater and travel.

McCLINTOCK, Barbara
1902-1992
American geneticist

A botanist who enrolled in college over her family's objections in 1919, Barbara McClintock was raised in Brooklyn, New York, and studied at Cornell University and worked alone for more than forty years as a research scientist at the Carnegie Institute of Washington. Her home and laboratory were at Cold Spring Harbor, Long Island, New York, where she planted corn each year and fertilized it according to her plan of genetic crosses, much as Gregor Mendel worked with the garden pea a hundred years ago. In the process, McClintock discovered mobile genetic elements that shed new light on recombinant DNA. Ultimately, her research increased understanding of human diseases like cancer and of how viruses work and bacteria can become resistant to drugs. She was awarded the Nobel Prize in physiology or medicine in 1983.

Barbara McClintock's discovery of "jumping genes" won her a Nobel Prize.

Flora MacDonald in 1979.

McCULLERS, Carson
1917-1967
American writer

A writer who focused on the mores and manners of the American South, Lula Carson Smith was born in Columbus, Georgia, and trained to be a musician. After a bout of rheumatic fever at 15, she gave up piano to write plays whose themes were "thick with incest, lunacy and murder". Her later stories and novels paid tribute to the downtrodden: loners, Southern blacks, and society's outcasts.

At 17 she took writing courses at Columbia University in New York, and at 20 she married Reeves McCullers, a troubled relationship that ended with his suicide in 1953. Her first book, *The Heart Is a Lonely Hunter* (1940), was a critical and financial success and later became a Hollywood film. She received fellowships from the Guggenheim Foundation and Yaddo, a writer's colony in Saratoga, New York, and was a member of the American Academy of Arts and Letters. Her later, best-known works include *Member of the Wedding* and *The Ballad of the Sad Café*.

MacDONALD, Flora
1926-
Canadian politician

Well-known for her energy and progressive stances, during her political career Flora MacDonald has campaigned for human rights, prison reform, abolition of the death penalty and abortion on demand. During the 1980s Flora MacDonald achieved distinction as Minister of Communications. From 1957 to 1966 she was Executive Director of the Progressive Conservative Headquarters, followed by a stint as National Secretary of the Progressive Conservative Association of Canada (1966-69). In 1972 she was elected Member of Parliament for Kingston and the Islands, and served successive terms as the Secretary of State for External Affairs, Minister for Employment and Immigration, and Minister of Communications. She also hosted a weekly television series called *North South* in 1990. As of 1992, she was appointed Chair of the International Development Research Center.

McKINNEY, Louise
1863-1933
Canadian suffragist and politician

McKinney, a leading figure in the Canadian Temperance Movement and an advocate of women's right to vote, was the first female member in any legislative body in the British Empire. Born Louise Crummy in Franksville, Ontario, she worked as a teacher in North Dakota, but returned to Canada after her marriage. In 1916 when she became a part of the leadership of the Non-Partisan League which sought public ownership of grain stores and flour mills. In 1917 she made history when she was elected the candidate for the League to the Alberta legislature, a position she held until 1921.

Illustrator Neysa McMein leads a women's suffrage parade in New York.

McMEIN, Neysa
1888-1949
American illustrator

An artist best-known for her pastel portraits of prominent American women that appeared in *McCall's* magazine and on the covers of the *Saturday Evening Post* and *Women's Home Companion*, Neysa McMein was born in Quincy, Illinois. She earned her way through the Art Institute of Chicago by writing music and playing the piano in a five-and-dime store. She later attended the Arts Students League in New York.

McMein was a war poster designer during World War I in both the United States and France and worked with the YMCA organization in France as well. She was a member of the Society of Illustrators and the Artists' Guild of the Authors' League of America, and her work was exhibited in galleries in Chicago and New York.

McPHERSON, Aimee Semple
1890-1944
American evangelist

Born Aimee Elizabeth Kennedy in Salford, Ontario, Canada, the future minister married evangelist Robert Semple at the age of eighteen and was ordained as a preacher of the Pentecostal Full Gospel Assembly in 1909. Widowed young during a missionary trip to China, she returned to the United States and joined the Salvation Army in 1912. She married Harold McPherson in 1916 and began her traveling revival tours all across the country. In 1921 she founded the International Church of the Foursquare Gospel, whose Angelus Temple in Los Angeles, California, attracted thousands. She was a gifted preacher who stressed fundamentalist principles including divine healing by faith and baptism in the Holy Spirit. She suffered a nervous breakdown in 1930 and her ministry was impaired by a series of court cases involving questionable financial transactions.

MADONNA
1958-
American singer, actress

A phenomenally successful contemporary entertainer whose erotic rock videos, world concert tours and tempestuous private life have earned her notoriety as well as popularity, Madonna is also shrewd at business and is known for her control of her own career.

Born Madonna Louise Ciccone in Bay City, Michigan, she abandoned a dance scholarship to the University of Michigan to go to New York in 1978. Her first album *Madonna* (1984) was a smash hit, with singles "Like a Virgin" and "Material Girl" soaring to the top of Billboard's charts. Her stage outfit of black bustier and garter belts, her shocking language and panoply of lewd gestures generated a cult following and vast publicity. Her 1985 film *Desperately Seeking Susan* and hit album *True Blue* (1986) brought more press attention. By 1989 she was the highest grossing woman in the entertainment business with a net worth estimated at $70 million. Her album *Blonde Ambition* was another success, heralded by a world concert tour which she recorded in the controversial film *Truth or Dare*. Her controversial book *Sex* was published in 1993.

MAKAROVA, Natalia
1940-
Russian dancer

A ballerina who combined classical finesse with a mysterious stage presence, Natalia Makarova was born in Leningrad, was graduated from the Vaganova School of Ballet in 1959 and joined the Kirov Ballet. In 1961 she was triumphant in her performance in *Giselle* at Covent Garden in London and went on tour throughout the United States. She also danced such Russian classics as *Aurora* and *Odette/Odile*. In 1970 Makarova defected from the USSR to join the American Ballet Theater in New York. She began performing in modern ballet by Anthony Tudor such as *Jardin Aux Lilas*, *Dark Elegies* and *Pillar of Fire* as well as the prima ballerina roles in *Swan Lake* and *The Sleeping Beauty*. In 1972 Makarova joined the Royal Ballet Company to dance several ballets by Kenneth Macmillan: *Manon*, *Das Lied von der Erde*, *Les Biches*, and a modern version of *Romeo and Juliet*. She also played the Black Queen in Ninette de VALOIS's *Checkmate*.

She retired from ballet in 1989 after performing with the Kirov for a year, and played a straight dramatic role in the London revival of *Tovarich* in 1991 and in a Moscow production of *Two For the Seesaw*.

Fundamentalist preacher Aimee Semple McPherson founded a church in 1921.

MALLON, Mary "Typhoid Mary"
1870-1938
Irish-American cook

Mary Mallon was the first known carrier of the bacteria which caused typhoid, a deadly disease at the turn of the century.

Irish immigrant Mallon worked as a cook in a number of private homes in New York. Although immune to the disease herself, she unwittingly transmitted it through her food preparations. A connection was made between Mallon and the typhoid outbreaks when a gifted epidemiologist noted a pattern of typhoid cases occurring in the households where she had worked.

When discovered as a carrier, Mallon was asked never to cook professionally again. She refused and had to be detained at a secluded hospital in the Bronx. Released after almost three years, she continued to cook in hotels and other institutions, not out of malice or ignorance, but because cooking was her passion. She was later readmitted to the hospital and lived out her life there.

Love her or hate her, most people have an opinion about Madonna, a pop star who maintains tight control of her own career.

MANDELA, Winnie (Nomzano)

1936-

South African political activist

In 1994, Winnie Mandela was elected president of the African National Congress's Women's League with 70 percent of the vote, showing that Winnie Mandela's years of organizing and fighting for South African freedom have not been forgotten.

A member of the Tembu royal house, Winnie Mandela has survived everything from her husband Nelson Mandela's 27-year jail sentence, to her own banning for eight years, to censure by the ANC for her outspokenness and unwillingness to toe a party line. In 1990, charges that she may have been party to the kidnapping and murder of a young man undermined her credibility. She and her husband, now president of South Africa, were subsequently divorced. Yet her election to the presidency of the ANC's Women's League makes her South Africa's most powerful and influential woman, and many people still see her as "the mother of the nation."

Winnie Mandela, president of the ANC's Women's League, with a group of children in Soweto.

MANKILLER, Wilma

1945-

Native-American chief

Wilma Mankiller became principal chief of the Cherokee Nation in 1985, making her the first female chief of a major Native American tribe.

Born in Talequah, Oklahoma, her family was relocated to San Francisco by the Bureau of Indian Affairs. Her involvement in Native-American rights began when she helped raise funds for the Indians who occupied Alcatraz Island in 1969. In the mid-1970s she reclaimed her grandfather's land in Oklahoma. She founded the Community Development Department of the Cherokee Nation in 1981 and was chief Ross Swimmer's running mate in 1983. As chief, she worked to counter stereotypes of Native Americans and brought the Cherokees' plight to national attention. She supported empowering Native Americans to solve their own problems. Afflicted with muscular dystrophy, she retired in 1994.

Ms. magazine voted her Woman of the Year in 1987. In her autobiography, *Mankiller – A Chief of Her People*, she recounts the obstacles she has overcome both professionally and personally to reach her present achievement.

MANSFIELD, Katherine

1888-1923

New Zealand writer

A short story writer who left her conventional Victorian background in New Zealand to join a group of avant-garde authors in London that included D.H. Lawrence and Virginia Woolf, Mansfield was born Katherine Beauchamp, the daughter of a successful entrepreneur who became director of the Bank of New Zealand, and attended Queen's College in London. Mansfield's first story collection, *Prelude* (1917), was published by the Woolfs' Hogarth Press. She also placed articles in *Rhythm*, a contemporary review edited by J. Middleton Murry, who became her husband in 1918 and was the subject of a subsequent novel, *The Man Without a Temperament.*

Mansfield suffered from tuberculosis and traveled restlessly in search of a cure. Despite her pain she wrote *Bliss and Other Stories* (1920) that recalled peaceful memories of her idyllic childhood in New Zealand. Mansfield followed a faith-healer to Fontainebleau, France, but died there of a hemorrhage at just 35.

MARALDO, Pamela

1947-

American health care administrator

Succeeding Faye Wattleton as president of the Planned Parenthood Federation of America in 1992, Pamela Maraldo moved to expand the organization's focus beyond reproductive rights toward comprehensive health services. Born in Wilmington, Delaware, Maraldo went to nursing school in New York (Adelphi University, 1970) and became a cardiovascular nurse at New York University Medical Center. She completed her master's degree at NYU (1976) while a research associate at the National Health Council, and from 1978 was director of public policy, then chief executive officer, of the National League for Nursing. She received her Ph.D. in 1985, when she was also named one of the top 12 executives of U.S. nonprofit organizations by *Savvy* magazine.

Wilma Mankiller (Cherokee) was the first woman chief of a major Native American tribe.

MARGRETHE II, Queen
1940-
Danish monarch

This much-loved monarch became Queen of Denmark on January 15, 1972, succeeding her father Frederick IX. When she was a child, the populace had voted to lift a ban on female monarchs, thus paving the way for her ascension. She studied abroad during the mid-60s, and so met her French diplomat husband, Prince Henrik of Denmark. Her children are Crown Prince Frederick, and Prince Joachim. An archaeologist, she writes for many scholarly journals, and is also a talented artist, best-known for her illustrations of J.R. Tolkien's *The Lord of the Rings*.

MARKHAM, Beryl
1902-1986
British aviator, writer

A free spirit and short story writer as well as an accomplished pilot, Beryl Markham was born in England and raised in Kenya by her father, a horse breeder and adventurer. She learned to train racehorses and to fly a plane, transporting mail, supplies, cargo and passengers between Sudan, Rhodesia, Kenya and Tanganyika. She flew the first solo flight across the Atlantic from east to west in September 1936, piloting a Vega Gull from England to Nova Scotia (where it crash-landed) in 21 hours and 25 minutes.

She wrote several books about living among the natives in East Africa and her experiences as a pilot and with thoroughbred racehorses, including *West with the Night* and *Straight On Till Morning*.

ABOVE: *British aviator Beryl Markham was the first person to fly solo across the Atlantic from east to west, in 1936.*

ABOVE: *The "rebel Countess," Sinn Fein leader Constance Markiewicz, practices her marksmanship at her home in Dublin.*

MARKIEWICZ, Countess Constance
1868-1927
Irish revolutionary

Daughter of an Irish baronet, Constance Gore-Booth became a principal leader in the Irish movement for independence. In 1898 she married a Polish landowner Count Casimir Markiewicz, and settled in the Ukraine, but she spent much time in Dublin, where she met many of the Irish Republican leaders. In 1908 she entered nationalist politics by joining Inghinidhe na hEireann, founded by Maud GONNE and Sinn Fein. Arrested after the Easter Rising of 1916 which she helped lead, she was released in the general amnesty of 1917, and became in 1918 the first woman to win election to the House of Commons. However, she followed Sinn Fein policy and refused her seat. She presided over the founding of the Fianna Fial in 1926, which sought to reform British-Irish relations constitutionally. A member of the first Dail (Irish Parliament) in 1923, she was reelected shortly before her death.

British ballerina Alicia Markova in rehearsal for Giselle *in 1957.*

MARKOVA, Dame Alicia
1910-
British dancer

Born Lilian Alicia Marks in London, she first performed at the Kensington Theatre in London and from the ages of 14 to 19, danced with Diaghilev's Ballets Russes, changing her last name to the Russian-sounding Markova. She later performed with Marie RAMBERT and then joined Ninette de VALOIS's Vic-Wells company, where she made her debut in *Giselle* in 1934 and soloed in the classic lead roles in *The Nutcracker* and *Swan Lake*. She formed a partnership with Anton Dolin that would endure throughout her career. From 1938 to 1941, the pair appeared with the Ballets Russes de Monte Carlo and then joined the American Ballet Theatre in New York, where Markova was the prima ballerina for seven highly successful seasons.

Markova was created a Dame of the British Empire and retired from the stage in 1963. She was Professor of Ballet and Performing Arts at the University of Cincinnati beginning in 1970, and still teaches master classes at the Royal Ballet School.

MARSH, Dame Ngaio
1899-1982
New Zealand novelist, Shakespearean director

Ngaio Marsh is renowned for her crisp detective novels featuring Roderick Alleyn of Scotland Yard – yet in this character's literary quips and allusions, Marsh reveals her first love, the works of William Shakespeare.

In 1920, Marsh acted with the Allan Wilkie Shakespeare Players in New Zealand, until 1928 when she moved to London for three years. Upon her return to New Zealand, she began to write. Her first murder mystery, *A Man Lay Dead*, appeared in 1933, and for almost 50 years her highly successful detective novels delighted audiences around the world. All the while, she directed Shakespearean productions for the first all-New Zealand Shakespearean Company, of which she was the director. She was honored with the title Dame Commander, Order of the British Empire in 1966, for her lively and multifaceted service to literature.

MARY, QUEEN
1867-1953
British monarch

Daughter of Prince Franz, Duke of Teck, and Princess Mary Adelaide, first cousin to Queen Victoria, she spent her childhood haunted by the debts of her parents. Queen Victoria pushed for her marriage first to the Duke of Clarence, heir to Edward VII, and then to his brother Prince George, whom she married. Their children were David (Edward VIII and heir to the throne), Albert (George VI), Mary, Henry, George and John. During World War I, Queen Mary gained great respect from her subjects as she tirelessly organized relief during the war. Never very close to her children, she turned away from her son Edward VIII when he married American divorcee Wallis SIMPSON. Her second son, George VI, became king.

A Dutch exotic dancer, Mata Hari was convicted of espionage and shot in 1917.

MATA HARI (Margaretha Geertruida Zelle)
1876-1917
Dutch convicted spy

An exotic dancer of remarkable beauty and a known *femme fatale* during World War I, Mata Hari was convicted of espionage and shot by a French military firing squad.

She performed in vaudeville throughout Europe but preferred doing private performances for a select clientele. Among this clientele were prominent military and government officials engaged in both sides of the conflict. Many of these men became her lovers. She was arrested by the French and charged with transmitting to the Germans secrets which had been confided to her during romantic trysts.

MEAD, Margaret
1901-1978
American anthropologist

A native of Philadelphia, Pennsylvania, Margaret Mead was educated at Barnard College and Columbia University. She became widely known for her studies of sexual roles and mores in South Pacific societies. Several of her books are considered classics, including *Coming of Age in Samoa* (1928), *Growing Up in New Guinea* (1930), and *Male and Female* (1949). Because she spent extensive time in the societies she studied (she learned seven Pacific languages), Mead acquired a reputation for reliable and detailed field reporting, although recently some of this work has been strongly criticized. She was one of the first to study the socialization of the young, as seen in her book

Culture and Commitment: A Study of the Generation Gap. She was curator of ethnology of the American Museum of Natural History from 1964 to 1969. The memoirs of her early years, *Blackberry Winter*, were published in 1972.

MEIR, Golda
1898-1978
Israeli politician and prime minister

At 70 years of age, when she thought herself retired, Golda Meir heeded her country's need and became prime minister of Israel (1969-74). Born Golda Mabovitch to Russian Jews, she emigrated with her family to the United States in 1906. She became involved in the Zionist movement, and with her husband and children emigrated to Israel in 1921. They lived in a kibbutz, which Meir loved for the comradeship, the manual work, even the discomforts, but which her husband hated. Eventually they separated as her passion for politics grew. By 1948 Meir's influence had grown so that she became one of the signatories of Israel's Declaration of Independence, and the first Israeli ambassador to Moscow. Her career included terms as Minister of Labor, chair of Israel's delegation to the United Nations from 1953 to 1966, and Secretary General of the Israeli Labor Party.

Golda Meir took over the premiership of Israel following the sudden death of Levi Eshkol in 1969. She resigned in 1974.

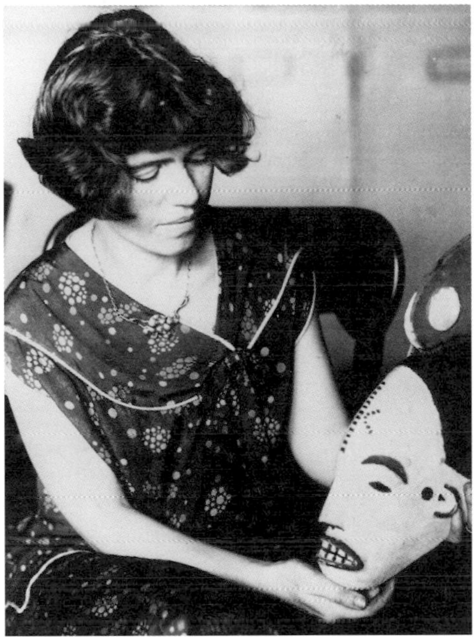

Anthropologist Margaret Mead's work in the South Pacific demonstrated cultural rather than biological determination.

MEITNER, Lise
1878-1968
Austrian physicist

The daughter of a Jewish lawyer in Vienna, Lise Meitner was one of the first women to receive a doctorate there, with a dissertation on radioactivity. She joined Max Planck's research team in 1907, when the eminent physicist was developing the quantum theory, and was appointed head of the department of radioactive physics at the Kaiser Wilhelm Institute in Berlin. There she and Otto Hahn made the first attempts to release latent energy from the atom's nucleus. Nazi persecution forced Meitner to emigrate to Holland and then to Stockholm, where she joined the Nobel Institute. There she pioneered nuclear fission, but dissociated herself from the research that produced the atomic bomb. In 1949 she became a Swedish citizen, after being appointed director of the Royal Institute of Technology. She served there until her retirement to Cambridge, England, in 1960.

MELBA, Dame Nellie
1861-1931
Australian operatic soprano

Helen Porter Mitchell was born near Richmond, outside Melbourne, Australia, and studied music locally before making her concert debut in Melbourne in 1884. Later she studied with Marchesi in Paris and made her operatic debut as Gilda in Brussels in 1887. The following year she sang at Covent Garden for the first time, as Lucia. Her repertoire eventually grew to 25 roles, including the title role in the opera *Hélène* which Saint-Saëns wrote for her. She was best known for her performances in *Lakmé*, *Faust* and *La Traviata*, all roles that used the bell-like purity of her voice. Her popularity in that golden era of opera is attested to by the inventions of Peach Melba and Melba Toast. She was created a Dame of the British Empire in 1918.

MENCHU, Rigoberta
1959-
Guatemalan human rights activist

Since the mid-1980s Menchu, a Quiche Indian, has publicized how the Guatemalan military and landowners have persecuted Guatemala's indigenous people in a 33-year civil war. Internationally recognized in 1992 when she became the first indigenous person to win the Nobel Peace Prize, she continues the work of her father, Vincente Menchu, founder of the Peasant Unity Committee who was killed by security forces for his struggle to secure land for the peasants. After the brutal killings of her family and the decimation of her village, Menchu fled Guatemala. Undaunted, she fights so that indigenous Guatemalan people will have land and education. In 1987 she set up a committee for reconciliation to push for negotiated settlement, and in 1991 created a foundation to secure the human rights and education of indigenous peoples throughout the Americas.

MERCOURI, Melina
1925-1994
Greek actress, politician

Mercouri was born in Athens into a political family – her grandfather was mayor of the city and her father the Minister of the Interior. She enrolled in the National Theatre Company and made her stage debut in 1944. She also made a number of films, most memorably *Never on Sunday* (1960), also starring and directed by Jules Dassin, whom she married in 1966. She repeated the role of the prostitute with the heart of gold who retold Medea to suit her own romantic fancies in the

Greek Minister of Culture Melina Mercouri visits the island of Rhodes in 1987.

Broadway musical *Ilya, Darling* in 1967. Her other films included *Phaedra* (1961), *Topkapi* (1964) and *Nasty Habits* (1976). She was an outspoken critic of the military junta of 1967, who stripped her of her property and citizenship. On its collapse in 1974, she returned triumphantly to Greece to run for Parliament. She lost by 92 votes, but won her seat in 1977. From 1983 to 1989 she served as Minister for Cultural Affairs, and succeeded in increasing subsidies for the arts, building libraries and promoting the preservation of national monuments. She campaigned actively for the return of antiquities to Greece, most prominently for the Elgin Marbles. She was reappointed to the position in 1993, and held it at her death.

MESSICK, Dale
1906-
American cartoonist

One of the few women to achieve major success as a cartoonist, Dale Messick created the comic strip "Brenda Starr" about a liberated woman reporter in 1940. Its first appearance was in a Sunday issue of the *Chicago Tribune*, and it achieved such popularity it became a daily comic strip feature in October 1945. Messick won the National Cartoonists Society silver plaque for Best Story Strip in 1975.

The character Brenda Starr pursued sensational news stories and romantic relationships with equal fervor, though her love affair with a mystery man remained elusive for over 30 years until their marriage in 1976. When Messick retired from cartooning, she handed down the strip to two women, illustrator Ramona Fradon and writer Mary Schmick. Brenda Starr now confronts contemporary criminals involved with international drug rings.

MIDLER, Bette
1945-
American singer, actress

A gutsy entertainer, Bette Midler was born in Paterson, New Jersey, and grew up in Hawaii. She moved to New York and sang in the chorus of the 1966 Broadway hit *Fiddler on the Roof* and in Greenwich Village clubs but made an unlikely debut as a headliner at the Continental Baths in New York, frequented by a largely homosexual clientele. By 1972 she was a well-known popular vocalist, and her debut album *The Divine Miss M* with singles like the Andrews' Sisters "Boogie Woogie Bugle Boy" sold over 100,000 copies a month.

Her first film role, in *The Rose*, was critically acclaimed and her rendition of the title song won a 1978 Grammy for Best Female Pop Vocal Performance. Midler went on a four-month concert tour in Europe that she recounted in her 1980 book *A View From a Broad* and a successful concert film *Divine Madness*. Midler's film career took off in the late 1980s with the popular movies *Down and Out in Beverly Hills*, *Ruthless People*, *Outrageous Fortune* and *Big Business*.

MILLAY, Edna St. Vincent
1892-1950
American poet

A feminist, political activist, playwright and poet whose sonnets symbolized the Jazz Age, Millay was raised by her divorced mother on the coast of Maine. A precocious talent, her first published poem appeared at 14, and at 20, her poem "Renascence" was a prize-winner in the *Lyric Anthology*. A sponsor financed her Vassar education after which she moved to Greenwich Village and wrote for *Vanity Fair*. She published the acclaimed volume of poems *A Few Figs from Thistles* in 1920, and went to Europe as a foreign correspondent for *Vanity Fair* in 1921. Millay won the first Pulitzer Prize for poetry in 1922 for her volume *The Harp-Weaver*. She married Eugen Boissevan in 1923 and bought a farm in Austerlitz, New York. A left-wing sympathizer, she was arrested at the protest against the Sacco and Vanzetti executions. In her later years the produced *A Buck in the Snow*, the love sonnets *Fatal Interview* and *Observations at Midnight* about her political views. A final anthology *Mine the Harvest* was published posthumously.

A 1931 photograph of acclaimed American poet Edna St. Vincent Millay.

DE MILLE, Agnes
1905-
American dancer, choreographer

The daughter of a successful New York playwright and the niece of Cecil B. de Mille, Agnes de Mille enrolled at the Theodore Kosloff Ballet School as a young girl. Her Broadway debut was in 1927 and she later danced in England with Marie RAMBERT, a protégé of Diaghilev. When de Mille returned to New York, her choreography was strongly influenced by Martha GRAHAM.

De Mille's original choreography revolutionized the rhythms and tempo of American musical theater in the Broadway productions of *Brigadoon, Carousel, Paint Your Wagon* and *Oklahoma!*. She received considerable honors, five times winning the New York Critics Award, as well as the Antoinette Perry Award and the Donaldson Award. She also garnered ten honorary university doctorates and was named Woman of the Year by the American Newspaper Women's Guild. Her books about dance include *Dance to the Piper, Promenade Home, The Book of the Dance* and her autobiography *Speak to Me, Dance with Me*, published in 1973.

MILLER, Lee
1907-1977
American photographer

A fashion photographer whose cool, sensuous images during the 1940s bore the imprint of the Surrealist movement, Lee Miller was born in Poughkeepsie, New York, and attended the Arts Students League in Manhattan. Her first career was as a fashion model for *Vogue* and other Conde Nast magazines as well as for the photographer Edward Steichen.

Miller was a studio assistant in the early 1930s in Paris to the Surrealist Man Ray, who became her mentor and lover. Before World War II, Miller left Paris for London, where she established her own photo studio with her brother Eric. She became head of *Vogue*'s London studios between 1940 and 1945, and was its war correspondent covering the fronts in France, Germany, Romania and Russia. She captured the war's surreal qualities in pictures that posed celebrities and models in front of burned-out buildings or with backdrops of ominous smoke and the twilight of bombs exploding. She is best known for her pictures of Dachau.

MILLET, Kate
1934-
American feminist, writer, sculptor

In 1970 with the publication of *Sexual Politics*, Kate Millet became a leading voice in the feminist movement. She explored the premise that male/female relationships were power-structured, and that this must change before women could obtain equality.

Born Katherine Murray in St. Paul, Minnesota, she was educated at the University of Minnesota (1956), Oxford (1958) and Columbia (Ph.D., 1970). In the early 1960s she married sculptor Fumio Yoshimura and lived in Japan, fostering her sculpting career. Returning to the United States in the mid-1960s, she became a National Organization of Women (NOW) member, and supported other women's liberation groups. Actively participating in feminist politics she demonstrated for passage of the Equal Rights Amendment (ERA).

Her books include *Sita* (1977), *Going to Iran* (1981), *The Loony-Bin Trip* (1990), and *The Politics of Cruelty: An Essay on the Literature of Political Imprisonment* (1994).

MISTRAL, Gabriela
1889-1957
Chilean poet, diplomat

Chilean poet Gabriela Mistral excelled in three careers: as an educator, as cultural ambassador and "Consul for Life" throughout Europe and the Americas, and as a poet, the first Latin American to win the Nobel Prize for literature (1945). In gem-like verses she captured the private passions and tragedies that haunted her life. Raised by her mother, also a teacher, Mistral began to write after the suicide of her first love in 1909. The theme of motherhood is developed in *Ternura* (1924) and tragically returned to in *Lagar* (1954) following the suicide of her nephew, whom she raised as a son. Beloved at home and abroad for her lyric skill and emotional honesty, Mistral embodied the nationalist aspirations of her country. Her tombstone reads: "What the soul is to the body is what the artist does for his people."

Dancer and choreographer Agnes de Mille as the Cowgirl in her ballet Rodeo *(1942), with music by Aaron Copland.*

MITCHELL, Joni
1943-
Canadian singer

A native of McLeod, Alberta, Roberta Joan Anderson began folk singing in her 20s in Toronto, but her singing and song-writing skills only began to receive attention after she married Chuck Mitchell and moved to Detroit in 1966. She then moved to New York, where established folk artists Tom Rush, James Taylor and Jackson Browne added her material to their repertoires. In 1968 Judy Collins's rendition of her song "Both Sides Now" hit the Top Ten. Mitchell's early albums *Clouds* and *Ladies of the Canyon*, whose covers were decorated with her own artwork (she studied commercial graphics at Alberta College of Art in Calgary), were big sellers. Songs like "Big Yellow Taxi" and "Chelsea Morning" were popular hits. In the mid-1970s Mitchell made a departure from her more upbeat, romantic tunes to the darker, experimental, jazzy songs of *The Hissing of Summer Lawns* (1975) and *Wild Things Run Fast* (1982).

MITCHELL, Margaret
1900-1949
American novelist

Apart from the Bible, Margaret Mitchell's Pulitzer Prize-winning novel *Gone With the Wind* is the best-selling book in history. The powerful images Mitchell created of the American South during the Civil War and her memorable characters, especially the gutsy Scarlett O'Hara, have become archetypes. The 1939 film version, with Clark Gable and Vivien Leigh, won ten Academy Awards.

Born in Atlanta, Mitchell grew up fascinated with the Civil War, and by age ten she knew all its dramas but one – that the South lost. Mitchell left Smith College after one year to care for her ailing father. Back in Georgia, she married twice and gained notice writing for the *Atlanta Journal-Constitution* – especially for her well-researched Civil War series – before undertaking her only novel.

Author Margaret Mitchell (center) with Gone With the Wind's *(l-r) Vivien Leigh, Clark Gable, David O. Selznick (director) and Olivia de Havilland.*

MITFORD, Jessica
1917-
British-born American investigative writer

Known for her investigative masterpieces, Mitford gained fame in the United States with her best-selling *The American Way of Death*, an exposé of the funeral business. Despite receiving criticism, she subsequently wrote other accusatory publications. A memorable account of the penal system, *Kind and Usual Punishment*, described "the sordid state of incarceration."

In her autobiography, *Daughters and Rebels*, she divulged her own family's eccentricities. Her father, Lord Redesdale, disapproved of formally educating girls and she received limited tutoring at home. In response to her constrained, privileged upbringing she found a voice as a protestor.

While executive secretary for Oakland's Civil Rights Congress she came under the scrutiny of the House Un-American Activities Committee. Despite being labeled as "communist" or "anti-Christian", she remained resolute.

Mitford has lectured and taught throughout the United States.

MOCK, Jerrie
1925-
American aviator

The first woman to fly solo around the world, in 1964, Geraldine Fredritz Mock was born in Newark, Ohio, and majored in aeronautical engineering at Ohio State University. She received her pilot's license in 1958 and managed airports in Illinois and Ohio. Her famous flight in a single-engine Cessna 180 followed a course of 22,858.8 miles in 29½ days with 21 stop-overs. When she landed at Port Columbus, Ohio, on April 17, 1964 she had set three other records as well: first to fly alone across the Pacific from west to east, first to fly a single-engine plane in either direction across the Pacific and the first woman to fly solo from coast to coast by going around the world. President Lyndon Johnson awarded her the Federal Aviation Agency's Gold Medal Award, and she was named Vice Chairman of the FAA's Women's Aviation Advisory Committee.

Mock is the mother of three children and has worked as a missionary in the jungles of New Guinea since her retirement from flying in 1969.

MODERSOHN-BECKER, Paula
1876-1907
German artist

A painter admired for her searching self-portraits and compassionate studies of elderly peasant women, Paula Becker was born in Dresden, Germany, and studied art in Bremen, Hamburg, and London. She settled in Worpswede, a small, rural artists' colony in Germany where she married artist Otto Modersohn.

Influenced by the French painter François Millet, she was also exposed to the post-Impressionists Van Gogh, Gauguin and Cézanne. Her affecting, introspective canvases of farm workers and pastoral landscapes have a primitive force. Though she died at 31 just after the birth of her daughter, she left a legacy of over 400 paintings. Her haunting self-images have large, staring eyes and planes of flat color.

Marilyn Monroe's "star quality" transcended her talents as an actress.

MONROE, Marilyn
1926-1962
American actress

She was born Norma Jeane Mortenson in Los Angeles, but later took her mother's name, Baker. She had an unhappy childhood in foster care, which she escaped through a teenage marriage. After a divorce she became a model and in 1946 was given a short term contract as Marilyn Monroe. In 1948 she posed for a nude calendar, after her contract had been dropped and she needed money. Her career then took an upturn and she appeared in *The Asphalt Jungle* (1950) and *All About Eve* (1950), revealing an extraordinary rapport with the camera. The studios apparently could not see past the sexy image, and played it up in subsequent films like *Gentlemen Prefer Blondes* (1953) and *How to Marry a Millionaire* (1953). Her parts in *The Seven-Year Itch* (1955) and *Some Like It Hot* (1959) showed her capable of playing comedy, but with a vulnerable edge. Her marriages to baseball star Joe DiMaggio and playwright Arthur Miller both ended in divorce, although Miller wrote the screenplay of her final film *The Misfits* (1961) for her. Her death by an overdose of barbiturates remains mysterious.

MONTESSORI, Maria
1870-1952
Italian educator

The first Italian woman to receive a Doctor of Medicine degree (University of Rome, 1894), Maria Montessori initially developed her educational method while working with mentally handicapped children. Revolutionizing modern education, the Montessori method emphasized freedom of expression, supported individual initiative and utilized sensory training.

In 1907 she acquired directorship of a "Casa dei Bambini" (day care center) and applied her principles to normal children. Critics questioned the method's informal structure; however, Montessori found remarkable success with all levels of students.

She devoted the remainder of her career to spreading her principles. She lectured, organized more centers and established training courses in her methods. Today Montessori schools are popular worldwide.

MOODY, Helen Wills
1906-
American tennis player

Helen Wills Moody won eight Wimbledon singles championships (1927-30, 1932-33, 1935 and 1938), a record that stood for over 50 years until Martina NAVRATILOVA took a ninth singles championship in 1990.

Born in Berkeley, California, she won her first national championship at 15 in 1921 and in 1923 took the U.S. women's singles finals at Forest Hills, the first of seven such triumphs (1923-25, 1927-29 and 1931). She entered the 1924 Olympics and was the first woman to win gold medals in both the women's singles and doubles, in which she paired with Hazel Hotchkiss to win the title. In both 1928 and 1929, Wills won the French, Wimbledon and U.S. singles titles without losing a set. She married Fred Moody in 1929.

Moody was a cool, elegant figure on the court whose strengths were a powerful serve and steady baseline game. She was named to the International Tennis Hall of Fame in 1959.

Maria Montessori's method of educating young children places emphasis on self-expression. It is popular worldwide.

Toni Morrison has won the Pulitzer Prize and the Nobel Prize for literature.

MOORE, Marianne
1887-1972
American poet

Born in St. Louis, Missouri, Marianne Moore graduated from Bryn Mawr College in 1909 and worked at the New York Public Library where she mingled socially with the avant-garde poets Ezra Pound, T.S. Eliot and William Carlos Williams.

Two early volumes of her verse were published, *Poems* in 1921 and *Observations* in 1924, and she was editor of the prestigious literary magazine *The Dial* from 1925 to 1929. Her precise and surprising style revealed a keen awareness of the natural world, particularly animals. Moore's *Selected Poems* were published in 1935, and she received the Pullitzer Prize in 1951 and the Bollingen Prize in 1953. An avid fan of the Brooklyn Dodgers baseball team, she often threw out the first ball to open the season.

MOREAU, Jeanne
1928-
French actress, director

Jeanne Moreau was born in Paris, and was a pupil at the Conservatoire Nationale D'Art Dramatique, and also trained with the Théâtre Nationale Populaire. She made her stage debut with the Comédie Française in *A Month in the Country* in 1948, and her film debut the same year in *Dernier Amour*. Her association with a number of the French New Wave directors brought her worldwide recognition in a series of films that portrayed her as world-weary sensual women. These included Louis Malle's *Elevator to the Scaffold* (1958) and Michelangelo Antonioni's *La Notte* (1961), but the film that really established her as a star was François Truffaut's *Jules and Jim* (1961), which became an international success. She proved to be a formidable director herself with *La lumière*, which she also starred in and wrote in 1976. Her later films include *La Femme Nikita* (1991), *Map of the Human Heart* (1993) and *The Summer House* (1944).

MORRISON, Toni
1931-
American writer

A prize-winning African-American author whose characters struggle for freedom amid racial persecution, Chloe Anthony Wofford was born in Lorain, Ohio, the daughter of working-class parents. She graduated from Howard University in 1953 and received a master's degree from Cornell. She married Harold Morrison, with whom she had two children before separating and moving to New York City. While senior editor at Random House, she worked on the autobiographies of black activist Angela Davis and boxer Muhammad Ali as well as the anthology *The Black Book* (1974), a collection of literature focusing on the black experience in America.

Her novels include *The Bluest Eye* (1970), *Sula* (1973), *Song of Solomon* (1977), *Tar Baby* (1981), *Beloved* (1987), which won the Pulitzer Prize, and *Jazz* (1992), which made her the first African-American to win the Nobel prize for literature. Morrison has taught writing and literature at Yale and Rutgers, and currently teaches at Princeton. She is a member of the American Academy of Arts and Letters.

MOSER-PRÖLL, Annemarie
1953-
Austrian skier

The youngest overall winner of the World Cup in alpine skiing, Moser- Pröll achieved this victory in 1971 and again in 1972. Considered the favorite for the gold medals at the 1972 Sapporo Winter Olympics, she finished second in the downhill, second in the giant slalom and fifth in the slalom, and was so disappointed that she retired in 1975 and skipped the 1976 Olympics. By the time Moser-Pröll went back to Olympic competition at Moscow's 1980 Winter Games, she had won four more World Cup titles. She finally achieved her goal of an Olympic Gold in the downhill event. Her total of 62 individual wins in major events is unsurpassed, and she also won record numbers of titles in both downhill and giant slalom.

MOSES, Grandma
1860-1961
American painter

A self-trained "primitive" painter, Anna Mary Robertson Moses did not begin her career until her late seventies. Born on a farm in upper New York State, she worked as a domestic in Virginia until she married a hired hand of one of her employers. Together they farmed in Eaglebridge, New York, and had ten children, of whom five survived.

When Anna's hands became too stiff to embroider, she switched to painting small oil canvases adapted from newspaper clippings of rural scenes. She displayed them at local fairs where they were spotted by the Manhattan dealer Louis J. Caldor. Three canvases were exhibited at the Museum of Modern Art in New York, and in 1940 Caldor arranged Moses's first solo exhibition in New York.

Sleigh rides in winter, autumn harvests, barnyard animals and farmers at work were the subject of the more than 2000 canvases Grandma Moses completed before her death at 101.

MUIR, Jean
1933-
British fashion designer

Jean Elizabeth Muir was born in London and studied at the Dame Harper School in Bedford before moving to London and becoming a salesgirl at Liberty's in 1950. She moved to Jaeger in 1956, and in 1961 opened a shop known as Jane and Jane. In 1966 she established her own design firm, Jean Muir. Her clothes are noted for their classic shapes and her use of jersey, which is tailored in designs that are soft and feminine. She produces similar designs with leather, especially suedes. She

Self-taught, Grandma Moses began painting in her late seventies.

was presented with a CBE in 1983. Following the development of her own career, she believes in technical training as a serious foundation for a designer, and that young designers should concentrate on craft more than on art.

MURDOCH, Dame Iris
1919-
Irish-born writer

A native of Dublin, Ireland, Iris Murdoch was raised in London, attended Badminton School and graduated with high honors from Oxford in 1942. A noted philosopher who has taught at Oxford, Murdoch is known for her formal, complex psychological novels which deal with such abstract concerns as good and evil, religious belief and the nature of sexuality. Her first novel *Under the Net* (1954) pitted its hero in a struggle for a concept of personal identity against other's intellectual opinions of him. *The Bell* (1958) portrays relationships in a religious community, while *A Fairly Honorable Defeat* (1970) examined problems of commitment in an irrational, modern world. Murdoch won the Booker Prize in 1975 for her novel *The Sea, The Sea*. Her play *Art and Eros* was produced at London's National Theatre in 1980. Her later novels include *The Message to the Planet* (1989), and *The Green Knight* (1994). She also published *Metaphysics as a Guide to Morals* in 1992.

MUSGRAVE, Thea
1928-
British composer, conductor

Thea Musgrave was born near Edinburgh, and received her B.Mus. from Edinburgh University. She also studied at the Paris Conservatoire with Nadia BOULANGER and at the Berkshire Music Center in 1959. Her early work was largely Scottish in inspiration, from her *Suite of Bairn Songs* composed in 1953 to her 1955 chamber opera *The Abbott of Drimock*. In the late 1950s her work became more abstract, using sound sequences played at random, the 12-tone scale, and incorporating pre-recorded tapes. She is probably best known for her operas, *The Decision* (1964-65), *A Christmas Carol* (1976) and *The Voice of Ariadne* (1972-73), based on the Henry James short story, *The Last of the Valerii*. In 1985 she composed an opera about Harriet TUBMAN, *Harriet, A Woman Called Moses*.

MYRDAL, Alva
1902-1986
Swedish sociologist, diplomat, writer

A major voice in the international disarmament movement, Alva Reimer Myrdal received the Nobel Peace Prize in 1982. She denounced the United States and Russia in *The Game of Disarmament: How the United States and Russia Run the Arms Race*.

She shared with her husband, Nobel Prize-winning economist Gunnar Myrdal, concerns about social and economic problems in her native Sweden. She taught in the adult education movement and was an expert on population problems. She encouraged greater participation by women in political and economic life and perceived social reform as being as vital as political and economic reform.

She was affiliated with the United Nations' Department of Social Affairs and the social sciences departments of United Nations Educational, Scientific and Cultural Organization (UNESCO). She served as ambassador to India and in Sweden's Parliament.

Her daughter Sissela Bok, a noted philosopher, recounts Myrdal's distinguished life in *Alva Myrdal: A Daughter's Memoir*.

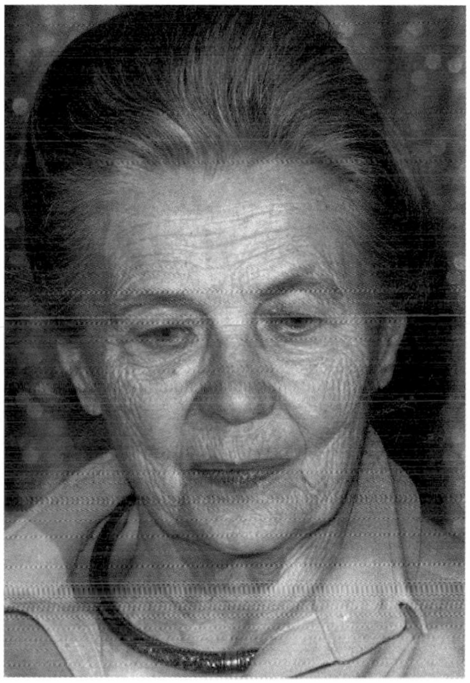

Nobel Peace Prize winner Alva Myrdal spoke out for nuclear disarmament.

N

Ax-wielding temperance advocate Carry Nation's work led to Prohibition with the passage of the Volstead Act in 1917.

Martina Navratilova celebrates after winning her sixth consecutive Wimbledon singles title, in 1987.

NATION, Carry
1846-1911
American temperance reformer, lecturer

Vehemently opposed to alcohol consumption, Carry Nation made a name for herself during the 1890s with her aggressive campaign against the use and sale of alcohol. Fueled by religious fervor and memories of an alcoholic first husband, she launched a powerful and emotional crusade for temperance.

In 1892 she co-founded the Texas branch of the Women's Christian Temperance Union (WCTU). Nation became famous for smashing liquor bottles in local saloons while singing hymns with great emotion. Often arrested, she remained steadfast in her mission, extending her activities to major cities across the United States and even traveling abroad with her message.

Nation did not live to see the prohibition of alcohol in the United States, in 1920. However, her dedication to the temperance movement will forever be recognized.

NAVRATILOVA, Martina
1956-
American tennis player

A legendary powerhouse on the women's tour, Martina Navratilova has won a record nine singles victories at Wimbledon and in 1993 topped the women's career earnings list with over $19.4 million. She has won well over 100 tournaments, including 18 grand slam titles. She was named the Female Athlete of the Decade for the 1980s by the National Sports Review, the Associated Press and United Press International.

Born in Prague, by 14 she was the 14-and-under national champion. By 1978 Navratilova had the number one ranking, and for the next 12 years was among the top three players in the world. Along with her nine Wimbledon singles titles, she won four U.S. Opens, three Australian Opens, and two French singles championships. She achieved the Grand Slam in 1984, and in November 1991 defeated Monica Seles for her 157th career title, tying Chris Evert for all-time championship victories. At the 1987 U.S. Open, Martina achieved the rare triple crown, winning the women's singles, the women's doubles (with Pam Shriver) and the mixed doubles with Emilio Sanchez.

Navratilova defected to the United States in 1975, becoming a citizen in 1981. A member of the Women's Sports Hall of Fame since 1984, the Women's Sports Foundation honored her with the first Flo Hyman Award for supporting women's advancement in sports in 1987.

NEGRI, Pola
1894-1987
Polish-born actress

Barbara Appolonia Chalupek was born in Janowa, Poland. Her family belonged to the impoverished nobility, which enabled her to be sent to the Imperial Academy of Dramatic Art. In 1918 she went to Berlin to appear in Max Reinhardt's pantomime *Sumurun*, and was then cast in films, working under directors like Ernst Lubitsch who cast her in

Louise Nevelson was elected to the American Academy of Arts and Letters.

Carmen (1918). One of her subsequent films, *Madame duBarry* (1919), was released in the United States as *Passion*, and it brought her a contract from Paramount in 1922. Her first film there was *Bella Donna* (1923), in which she starred as an exotic worldly woman, Hollywood's only part for European actresses at that time. She also starred in *Forbidden Paradise* (1926) and *Hotel Imperial* (1927), considered the best movie she made in Hollywood. By 1928 her Hollywood career was over. She returned to Germany in 1935 and made other films, although her last film, *The Moon Spinners* (1964), was made for Walt Disney.

NEVELSON, Louise
1899-1988
American sculptor

Louise Berliawsky was born in Kiev and emigrated with her family to Rockland, Maine. She attended the Arts Students League in New York, and married Charles Nevelson in 1920, with whom she had one son. She studied with Hans Hoffman in Munich in 1931 and with the muralist Diego Rivera in Mexico. Her early pieces combined interests in surrealism and constructivism.

Using wood, plexiglass, mirrors, aluminum and steel, Nevelson became known for her room-sized environments intended to be mystical inner sanctums: Her archetypal masterpiece *The Palace* was a 12-foot walk-in chamber at the Museum of Modern Art in 1977. Its black, hieroglyphic wooden walls reflected from a floor of mirrors. She also designed the all-white *Chapel of the Good Shepherd* at the Citicorp Center in New York.

NIDETCH, Jean
1923-
American entrepreneur

Jean Slutsky was born in Brooklyn, New York, and was overweight even as a child. When she reached 214 pounds she went to an obesity clinic, which gave her a diet, but she binged on cookies and cake secretly. Too ashamed to confess this behavior to her doctor or diet counselor, Nidetch got together with six overweight friends and they set up sessions to help one another stay on their diets. Within a year, with the encouragement of her friends, Nidetch lost 68 pounds. She increased the number of sessions, and inspired a number of friends and members of her family to lose weight. One friend suggested she open a business. She started Weight Watchers in 1963, which has proven to be one of the most successful diet systems, combining dieting and the encouragement of peers. The *Weight Watchers Cook Book* appeared in 1966, and the business has kept abreast of trends by marketing special frozen dinners and diet drinks and including exercise programs.

NILSSON, Birgit
1918-
Swedish dramatic soprano

Marta Birgit Nilsson was born on her family farm in Västra Karup, Sweden. She studied at the Royal Academy of Music in Stockholm, and made her debut as Agathe in *Der Freischutz* in 1946, having learned the part in three days. She made her formal debut in Verdi's *Macbeth* later the same year. She continued to study and expand her repertoire, singing her first Brunnhilde in Stockholm in 1954. She made her debut at the Metropolitan Opera as Isolde in 1959, and received a 15-minute ovation. Her repertoire includes the great Wagnerian roles, as well as Strauss's Elektra and Puccini's Tosca and Turandot. Her voice was phenomenal in size and power, and her gift of perfect pitch allowed her to use it without the fear of flatting. She is generally considered the finest Wagnerian singer of her era, and was honored by the Swedish king with an appointment as Hovsångerska (Courtsinger). She retired in 1982, and now teaches master classes.

NIN, Anaïs
1903-1977
American writer

A diarist who investigated the female psyche in lyrical language, Nin was born in Paris, the daughter of a French-Danish singer and a world famous Cuban pianist, Joachim Nin. She went on glamorous, transcontinental tours with her father as a child and was so bereft when he left her mother, she began her diaries as a letter to him to assuage her sense of separation.

Nin continued the correspondence through her maturity, plumbing her personal experiences and the nature of eroticism in a forthright, spontaneous style. She lived in Paris in the late 1920s, working as an artist's model and a Spanish dancer. She associated with the American writers Henry Miller and Lawrence Durrell and studied psychoanalysis with Dr. Otto Rank, exploring the bonds between identity and sexuality.

Forced to leave Paris at the outset of World War II, Nin settled in Greenwich Village and submitted stories and reviews to the *New Yorker* magazine beginning in 1940. Her novels, which expand upon certain passages of the diaries, include *Winter of Artifice* (1939), *A Spy in the House of Love* (1954) and *Seduction of the Minotaur* (1959) among others. *Delta of Venus: Erotica* was published in 1977.

NOCE, Teresa
1900-
Italian socialist, writer

An international organizer who was key to the creation of the Italian Republic, Noce joined the Socialist Party in 1919 and the Communist Party in 1921. She traveled back and forth from Italy to France, and was a leader in the strikes of women workers in the early 1930s as well as a participant in international organizations of women against fascism. During World War II, she was a member of the French Resistance until she was captured. In 1947 she founded the journal *La voce dei tessili* (*The Voice of the Textile Workers*) while secretary for the Federazione Impiegati Operai Tessili. Her writings include novels detailing her experience as a young worker and in the concentration camps.

NOOR AL-HUSSEIN (Lisa Halaby)
1951-
American-born Queen of Jordan

In 1978 Lisa Najeeb Halaby. an American-born, Princeton-educated architect married Hussein ibn Talal, the King of Jordan. Born in Washington, D.C., the daughter of an Arab-American father, she credits him with her great appreciation of Islam. In 1976 she helped to design plans for Arab Air University and worked in the New York City office of Royal Jordanian Airlines. During this time she met King Hussein. On becoming queen, she decided to focus on bettering educational resources and development, especially for women, and works to preserve and celebrate Jordan's cultural heritage.

N

NORMAN, Jessye
1945-
American operatic soprano

Jessye Norman was born in Augusta, Georgia, and began to study voice at Howard University, where she was graduated with honors in 1967. She received her Masters from the University of Michigan in 1968, the same year she won first prize in the Munich International Music Competition. She made her debut as Elisabeth in *Tannhäuser* at the Berlin Deutsche Oper in 1969, and she signed a three-year contract with that house. She expanded her repertoire by singing throughout Europe, at concert halls, music festivals and other opera houses. She made her American debut as Aida at the Hollywood Bowl in 1972, and her Metropolitan Opera debut as both Cassandra and Dido in Berlioz's *Les Troyens* in 1983. She was also invited to sing La Marseillaise at the bicentennial celebration of the French Revolution in 1989.

One of the most versatile and popular concert and operatic singers of the 1990s, her repertoire ranges from Purcell to Richard Rodgers, and from opera to lieder and art songs to spirituals. She has won numerous Grammys for recordings of all kinds, although the album of spirituals she recorded with Kathleen Battle was probably the most popular.

Soprano Jessye Norman in Berlioz's Les Troyens *at the Met in 1983.*

NORTON, Eleanor Holmes
1937-
American government official

The first woman to chair the Equal Employment Opportunities Commission (1977-1983), Washington native Norton began her legal career as assistant legal director of the American Civil Liberties Union in New York City. Her first case defended the first amendment rights of a white supremacist group, for she refuses to allow her gender or race to determine the struggles that she wages. In 1970 she was appointed chair of the NYC Commission on Human Rights, and campaigned against segregationist housing bills, sex discrimination in the workplace and lack of minority representation in the media. In 1973 she became cofounder of the Black Feminist Organization, and in 1977 President Carter appointed her chair of the EEOC. In 1990 she was elected to the House of Representatives on behalf of Washington, D.C.

NOVELLO, Antonia C.
1944-
American physician, former U.S. Surgeon General

In 1990 Antonia C. Novello became the first woman appointed Surgeon General of the United States, and the first Hispanic-American. Born in Fajardo, Puerto Rico, Antonia Coello was a sickly child, and dreamed of being a children's doctor, which she achieved in 1970. She earned her Masters in public health from Johns Hopkins University in 1982. From 1978 to 1990 she worked in the U.S. Public Health Service at the National Institutes of Health. As Surgeon General she focused on the health care of minorities, women and children, and pressured cigarette and alcohol companies to stop campaigns that subtly targeted young people. In 1993, when she was replaced by Joycelyn ELDERS under the Clinton administration, she became a special representative to UNICEF dealing with the health needs of women, children, and adolescents.

NYEMBE, Dorothy
1930-
South African activist

Dorothy Nyembe has long fought against the oppression of black South Africans, and been repeatedly imprisoned for that resistance. After taking part in the Defiance Campaign of 1952, in which thousands defied pass laws, curfews, and entered places where blacks were not permitted, she was jailed for two years. In 1956 she led the Natal women who protested the pass laws. In 1963 she was sentenced to three years in jail on charges of furthering the aims of the African National Congress (ANC), a banned organization. Herself banned in 1963, and again in 1968, she was convicted under the Terrorism Act and the Suppression of Communism Act, and was not released from jail until 1984. She remains active in the movement.

O

OATES, Joyce Carol
1938-
American writer

Prolific writer Joyce Carol Oates has been criticized more for the quantity of her output – more than a book a year – than for its quality. Luckily for her wide readership, she hasn't let that discourage her. Through essays, short stories, novels, plays and poetry, she has woven a complex literature of modern American life – its violence, psychology and moral ambivalence. Her powerful novel *them* was among the first to draw attention, winning the National Book Award in 1969. Recent works such as *Black Water* (1992) and *Haunted: Tales of the Grotesque* (1994) have graced the bestseller lists with their gothic-realist mix of current history and imagination.

Born in Millersport, New York, Oates began writing as a college student at Syracuse University and University of Wisconsin at Madison. She has had a distinguished academic career, and currently teaches at Princeton University.

O'BRIEN, Edna
1936-
Irish novelist, playwright

A prolific and controversial writer, Edna O'Brien made her mark with the publication of her first novel *The Country Girls* in 1960. This popular coming-of-age story was banned in her native Ireland, as were her next six books, for its graphic treatment of sex and defiant (if often lonely) independence of the women protagonists.

O'Brien raised her two sons in London while supporting herself by writing novels, short stories, plays, screenplays and juvenile literature. Her works continue to sell well, beloved for their immaculate prose, where the pain of her own family life is tempered with earthy humor and sensually detailed landscapes of Ireland. Her most recent works are *Time and Tide* (1992) and *House of Splendid Isolation* (1994).

Sandra Day O'Connor was appointed U.S. Supreme Court Justice in 1981.

O'CONNOR, Flannery
1925-1964
American writer

A writer in the Southern Gothic tradition, Mary Flannery O'Connor was born in Savannah, Georgia. When she was a teenager her father died of lupus, the same crippling blood infection O'Connor contracted in her early twenties. Elements of the macabre and the grotesque are woven into her fiction, and her characters' lives are laced with sorrow, guilt and desperation.

O'Connor attended the University of Iowa, where she won the Rinehart-Iowa Prize for a work-in-progress *Wise Blood* published in 1952. After receiving her master's degree, O'Connor returned to her mother's farm in Georgia, where she raised chickens and peacocks.

O'Connor is best known for her novel *The Violent Bear It Away* (1960) and a short-story volume *Everything That Rises Must Converge* published after her death in 1965. A compilation of her correspondence was produced in 1978, tracing friendships with the poet Robert Lowell, the editor Robert Giroux and the writer Caroline Gordon.

O'CONNOR, Sandra Day
1930-
American lawyer, politician, U.S. Supreme Court Justice

Sandra Day O'Connor, the first woman appointed U.S. Supreme Court Justice, was born in El Paso, Texas, and was graduated *cum laude* from Stanford University. When she graduated from Stanford Law School in 1952, no law firm would hire her because she was a woman, so she ran her own – then entered public service. From 1960 to 1965 she worked for the Republican Party on the county precinct committee, then served as assistant attorney general in Arizona. She served two terms in the Arizona state legislature, and in 1972 when she was elected majority leader of the Arizona state senate, she became the first woman to serve in such a position. There she gained a reputation as a conservative, although she voted in favor of the Equal Rights Amendment. She served on the Maricopa County Superior Court starting in 1974, and on the Arizona Court of Appeals from 1979 until her appointment to the high court bench in 1981.

O'KEEFFE, Georgia
1887-1986
American painter

Perhaps the most influential American woman painter of the twentieth century, O'Keeffe was born in Sun Prairie, Wisconsin, took classes at the Art Institute in Chicago and the Arts Students League in New York, and taught art for several years in rural Texas and Virginia. In 1924 she married Alfred Stieglitz, the avant-garde photographer who staged her first solo show at his Gallery 291 in Manhattan. They lived in Manhattan and summered in Lake George, New York, and O'Keeffe employed some of Stieglitz's stylistic techniques – crisp, hard-edge forms, close-up views and cropped images – in her canvases.

Following visits to the Southwestern art colony in Taos, New Mexico,

O'Keeffe moved to New Mexico where she became a member of a coterie of artists and writers that included Mabel Dodge Luhan, D.H. and Frieda Lawrence, Marsden Hartley and John Marin. She lived alone at Ghost Ranch in Abiquiu for 40 years after Stieglitz's death, maintaining a spartan regime.

Her best-known works are large, sensual flower studies and landscapes that incorporate desert plains, bleached animal bones, pale adobe buildings and fathomless blue skies. Throughout her life she was a financial success, and she garnered significant critical acclaim before her death at 98.

O'LEARY, Hazel R.
1937-
American business executive, lawyer, government official

Born in Newport News, Virginia, O'Leary graduated Phi Beta Kappa from Fisk University in 1959 and received her law degree from Rutgers University in 1966. She served in the Carter administration's Department of Energy as an administrator for conservation and the environment. Appointed Secretary of Energy in President Clinton's Cabinet in 1993, Hazel O'Leary declared it her mission to solve the problem of radioactive waste. As executive vice president of Northern States Power Co., in Minneapolis, she had supported the establishment of a bitterly contested nuclear waste dump, but at the Department of Energy she quickly made it clear that not only would the department thoroughly investigate 40 years of government-sponsored human radiation experiments, opening previously secret files to the public, but that she would not press for a new generation of commercial reactors.

ONASSIS, Jacqueline Kennedy
1929-1994
American editor, former First Lady of the United States

Wife of President John Kennedy, Jacqueline Bouvier Kennedy represented the United States' vision of royalty – chic, beautiful and elegant. After graduating from George Washington University in 1951, she worked for the *Washington Times Herald* photographing and interviewing poeple. One of her interviewees was Senator John F. Kennedy, who became her husband in 1953. As First Lady, she made the White House "a showcase for American art and history," and became a model of fashion and style around the world. When Kennedy was assassinated, the nation credited Jackie's dignity and grace with guiding it through the tragedy. She remarried Greek shipping magnate Aristotle Onassis in 1968. After his death, she returned to the United States and became an editor for Viking and later Doubleday, using her finely-tuned aesthetic sense to cultivate the books of Naguib Mahfouz, Michael Jackson, and Bill Moyers' celebrated interviews with Joseph Campbell.

A symbol of American charm and grace: Jacqueline Kennedy Onassis in 1992.

ONO, Yoko
1933-
American singer, songwriter, performance artist

Yoko Ono was born into a wealthy banking family in Tokyo where she was raised and educated before attending Sarah Lawrence College. A member of the avant-garde conceptual art world after graduation, Ono met Lennon at a gallery reception for her work in London, and married him in 1969.

Their first musical effort together was the 1968 album *Unfinished Music # 1: Two Virgins* and the couple appeared nude on the album cover. After the Beatles broke up, Ono and Lennon created The Plastic Ono Band, releasing a successful single "Give Peace a Chance". They recorded a number one Billboard hit "Instant Karma" in 1970. They also made controversial documentary films such as *Rape*. Their album *Double Fantasy* was released just before Lennon was tragically shot and killed on December 8, 1980. Ono's 1981 album *Seasons of Glass* was testimony to her loss, followed by *It's Alright* of 1982, a work of resolution. She went on tour in 1985 to promote her album *Starpeace*, but she has mainly de voted her time to charitable causes and the legacy of her talented husband.

Painter Georgia O'Keeffe was a pioneer of modernism in the United States.

Vijaya Pandit, president of the U.N. General Assembly, 1953-54.

PAGLIA, Camille
1947-
American writer, educator, anti-feminist

Paglia's controversial best-seller *Sexual Personae: Art and Decadence from Nefertiti to Emily Dickinson* (1990) made her the feminist movement's number one enemy. The views she set forth were reactionary and a backlash to liberal feminism. Her theory stressed the truth in gender stereotyping and affirmed a biological basis to sex differences.

Born in Endicott, New York, Paglia was graduated from SUNY Binghampton in 1968 and received her Ph.D. from Yale in 1972. *Sexual Personae* was developed from her doctoral dissertation. A flamboyant professor at the University of Pennsylvania, she has also published *Essays: Sex, Art and American Culture* (1992).

PANDIT, Vijaya Lakshmi
1900-1990
Indian freedom fighter, politician

The first woman to serve as President of the United Nations General Assembly, in 1953, Vijaya Pandit has been called the "virtual chief of one of Asia's most important political dynasties." Sister of Jawaharlal Nehru, the first prime minister of independent India, she fought actively for India's independence, and was arrested and jailed several times by British colonial authorities. In 1937, she was the first congresswoman to be appointed a provincial minister. During the independence movement she was a self-made ambassador to the United States, and spoke eloquently for their cause. After India achieved independence in 1947 she was ambassador to the USSR (1947-49), the United States (1949-51), and was High Commissioner to Britain (1955-61). She headed the Indian delegation to the UN from 1946 to 1951. She emerged from retirement in 1975 to oppose her niece Indira GANDHI's crackdown on civil rights, and was key to Gandhi's failure to win reelection. Her memoirs, *The Scope of Happiness*, were published in 1979.

PANKHURST, Emmeline
1858-1928
PANKHURST, Dame Christabel
1880-1958
PANKHURST, Estelle Sylvia
1882-1960
PANKHURST, Adela Constancia
1885-1961
British suffragists

Emmeline Pankhurst was imprisoned several times during her militant fight for women's suffrage in Britain.

The Pankhurst family is remembered for their zealous battles to win suffrage for women in England and for setting a new standard for how these battles might be waged. Emmeline Goulden Pankhurst, mother of Christabel, Sylvia and Adela, was herself the daughter of radical reformers. She married Richard Pankhurst in 1879, and together they worked on the Manchester Women's Suffrage Committee and Married Women's Property Committee. She and her daughters founded the Women's Social and Political Union (WSPU) in 1903. The WSPU became known for its dramatic actions that included marches, clashes with the police, and attacks on property. Emmeline and Sylvia were often arrested, using hunger and thirst strikes to strengthen their position.

During World War I Emmeline and Christabel focused their energies on rallying support for the war, while Sylvia, who bitterly opposed the war, did relief work and joined with the Women's International League for Peace and Freedom. Adela emigrated to Australia in her early twenties, joined the Australian Socialist Party, and founded the Australian Women's Guild of Empire. In 1917, Emmeline reformed the WSPU as the Women's Party, fielding 16 candidates for the 1918 election. Their bids were unsuccessful, but that year women over the age of 30 won the vote. Ten years later, thanks in large part to the Pankhursts' tireless efforts, British women achieved full suffrage.

PARKER, Bonnie
1910-1934
American outlaw

Born and raised in Rowena, Texas, Bonnie Parker gained infamy as the girlfriend and accomplice of Clyde Barrow. Together they were known simply as Bonnie and Clyde. Her mundane life changed forever in 1930, when she met Clyde and they embarked upon a crime spree. Primarily petty thieves, Bonnie and Clyde were both expert marksmen and she was the official getaway driver. They were despised by other noted criminals of the time for their ruthlessness, and were considered vicious killers who lacked moral conscience.

Despite their villainy, they were able to elude capture until 1934, when they were killed in an ambush with the Louisiana police.

PARKER, Dorothy
1893-1967
American writer

A master of witty repartee, Dorothy Rothschild grew up on Manhattan's Upper West Side and began her career as a copywriter for *Vogue* and a drama critic for *Vanity Fair*. She was the only female member of the famous Round Table of writers and humorists who met for lunch at New York's Algonquin Hotel in the 1920s, a set including literary luminaries George S. Kaufmann, Alexander Woolcott, Frank Case and Robert Benchley. Her reviews appeared in the *New Yorker*, a magazine edited by another Round Table member, Harold Ross, from 1926 to 1955.

Parker married a banker, Edward Parker, in 1917 but divorced him in 1928, keeping his name which had become her byline. She had a turbulent marital relationship with a bisexual writer, Alan Campbell, but remained with him until his death in 1963. The couple wrote screenplays in Hollywood for as much as $5000 a week in their heyday, but were later blacklisted for their antifascist and leftist views.

Dorothy Parker with fellow Algonquin Round Table members Alexander Woolcott (left) and Frank Case, 1938.

PARKS, Rosa
1913-
American civil rights activist

Rosa Parks was born in Tuskegee, Alabama, and became secretary for the National Association of Colored People (NAACP) and a member of the Union of Sleeping Car Porters in Montgomery. She became world famous for her heroic refusal to give a white man her seat on a segregated Montgomery, Alabama, bus, on December 1, 1955, a move which launched the victorious year-long Montgomery bus boycott. As a result, Parks was fired from her job, and she moved to Detroit where she became special assistant to Congressman John Conyers for 25 years. In 1988, she founded the Rosa and Raymond Parks Institute for Self-Development. In 1993 she published the account of her life, *My Story*.

PARTON, Dolly
1946-
American singer, songwriter, actress

Dolly Parton's songwriting talents and business savvy have carried her beyond the realm of country music. She was born in Locust Ridge, Tennessee, the fourth of 12 children who lived in a two-room shack. Parton's singing career was launched with two 1967 country hits, "Dumb Blonde" and "Something Fishy". She partnered with country singer Porter Wagoner, recorded several popular singles and toured with his road show until 1974. She went solo and scored a succession of hit records, several of which crossed over into the popular song genre. Among her better known titles are "All I Can Do", "Starting Over Again", "Blue Ridge Mountain Boy", "Just Because I'm a Woman", "Heartbreaker" and "9 to 5". Parton wrote the last song as the title track for a 1980 movie in which she starred with Jane Fonda and Lily Tomlin. A number of female vocalists, notably Linda Ronstadt, Olivia Newton-John and Emmylou Harris, have made successful recordings of songs she wrote. Parton won the Grammy for Best Popular Song in 1994 for her single "I Will Always Love You", sung by Whitney Houston. Her theme park Dollywood is in Tennessee.

PAUKER, Ana
1893?-1956
Romanian politician

In 1947, Ana Pauker was appointed Foreign Minister of Romania, the world's first woman in such a post, and the Vice-Premier. Daughter of a Jewish Moldavian butcher, Pauker joined the underground Communist Party in 1921, and was imprisoned many times during her building of the party. In 1940, after her release from prison in an exchange of prisoners between the Soviet Union and Romania, she moved to the Soviet Union. During World War II she organized Romanian war prisoners into a Red Army unit, leading them victoriously into Romania in 1944. In 1946 she led the first National Congress of Anti-Fascist Romania Women in launching a plan for reconstruction, education, peace and social progress. Although purged from the party in 1952 on charges of deviationism, she still maintained influence until her death.

PAUL, Alice
1885-1977
American suffragist

Born in Mooretown, New Jersey, to a Quaker family, Alice Paul was graduated from Swarthmore College and received her Ph.D. from the University of Pennsylvania. A radical activist for women's suffrage and equal rights, Paul was the original author of the Equal Rights Amendment (ERA). Impressed with Emmeline PANKHURST's dramatic public demonstrations that even included attacks on property, she later applied their methods to call attention to the ERA in the United States. She joined the National American Women's Suffrage Association, but found their methods too gradual, and broke off to start the Congressional Union for Women's Suffrage, out of which sprang the Women's Party. After the passage of the 19th amendment granting women the vote, she focused on equal rights for women, and authored the ERA in 1916. Although the act was never ratified, she was instrumental in getting the UN Charter to acknowledge that women's rights are equal to those of men.

PAVLOVA, Anna
1883-1931
Russian dancer

A legendary ballerina, noted for her exquisite style and effortless grace, Anna Pavlova was born in St. Petersburg, the daughter of a laundress. She joined the Imperial Ballet at 10 and performed at the Tsar's coronation in 1896 at 13. The first prima ballerina to appear outside Russia when she traveled to Scandinavia, she later left Russia with Diaghilev's Ballet Russes on tour in Europe in 1909.

Pavlova broke away from Diaghilev to form her own company, and toured the world. She first danced with partner Mikhail Mordkin at the Metropolitan Opera House in 1910, and she became a popular sensation and inspiration to American dancers who saw her on tour from 1912 to 1926. The choreographer Fokine composed the ballet *Les Sylphides* for her, and she is associated with her famous role of the dying swan.

Russian ballerina Anna Pavlova in the title role of The Dying Swan.

Pavlova married her accompanist André Darmide in 1924 and she continued performing until her death.

PAYSON, Joan Whitney
1903-1975
American philanthropist, sportswoman

Joan Whitney, born in New York, was the daughter of the third richest man in the United States. She went to Barnard College, and to business school, and married Charles Shipman Payson in 1925. She and her husband gave financial backing to many Broadway plays and films, including *A Streetcar Named Desire*, *Rebecca* and *Gone With the Wind*. She was also a founder of the Museum of Modern Art. Her mother had instilled in her a love of sports, taking her to see the Giants play baseball at the Polo Grounds and to the track at Saratoga during the season when any of their horses from Greentree Stables were running. In the early 1960s Joan Payson tried to buy the Giants to keep them from leaving New York, but the owner wouldn't sell. In 1962 she put up 85 percent of the money to found the New York Mets, and persuaded Casey Stengel to come out of retirement to manage the new baseball team. Mrs. Payson was also the president of the Helen Hay Whitney Foundation and the co-owner (with her brother Jock) of Greentree Stud, Inc. and Greentree Stables, at the time of her death.

PECK, Annie Smith
1850-1935
American alpinist

The first person to climb the north peak of 21,812-foot Mt. Huascarán in Peru, the highest altitude ever reached in the western hemisphere in 1908, Annie Smith Peck was born in Providence, Rhode Island. Peck received her undergraduate and master's degrees in Classics at the University of Michigan and was the first woman admitted to the American School of Classical Studies in Athens in 1885.

By 1900 Peck had climbed over 20 major peaks and represented the United States at the Paris Congrès Internationale de l'Alpinisme. Peck wrote several mountaineering guidebooks and travel chronicles, including *A Search for the Apex of South America* (1911), *The South American Tour* (1913) and *Industrial and Commercial South America* (1922). At 61, she was the first person to climb Mt. Coropuna in Peru (21,250 feet), leaving a pennant with the logo "Votes for Women" at the summit. Her last mountain ascent, at 82, was New Hampshire's Mt. Madison (5,380 feet).

PEDERSEN, Helga
1911-
Danish lawyer, politician

A supporter of prison and penal reform and improvement of women's legal status, Helga Pedersen became the first woman judge at the European Court of Human Rights in 1971. Before that, her distinguished career included service as a Member of Parliament from 1950 to 1964, followed by her appointment as supreme court justice. A UNESCO delegate from 1949 to 1974, her many awards include the gold medal from the Association of World Peace Through Law.

PENNINGTON, Mary
1872-1952
American bacteriologist

A native of Nashville, Tennessee, Mary Engle Pennington received a Ph.D. in chemistry from the University of Pennsylvania in 1895. She opened her own clinical laboratory in Philadelphia and did extensive research in bacteriology, developing procedures to ensure the purity of milk. She worked closely with Philadelphia's bacteriological laboratory to develop national standards of milk inspection and began to study refrigeration. The Department of Agriculture appointed her to head its new food research laboratory in 1907 and she traveled all over the country setting standards for refrigerated train cars. Pennington became a pioneer in the safe techniques of freezing foods, and was the first woman member of the American Society of Refrigerating Engineers.

PEREY, Marguerite
1909-1975
French chemist

Frustrated by poverty in her hope of becoming a doctor, Marguerite Perey jointed the staff of the French Radium Institute, headed by Marie CURIE, at the age of twenty. Beginning as a junior laboratory assistant, she rose rapidly as a result of her brilliant work. She discovered the element actinium K – which she called francium, in honor of her country – and became a professor of nuclear chemistry at Strasbourg University, where she also directed the Nuclear Research Centre. Perey was the first woman to become a member of the Académie des Sciences, in 1962, and was awarded the Legion of Honor. Like Marie Curie and her daughter, Irène JOLIOT-CURIE, Perey died of leukemia incurred by working with radioactive substances before the danger was known.

PERKINS, Frances
1880-1965
American government official, labor activist

The first woman to serve in the Cabinet, Perkins was responsible for creating unemployment insurance, the minimum wage and maximum hours. A graduate of Mount Holyoke College, she taught chemistry in Chicago before moving into settlement work at Hull House. In 1910 she received a masters degree from Columbia, and began working for women's suffrage and labor rights in New York. In 1911 she witnessed the Triangle Shirtwaist Factory fire, a landmark for exposing unsafe conditions and worker abuses because the 146 workers died due to the managers' custom of keeping factory doors locked. She worked on the committee to investigate the fire, and in 1918 she became the first woman appointed to the New York State Industrial Committee, becoming chairman in 1926. She served as State Industrial Commissioner until 1933, when Franklin Delano Roosevelt appointed her Secretary of Labor, a position she held until 1945. From 1945 to 1952, she worked on the Civil Service Commission.

Eva Perón was much loved by the people of Argentina for her concern for working people and for the poor.

PERÓN, Eva
1919-1952
Argentinian political leader

Eva Perón, the first Presidenta of Argentina, always wanted to be a star. "Evita" fled the small town where she grew up to make a future in the city of Buenos Aires. When she met Colonel Juan Perón, her future husband, she was working as a radio actress. Smitten by her beauty, he married her in 1945. In 1946 he became president, and she became enormously popular among the working people for she listened to them, empathized with them, and ceaselessly donated money, food and medicine. A sweetener of bitter pills, she used charity to regain worker loyalties after the government broke a sugar workers' strike in 1949. Concerned with the plight of women, she gained women the vote. In 1951 she wrote *My Life's Work*, and died of cancer the following year at the age of 33. A popular Broadway musical, *Evita*, was based on her life.

PIAF, Edith
1915-1963
French singer, songwriter

A nightclub chanteuse whose songs about heartbreak were delivered in a husky, throbbing voice, Piaf was born Edith Giovanna Gassion in Paris. Abandoned by her mother, she was raised by her paternal grandfather in a Norman village. Her father was a circus acrobat who took her on tour and encouraged her to sing in cafes and the circus. Her first nightclub appearance was at Gerry's in Paris wearing a tattered sweater and skirt, an outfit that suggested the name "Piaf", a colloquial French word meaning sparrow, to her employer. She sang in cafes, theaters and films, christening her international career with the ballad "La Vie En Rose", a song she wrote herself. She also composed "If You Love Me (I Won't Care)" and "Just Come Home".

PICKFORD, Mary
1893?-1979
Canadian actress

Gladys Mary Smith was born in Toronto and became a child actress in the United States, working for David Belasco. At the age of 16 she joined the Biograph Company in New York, and worked with D.W. Griffith. Her early films included *Her First Biscuits* (1909) and *The New York Hat* (1913), written by Anita Loos. In 1916 she founded the Mary Pickford Company, preferring not to be under contract to any particular studio, and taking advantage of her popularity to stay employed. In 1919 she joined Douglas Fairbanks, whom she soon married, Charlie Chaplin and D.W. Griffith to form United Artists. She continued to capitalize on her youthful appearance in popular films like *Pollyanna* (1919), *Little Lord Fauntleroy* (1921) and *Tess of the Storm Country* (1922). She won the first Academy Award for Best Actress for *Coquette* (1929), and retired several years later. In 1975 she was awarded a special Academy Award "in recognition of her unique contributions to the film industry and the development of film as an artistic medium."

Mary Pickford was Hollywood's most popular star from 1912 to 1928.

Prime Minister-designate Maria de Lourdes Pintassilgo of Portugal in 1979.

PINTASSILGO, Maria de Lourdes
1930-
Portuguese politician

All her life, Pintassilgo has been a passionate spokesperson for women's rights and leftist issues. She studied chemical engineering in college, and went on to become the head of the documentation center, Companhia Uniao Fabril (CUF) (1954-60). She founded the National Commission on the Status of Women (1970-74), and from 1971 to 1972 was a member of the Portuguese delegation to the United Nations General Assembly. After the 1974 revolution she was Secretary of State for Social Security, followed by a stint as Minister of Social Affairs, during which she established a committee on the status of women. She has also served as Caretaker Prime Minister (1979-80) and since 1990 has been on the National Council of Ethics for Live Sciences.

PLATH, Sylvia
1932-1963
American poet, novelist

Sylvia Plath was born in Boston, Massachusetts. She won a scholarship to Smith College but following a summer internship as a guest editor for *Mademoiselle* magazine, she suffered a breakdown and tried to commit suicide. Her novel *The Bell Jar*, published in 1963 under a pseudonym, included an account of her hospitalization, which included shock treatment therapy.

Plath graduated *summa cum laude* from Smith in 1955, winning a Fulbright scholarship to Cambridge University. Studying in London she met the British poet Ted Hughes, whom she married in 1956. Hughes's intellectual support and encouragement at first inspired Plath's craft, and a volume of poems *The Colossus* appeared in 1960. They had two children before separating in 1962. Plath continued to write poems at a feverish pace, and the volume *Ariel* (published posthumously in 1965) was a critical success. *Letters Home*, edited by her mother, were published in 1975. Plath committed suicide in February 1963.

PLISETSKAYA, Maya
1925-
Russian dancer

A renowned Soviet ballerina, Maya Plisetskaya was born in Moscow on November 20, 1925 and graduated from the Moscow Choreographic School in 1943. She was immediately accepted as a member of the ballet troupe of the Bolshoi Theater and danced her first principal role as Masha in *The Nutcracker*. Her artistry was well-suited to interpretations of the modern composers Tchaikovsky, Glazunov and Bizet. Her temperament found its highest expression in lyrical and heroic roles such as Odile in *Swan Lake*, the mistress of Copper Mountain in Prokofiev's *The Stone Flower*, Aurora in Tchaikovsky's *The Sleeping Beauty*, Kitri in Minkus's *Don Quixote* and Carmen in Bizet's *Carmen Suite*.

Plisetskaya was named People's Artist of the USSR in 1959 and received the Lenin Prize in 1964. She staged the ballet *Anna Karenina*, based on Tolstoy's novel, at the Bolshoi Theater in 1972. During her career she toured internationally, including the United States, France, Italy, Great Britain and Canada.

PORTER, Katherine Anne
1890-1980
American writer

A Pulitzer Prize winner and recipient of the National Book Award for her *Collected Stories* of 1965, Porter is best-known for her pre-World War II saga *Ship of Fools*. Porter was born in Indian Creek, Texas, and raised by her grandmother. She attended convent schools before running away to get married at 16. She divorced at 19 and went to Chicago to work as a journalist, a career she pursued in Fort Worth and Denver before a stint as a ghostwriter in New York prior to World War I.

Porter lived in Mexico during the war and sold a short story "Maria Concepcion" to *Century* magazine. A Guggenheim Fellowship financed her return to Mexico, a period described in her collection *Flowering Judas* (1928). A second marriage to a foreign attachè took her briefly to Europe, and she later married a third time, to a professor at Louisiana State University, and lived for several years in Baton Rouge. Her novel *Noon Wine* of 1937 won the Book of the Month Club Award, *Pale Horse, Pale Rider* appeared in 1939, and her last book, *The Never-Ending Wrong*, was published in 1977.

PORTER, Sylvia
1913-1991
American economic journalist

Sylvia Feldman was born in Patchogue, New York, and studied English literature and history at Hunter College until the Depression wiped out her mother's small fortune. Sylvia turned to economics, and graduated *magna cum laude* in 1932. She worked for an investment counseling service and a brokerage firm on Wall Street before taking a graduate course at NYU's School of Business Administration. Starting in 1935, she wrote a financial column in the *New York Post*, writing as S.F. Porter because the editor thought that people wouldn't take financial advice from a woman. She made financial information accessible to the public, and exposed a bond racket in 1936. She wrote her first book, *How to Make Money in Government Bonds*, just before World War II, but is best known for her *Income Tax Guide*, which has been published annually since 1960. Her other major work, which is continually updated, is *Sylvia Porter's Money Book*, first published in 1975, three years before she shifted her column to the *Daily News*.

POST, Emily
1873-1960
American writer

The *grande dame* of American etiquette, Emily Post was born into an affluent Baltimore family and had been brought up with the manners associated with having

Soprano Leontyne Price in the title role of Tosca *at the Met.*

privilege. She traveled throughout Europe and socialized with titled gentry.

In order to support her family after a divorce, she began writing professionally. Her fictional pieces were well-received. When she was first approached to write about etiquette, she opposed the idea. However, *Etiquette: The Blue Book of Social Usage* (1922) was an immediate hit. A best-seller, it was revised and modified ten times during Post's lifetime. Her other career endeavors included a radio show on gracious living and her first love, interior decorating.

POTTER, Beatrix
1866-1943
British children's writer and illustrator

The author of the beloved Peter Rabbit children's books, Helen Beatrix Potter was born into a well-to-do family in London where her father was a barrister. Potter had little formal art training but was often taken on gallery tours in London. She kept a rabbit, Benjamin Bounce, on the third floor of their London flat along with a menagerie of lizards, turtles, frogs and salamanders which she used as models for her sketches.

When she was 24, she began selling her drawings as greeting cards and verse illustrations. *The Tale of Peter Rabbit* was first published in 1902. By 1913 she had produced 17 children's stories, and her characters Peter Rabbit, Jeremy Fisher, Squirrel Nutkin and Jemima Puddleduck quickly became household names. *The Tale of Peter Rabbit* has sold over 60 million copies in English and has been translated into 15 languages. Potter died of bronchitis in 1943, leaving her 4000-acre Lake District property to The National Trust.

PRICE, Leontyne
1927-
American operatic soprano

Mary Violet Leontyne Price was born in Laurel, Mississippi, and began piano lessons when she was three. At the age of nine she heard Marian ANDERSON sing, and was inspired to follow in her footsteps. From Wilberforce College in Ohio, she went to Juilliard in 1948. She sang in a revival of *Four Saints in Three Acts* in 1952 and sang Bess in Ira Gershwin's revival of *Porgy and Bess* that year, which toured the United States and Europe. She made her operatic debut in 1957 in San Francisco, and sang her first Aida the following year in Vienna. She joined the Metropolitan Opera in 1961 as Leonore in *Il Trovatore*, and was chosen by the composer to sing Cleopatra in Samuel Barber's *Antony and Cleopatra*, the opera that was commissioned for the opening of the new Met in 1966. She was also the first black woman to sing at La Scala, in 1959. She received the Presidential Medal of Freedom in 1964. Her farewell performance at the Met as Aida in 1985 was broadcast live on television.

PRIESAND, Sally
1946-
American rabbi

A native of Cleveland, Ohio, Sally Priesand received a B.A. and an M.A. degree in Hebrew letters from Hebrew Union College-Jewish Institute of Religion in Cincinnati. In 1972 she became the first woman in Reform Judaism to be ordained as a rabbi. She spent four years at New York City's Free Synagogue and three at Temple Beth El in Elizabeth, New Jersey. In 1981 she became spiritual leader at Monmouth Reform Temple in Tinton Falls, New Jersey. She has served as chairman of the Task Force on Women in the Rabbinate and in 1975 published *Judaism and the New Woman*.

Q

QUANT, Mary
1934-
British fashion designer

Born near London, Mary Quant studied at Goldsmith's College of Art, and in 1955 opened a boutique Bazaar in Chelsea. Her partner Alexander Plunket-Greene became her husband two years later. She began to design and make clothes for the shop when she became frustrated by her inability to buy the sort of clothes she wanted to sell. Her designs, featuring geometric simplicity and short skirts made in bold colors and unusual fabrics, became extremely fashionable in the early 1960s, and became an identifiable part of the "Chelsea Look" and Swinging London. Her subsequent line of clothes developed into a multi-million dollar international fashion industry. Mary Quant was awarded the OBE in 1966, the first woman fashion designer to be so honored. In the 1970s she broadened the line to include cosmetics, in readily identifiable cases, and textiles.

ABOVE: *Jane Bryant Quinn writes a popular syndicated column on personal finance.*
ABOVE RIGHT: *Fashion designer Mary Quant displays her OBE after receiving it at Buckingham Palace in 1966.*

QUINN, Jane Bryant
1939-
American journalist, financial expert

Jane Bryant Quinn was born in Niagara Falls, New York, and attended Middlebury College. After graduation she went to New York and took a job in the *Newsweek* mailroom. The following year, she went to work as a writer for *Insider's Newsletter*, eventually rising to co-editor before joining *Business Week* in 1967. She began to write financial columns for the *Washington Post* in 1973, and was syndicated the following year. In 1974 she began her column in *Woman's Day*, which allows her to reach a wider audience with her no-nonsense, jargon-free advice. She is the author of several books on personal finance, including *Everybody's Money Book* (1979) and *Making the Most of Your Money* (1991).

R

RAMBERT, Dame Marie
1888-1982
Polish dancer, teacher

A native of Warsaw, Cyria Ramburg originally went to Paris to study medicine but when she saw Isadora DUNCAN dance, she decided upon her future profession. She danced barefoot in performances in Paris, and then went to study in Geneva with Emile Dalcroze, a pioneer in eurythmics. Diaghilev watched her dance in 1911 and invited her to join his ballet corps based in Monte Carlo.

Calling herself Marie Rambert, the dancer settled in London in 1915 and married the noted British playwright, Ashley Dukes, with whom she had two children. In 1920 she began a club called the Camargo Society and founded a school and tiny theater where she introduced choreography by Frederick Ashton, Anthony Tudor, Andre Howard and William Maurice. It was a popular and critical success, and spawned the Ballet Rambert, which toured extensively. Beginning in 1966, the corps departed from a strictly classical repertoire to include innovative modern dance choreography, some of it created by its own performers. Along with Dame Ninette de VALOIS, Rambert is considered one of the pioneers of modern British ballet.

Rambert was created a Dame of the British Empire in 1962. She translated Galina ULANOVA's autobiography and later she wrote her own autobiography *Quicksilver*.

RANKIN, Dame Annabelle
1908-1986
Australian politician

Australia's first female ambassador, Rankin was born in Brisbane, and began her public career during World War II when she served as YWCA Assistant Commissioner in charge of welfare work for women's services. She organized the Junior Red Cross in 1946, and that same year became a member of the Senate. From 1947 to 1949 she served as Opposition Chief Whip, and in 1947 became a Member of Parliament's Standing Committee (1950) and served as Government Whip (1951-66). As Minister of Housing from 1966 to 1971, she was the first woman in Australia to head a federal department, with yet another first being her appointment as ambassador to New Zealand from 1971 to 1975. In line with her social concerns, she was vice-president of the Multiple Handicapped Children's Association, and patron of the Cystic Fibrosis Association.

Vanessa Redgrave as Sylvia Pankhurst in Oh What a Lovely War *(1968).*

RANKIN, Jeannette
1880-1973
American politician

Jeannette Rankin never faltered from her conviction that war in any form is wrong. A native of Missoula, Montana, she taught and worked as a social worker in Seattle, and then campaigned in western states for women's right to vote. In 1917 she became the first female member of Congress (D-Montana), and was the only representative to vote against U.S. entry into World War I. Because of her stance against the war, she lost re-election in 1919, and so continued her activism with the Women's International League for Peace and Freedom. Re-elected to Congress in 1940, she refused to vote for entry into World War II, which ended her career. During the 1950s she traveled throughout the third world speaking out against American foreign policy, and in the 1960s she opposed the war in Vietnam.

RAY, Dixy Lee
1914-1994
American scientist, politician

Born in Tacoma, Washington, Dixy Lee Ray had a long and productive career as a scientist before she was elected governor of Washington State in 1977. She studied zoology at Mills College and spent three decades teaching, becoming an expert on crustacea and on the organisms that attack wood underwater, causing damage to wharves, boats, and dry docks. She was among the first to warn of pollution in the oceans caused by pesticides and radioactive materials. She was an advisor to the National Science Foundation and served aboard the Stanford University research ship that plied the Indian Ocean. She also served as a member of the Atomic Energy Commission during the Nixon administration (1973-75). Her books include *Trashing the Planet* (1991) and *Environmental Overkill* (1993).

REDGRAVE, Vanessa
1937-
British actress

Londoner Vanessa Redgrave was born into the theatre, as both of her parents, Michael Redgrave and Rachel Kempson, were actors. She attended The London Central School of Speech, Music and Drama, and made her first film, *Behind the Mask*, in 1958, the same year she made her London theater debut opposite her father in *A Touch of the Sun*. She became a member of the Royal Shakespeare Company, but first attained international recognition for *Morgan* (1965), for which she was nominated for an Academy Award and *Blow-Up* (1966). At the same time, she was becoming well-known for her espousal of left-wing causes, especially that of the Palestinians. Nominated for several Academy awards, she won the Academy Award for Best Supporting Actress in 1977 for her performance in *Julia*, and has appeared on stage in plays by Ibsen, Tennessee Williams and Chekhov, among others. She has also appeared in several Merchant-Ivory films including *The Bostonians* (1984) and *Howards End* (1993).

REITSCH, Hanna
1912-1979
German aviator

Born in Bonn, Hanna Reitsch flew from the age of eighteen, when she learned to pilot a glider, a popular form of flying in Germany between the wars. She learned to fly a motorized plane in 1935, when the Luftwaffe began to rebuild its force. Reitsch became the first female test pilot for the German forces and was awarded the Iron Cross in 1942 for her contributions to civilian flying. She set more than 40 altitude and endurance records in powered and motorless aircraft. She survived several crashes, including that of a Dornier bomber she purposely flew into a balloon cable, and the sensitive rocket-engined Messerschmidt Me163. She is best known for the flight she made into Berlin at the end of the war, supposedly to rescue Hitler, and she was one of the last people to see him alive. Cleared of any suspicion of war crimes by the Americans, although she had been involved in testing the prototype of the V-1, Reitsch continued to fly. In 1962 she set up a National School of Gliding in Ghana for President Kwame Nkrumah. Her autobiography *Flying Is My Life* was published in the United States in 1954.

RENO, Janet
1938-
American lawyer, Attorney General of the United States

From high school debating champion to big-city prosecutor, Janet Reno is a steely-nerved lawyer with a drive to be the best. In 1993, that best became exceptional indeed, when she was appointed the first female to be U.S. Attorney General. Born in Miami, Florida, she graduated from Cornell and Harvard Law School, where she was one of 16 women in a class of over 500. From 1963 to 1971 she worked as a lawyer in private law firms, achieving her first political appointment in 1971. As administrative assistant state attorney in Florida, her impressive performance led to her appointment as the first woman to head a county prosecutor's office. As Attorney General, she drew praise for assuming full responsibility for the tragic end to the Branch Dravidian complex in Waco, Texas. She advocates seeking alternatives to imprisonment and the death penalty, and has spoken out vehemently against violence on television.

U.S. Attorney General Janet Reno shows a child's letter protesting violence on TV.

RHYS, Jean
1894?-1979
British novelist, short story writer

Daughter of a white Dominican woman and a Welsh doctor, Jean Rhys's Caribbean childhood reverberates through her fiction, especially her most successful book, *Wide Sargasso Sea* (1966).

Born Gwen Williams on the island of Dominica, and later educated in England, Rhys worked in vaudeville as a young woman. With her first husband Jean Lenglet, she moved in the literary circles of Budapest, Vienna and Paris, where she met her literary mentor Ford Madox Ford. Her first novel *Quartet* portrays her relationship with Ford and his wife. She returned to England in 1934 and worked as a writer, translator, tutor and model. Despite economic difficulties and three rocky marriages that tinged her writing with bitterness, Rhys uniquely captures a woman's view of a world filled with sensual delights and fundamental injustices.

RICHARDS, Ann
1933-
American politician

Born Dorothy Ann Willis in Lakeview, Texas, Richards graduated from Baylor University in 1954 and earned a teaching certificate at the University of Texas at Austin while her husband studied law. When David Richards declined to run for Travis County commissioner in 1975, she was selected as the candidate, was elected, and became particularly effective at providing human services in the county. The stress of public life and a period of alcohol abuse led to separation and then divorce. In 1982 she achieved statewide office as Texas treasurer and in 1984 was chosen by the Democratic national leadership to second the presidential nomination of Walter Mondale. A new voice on the national scene, Richards was keynote speaker at the 1988 Democratic convention, where she described Republican candidate George Bush as having been "born with a silver foot in his mouth." In 1990 she won a hard-fought runoff campaign for governor of Texas.

R

RICHIER, Germaine
1904-1959
French sculptor

A sculptor with a fascination for natural processes of birth and decay and a strong spirit of experimentation, Richier was born and raised on a farm near Arles in southern France. Although her father opposed her interests, claiming "women are not made for art", Richier attended the Montpelier École des Beaux Arts in 1922 and in the 1930s began to receive awards for her bronze busts and figural studies.

A seminal work that employed spectral, corroded pieces of bronze was *Batman*, a transmogrified character. Her work was also related to the attenuated figures of Alberto Giacometti – both artists studied with Antoine Bourdelle, a former pupil of Rodin.

In the 1950s she added paint and even broken glass to her work, which evolved in novel ways throughout her life. She had a major show at the Women Artists of Europe Exhibition in Paris in 1936 and won the sculpture prize at the São Paolo Biennale in 1951.

RIDDLES, Libby
1957-
American dogsledder

The first woman to win the arduous, 1100-mile Alaskan Iditarod Trail Sled Dog Race (1985), Riddles was born and raised in Minnesota and lives in Alaska.

The Iditarod follows a turn-of-the-century overland mail and cargo route, crossing wilderness territory from Anchorage northwest to Nome. It encompasses numerous rivers, two mountain ranges and parts of the frozen Bering Sea. Temperatures range from −50°F. to just 40°F. and winds on course have reached 140 miles per hour.

Contestants are allowed 18 dogs but Riddles used only 13 in her victory run, her third attempt at the Iditarod. She finished in a little over 17 days, three hours before the second place finisher, and she earned $50,000 for her triumph. The Women's Sports Foundation named her Professional Sportswoman of the Year in 1985. She is the author of *Race Across Alaska* (1988).

RIDE, Sally K.
1951-
American astronaut

One of the first female astronauts in the U.S. space program, Rides was one of six women selected by NASA for the space shuttle program in 1978. Ride was born in Los Angeles, and received her bachelor's, master's and doctoral degrees in physics from Stanford University. She became the first American woman in space aboard the orbiter *Challenger*, launched on June 18, 1983. She flew a second satellite mission in October 1984, and headed the Ride Commission which investigated the explosion of the space shuttle *Challenger* in 1986.

In 1987 she became a Science Fellow at the Stanford University Center for International Security and Arms Control, and in 1989 she joined the faculty of the University of Calironia, San Diego, as a professor of physics. She is also Director of the California Space Institute, a research institute at the University of California.

RIEFENSTAHL, Leni
1902-
German actress, film director

Born in Berlin, Helene Bertha Amalie Riefenstahl studied to be a dancer, but soon turned to film, starring in several good German silents including *The White Hell of Pitz-Palu* (1929). In 1932, she formed her own company, directing and starring in *The Blue Light*. When the Nazi Party rose to power, Riefenstahl became a favorite of both Hitler and Goebbels, although she always maintained that the affection was one-sided. She did, however, direct the brilliant documentary on the Nuremberg rallies, *The Triumph of the Will* (1936). Her next film, *Olympia* (1938), a survey of the 1936 Olympic Games in Berlin, is considered the best sports movie ever made, for its sheer visual beauty. Both of these films were responsible for her being blacklisted after the war, and she did not complete her next film, *Tiefland*, until 1952. Subsequent works were never completed or released, and her film, *Nuba* (1977), became a beautiful book of photographs *The Last of the Nuba*. She has since turned to the still camera and produced several other books, including her memoirs.

German film director Leni Riefenstahl.

Ireland's president, Mary Robinson, advocates social reforms such as the right to abortion and divorce.

RILEY, Bridget
1931-
British painter

An influential leader of the Op Art movement, Bridget Riley is known for her smooth, flat paintings in black-and-white whose patterns create optical illusions.

Born in London in 1931, she attended the conservative Goldsmiths College of Art and the Royal College of Art. Thereafter she worked as a teacher and commercial artist and studied the visual effects created by the pointillist, Georges Seurat. In the 1960s she began to devise her precise, orderly and hypnotic canvases stripped of color, narrative or subject matter.

Her international reputation soared when her work *Fall*, a mesmerizing series of lines resembling carefully combed tresses, appeared in "The Responsive Eye", a seminal show of 1960s artists held in 1965 at the Museum of Modern Art in New York. She has expanded her repertoire to include a multicolored palette and varied shapes that resemble textile weavings.

RINGGOLD, Faith
1930-
American artist

Faith Willi Jones was born in Harlem, New York, and received her bachelor's and master's degrees from City College of New York where she studied with the modern painter, Robert Gwathmey. During the 1960s the civil rights movement inspired her themes. She employed the American flag and cubist motifs derived from African art to portray such bitter realities of her ancestral past as slave rape. In 1973 she began creating soft fabric sculptures such as dolls, masks, and quilts, the process of which evoked traditional spheres of women's work. Since 1986 Ringgold has also produced performance art, which has encouraged audience participation and included music by Aretha FRANKLIN and Billie HOLIDAY. She has taught at the University of California, San Diego since 1984, and has published a number of essays and several books, including *Tar Beach* (1991).

RIVERA, Chita
1933-
American dancer, actress

Dolores Conchita Figuero de Rivera was born in Washington, D.C., and won a scholarship to the School of American Ballet in New York. In 1952, though, her first job was touring in the chorus of the company of *Call Me Madam*. She returned to New York as a principal dancer in *Guys and Dolls*. Rivera was encouraged by Gwen Verdon, when she was in the chorus of *Can-Can* (1954), to study singing and acting. She did, and created the role of Anita in *West Side Story* in 1957, for which she received her first Tony nomination. She has received six more nominations, for shows as different as *Bye, Bye Birdie* in 1960, *Chicago* in 1975 and *The Kiss of the Spider Woman* in 1993. She won a Tony for her performance in *The Rink* in 1984.

ROBINSON, Mary
1944-
Irish politician, president

Ireland's first female head of state, Robinson has made the role of president into one that champions the welfare of those on the edges of Irish society: prisoners, abused women, rural areas, gays and lesbians, and has championed the right to divorce and woman's right to an abortion. A mediator, she has also nurtured links with traditional women's groups, saying "If feminists don't value the work of women who stay at home, how is society going to value it?" Educated at Trinity College, Dublin, and in law at Harvard College during the 1960s, from 1969 to 1989 she served on the Seanad (Senate) as Labour representative, and is the first Irish chief of state to meet with the British monarch since Ireland's founding in 1949.

RODDICK, Anita
1943-
British retail entrepreneur

Anita Lucia Perella was born in Littlehampton, Sussex, and attended the Newton Park College of Education, with the idea of becoming a teacher. Instead, she took a job with the women's rights department of the United International Labor Organization in Geneva. After a year there, she took a leave of absence to travel around the world. This trip introduced her to many different cultures, and many of the rituals and customs of the third world. After her return to Britain, she married Gordon Roddick, an artist. She opened the first Body Shop in Brighton, selling cosmetics made from natural ingredients, some of which she had discovered on her trip. As the shops became more successful, though much imitated, Roddick realized she could use the business to aid social and environmental causes as well as to give business and thus a measure of independence to third world communities.

Body Shop went public in 1984 and the stock increased 50 percent by the following day. The company now has over 300 stores, many of them franchised, all over the world. Anita Roddick received an OBE in 1992.

First Lady Eleanor Roosevelt became "First Lady of the World" when President Harry S Truman appointed her U.S. delegate to the United Nations.

ROGERS, Ginger
1911-
American actress, dancer

An actress, singer and dancer whose film partnership with Fred Astaire is one of Hollywood's finest legacies, Ginger Rogers was born in Independence, Missouri. As a young girl, she won a Charleston contest in Texas and toured with her own vaudeville act as a teenager. She appeared in several unremarkable Hollywood films before gaining notice when she danced the Carioca with Astaire in *Flying Down to Rio* (1933). Their films together included the hits *The Gay Divorcee* (1934), *Top Hat* (1935), and *The Barkeleys of Broadway* (1949).

Rogers also starred in a number of plays and movies on her own, notably *Kitty Foyle* (1940) for which she won an Oscar for her title role performance. Other roles that showcased her talents (she appeared in 73 films in all) were in the films *42nd Street*, *Lady in the Dark*, and *Oh Men! Oh Women!*. Rogers also played Dolly Levi in the Broadway production of *Hello, Dolly* and appeared on the London stage in the 1960s in *Mame*.

ROOSEVELT, Eleanor
1884-1962
American diplomat, humanitarian, former First Lady of the United States

Eleanor Roosevelt is best remembered for her work on behalf of women, children, the poor, and African-Americans. Born into a wealthy family, and a niece of former president Theodore Roosevelt, a sense of duty and obligation was instilled in her from her youth. She fell in love with her distant cousin, Franklin Roosevelt, and they married in 1904. After he contracted polio in 1921, Eleanor determinedly saw to it that he would be able to continue his political career. She revived her activism in women's settlement houses, and began traveling, speaking and writing on what she learned were people's day-to-day issues. When he became president in 1933, FDR came to rely on her to evaluate his own perceptions and the official reports that he read. In 1945 President Harry S Truman made her the American delegate to the United Nations. Instrumental in creating the 1948 Universal Declaration of Human Rights, for the rest of her life she would be an advisor to presidents, and a spokesperson for human rights and justice.

ROSENBERG, Ethel Greenglass
1915-1953
American convicted spy

Ethel and Julius Rosenberg are the only persons ever executed for treason during peacetime in the United States.

Born in New York's Lower East Side to Jewish parents, Ethel Rosenberg espoused left-wing politics. The event which led to her arrest and conviction was testimony offered by her brother, David Greenglass. His work on an atomic bomb project at Los Alamos gave him access to privileged information. He alleged that the Rosenbergs, in their capacity as spy ring leaders, directed him to pass secret information to the Soviets. The Rosenbergs adamantly professed their innocence; however at the height of the Cold War, they were convicted in 1951. They were executed on June 19, 1953, at Sing Sing Prison.

The Rosenberg trial aroused international interest, yet despite protests President Dwight Eisenhower refused to exercise clemency. Historical evaluations have suggested that anti-Semitism played at least as great a role in their execution as their left-wing views.

ROSENTHAL, Ida
1886?-1973
American fashion designer

Ida Cohen was born in Minsk, and went to school in Poland, before emigrating to the United States in 1905. The following year she married William Rosenthal, a sculptor. She worked in the dress business, first in wholesale and later in retail, as many women began to buy their clothes ready-to-wear rather than making them at home. Rosenthal realized that such clothes would fit better if the underwear really held the body, and developed a brassière, which with the aid of her husband the sculptor was designed to be made in standardized sizes. Together they founded the Maiden Form Brassière Company in 1922. Mrs. Rosenthal remained on the board of the company, which became Maidenform, until her death. She and her husband donated some of the profits from their invention to help found the Albert Einstein College of Medicine.

ROSS, Diana
1944-
American singer, actress

Raised in a Detroit housing project, Diana Ross studied design, cosmetology and modeling as a teenager. She also joined a singing group with her neighbors, Florence Ballard and Mary Wilson, who called themselves the Primettes. Scouted by Smokey Robinson for Motown Records, they sang back-up for Martha Reeves and the Vandellas before changing their name to the Supremes. They teamed up with the Holland-Dozier-Holland songwriting crew and scored nine consecutive top singles between 1964 and 1967 including "Baby Love" and "Stop in the Name of Love". Ross changed the group's billing to Diana Ross and the Supremes in 1967 and broke away to pursue her own acting and singing career in 1969.

Ross was nominated for an Academy Award for her starring role as Billie HOLIDAY in *Lady Sings the Blues* in 1972. She sang a hit duet with Lionel Ritchie called "Endless Love" in the early 1980s, and continues to be a popular personality.

RUBENSTEIN, Helena
1870-1965
Polish cosmetics entrepreneur

Born in Cracow, Poland, Helena Rubenstein studied at the University of Cracow and in Switzerland before she went to stay with relations in Australia in 1902. When she noticed that some skin cream she brought with her protected her skin against the harsh Australian sun, she had several cases sent out and opened a successful shop there. Several years later she returned to Europe and opened her first European salon in London in 1908 promoting Creme Valeaze, a skin cream she had manufactured according to a formula developed by a chemist, Jacob Lukusky. World War I caused her to move to New York, where she began her great rivalry with Elizabeth ARDEN. Rubenstein developed and sold the first tinted face powder and foundation, and pioneered the use of silk in cosmetics. She also used methods of mass production and wide marketing to attract customers who were intimidated by the Arden mystique.

Cosmetics maven Helena Rubenstein had a lifelong rivalry with Elizabeth Arden.

Wilma Rudolph recovered from disabling childhood diseases to win three Olympic track and field gold medals.

RUDKIN, Margaret
1897-1967
American entrepreneur

Margaret Fogarty was born in New York, and worked in banking and a brokerage house before her marriage to Herbert Rudkin in 1923. They moved to Connecticut, where Margaret Rudkin started baking stone-ground whole wheat bread for her asthmatic son when she couldn't buy it locally. Friends began to ask her to bake more, and she sold some in small stores before she opened the mail-order business that she named after their house, Pepperidge Farm. The business which began in their garage soon moved to a plant in Norwalk, Connecticut, which is still the corporate headquarters. The company added frozen pastries and cookies to the line before the Rudkins sold it to the Campbell Soup Company in 1960. Margaret Rudkin was retained as the president of Pepperidge Farm and became a director at Campbell Soup.

RUDOLPH, Wilma
1940-1994
American track and field athlete

The first woman runner to win three gold medals at an Olympic Games, Wilma Rudolph was born in St. Bethlehem, Tennessee, and contracted pneumonia and scarlet fever as a child which left her unable to walk until the age of 8. Her family's ministrations, including weekly physical therapy sessions 90 miles away in Nashville, helped enable her to become an accomplished athlete by the time she was 14. She set a state high school basketball record by scoring 803 points in 25 games, and at just 16 was a member of the bronze medal-winning 4 × 100 meter relay team for the U.S. at the 1956 Olympics.

Rudolph was a student at Tennessee State University when she won three gold medals at the 1960 Rome Olympic Games. She set a world record of 11.0 seconds in the 100 meter sprint, won the 200 meter dash, and was a member of the gold medal-winning 4 × 100 meter team relay. The Associated Press named her Athlete of the Year in 1960. and she received the James E. Sullivan Award in 1961 for the top amateur athlete in America.

RUSSELL, Dora
1894-1986
British feminist, educator, pacifist

An early campaigner for reproductive freedom and Margaret SANGER's colleague, Russell co-founded the Worker's Birth Control Group in 1924.

Born Dora Winifred Black, she was educated in England at Girton. In 1917 she accompanied her father to New York as his secretary, where he served as head of the British Mission. She married Bertrand Russell in 1921. With her husband she developed the Beacon Hill School, which supported a permissive approach to education. During the 1950s she actively supported nuclear disarmament and inspired the creation of a women's caravan throughout Europe to protest the Cold War. Committed to pacifism, she led a nuclear disarmament rally at age 89.

RYDER, Sue
1923-
British social worker

Motivated by her religious convictions, Sue Ryder (Baroness Ryder of Warsaw in Poland and Cavendish in the County of Suffolk) devoted her life to relieving the suffering of others. During World War II she assisted partisan groups in occupied Europe. After the war, her energies went toward relief in Northern Africa and Italy. In 1953 she opened a home in Suffolk, England, for concentration camp survivors and extended its mission to include the physically and mentally ill. She has founded 16 Sue Ryder Homes in Britain and others in eastern Europe and India. She is married to Leonard Cheshire, British war hero and founder of the Cheshire Homes for the disabled. Her autobiographies are *And The Morrow Is Theirs* and *Child Of My Love.*

S

SABIN, Florence R.
1871-1953
American histologist

A native of Central City, Colorado, Florence Sabin studied at Smith College and Johns Hopkins University Medical School, where she became the first woman graduate in 1900. She became a faculty member and researcher there in 1902 and a full professor of histology in 1917. She determined the origin of red corpuscles and joined the Rockefeller Institute for Medical Studies in 1925. As head of the department of cellular studies, she conducted research on tuberculosis that led to passage of the Sabin Health Bills by the state of Colorado. A 90 percent drop in the death rates from tuberculosis, and major inroads against syphilis, resulted from this legislation.

SACHS, Nelly
1891-1970
German poet, playwright

"Writing was my mute outcry," explained Jewish poet Nelly Sachs, whose work painfully and profoundly confronts the Holocaust.

Sachs was born and raised in Berlin, where she wrote plays and light verse. In 1940 she and her mother fled to Sweden, through the help of writer Selma LAGERLÖF, with whom Sachs had corresponded since childhood. The rest of her family perished in the concentration camps. An intensely private person, Sachs supported herself as a translator and, already past 50, began to write poetry in earnest. Her four volumes of poetry, which include *Journey into the Dust-Free Zone* (1961) and *Figures in the Sand* (1962), drew notice not just for their descriptions of agony in the death camps, but for the mystical possibility of redemption they suggest. Poet Stephen Spencer described Sachs' work as "apocalyptic hymns rather than modern poetry." Sachs won the Nobel Prize for literature in 1966, shared with Israeli author Shmuel Yosef Agnon.

A writer of poetry, novels, and biography, Vita Sackville-West is probably best known for her letters, particularly those she exchanged with Virginia Woolf.

SACKVILLE-WEST, Vita
1882-1962
British writer

Prolific author and poet Vita Sackville-West is as famous for her unconventional life as for her writing, in particular her passionate friendship with Virginia WOOLF. Woolf's novel *Orlando* is dedicated to Sackville-West, upon whom the gender-switching protagonist is said to be based.

Sackville-West defied traditional sex roles in her essays and novels, as well as in her personal life. Despite constant love affairs, her marriage to Harold Nicolson thrived on affection, companionship and a passion for gardening. The gardens she designed at Knole, her family's great house in Kent, and Sissinghurst Castle earned her an international reputation for landscape design. Her award-winning long poem *The Land* (1927) unites her love of the English countryside with accurate portraits of country folk, a saga of earthy humor and wisdom.

SAGAN, Françoise
1935-
French novelist

Sagan is noted for her highly successful, essentially autobiographical novel *Bonjour Tristesse*. Born Françoise Quoirez, she was raised in Lyon, France, during World War II and after failing the entrance examination to the Sorbonne at 18 began writing the novel. A tale of an unhappy teenager determined to dissuade her widower father from remarrying, the book was an instant success when it was published in 1954 and was awarded the Prix des Critiques. It appeared in the U.S. in 1955 and was translated into 20 languages and was made into a popular film by director Otto Preminger in 1957.

Sagan's other novels include *A Certain Smile* (1956), *Aimez-Vous Brahms?* (1959), the autobiographical *Responses* (1980), *The Painted Lady* (1983), *A Reluctant Hero* (1987) and *Evasion* (1993). She has also written plays and collaborated on a ballet with the composer Michel Magne.

ST. DENIS, Ruth
1878-1968
American dancer, choreographer

A pioneer modern dancer who profoundly influenced the course of modern dance, Ruth Denis was born in New Jersey. The daughter of a doctor and an engineer, she began earning her living dancing in vaudeville during the 1890s where she met dancer Ted Shawn, whom she married in 1914. Together they founded Denishawn in Los Angeles, the first American dance school with a curriculum and a standard of achievement. They embraced all styles of movement, from classical ballet to Eastern dance. She choreographed original works such as

Birth control activist Margaret Sanger (sixth from left) in Brooklyn in 1917.

"White Jade", "Radha – the Hindu Temple Dance", "Cobra", "Yogi" and the "Dance of Siva". These were a cultural cross of theatricality and religious mysticism that employed sumptuous color and light with elaborate costumes and stage scenery. Denishawn went on tour nationally from 1923 to 1929 and the company included Martha GRAHAM and Doris Humphrey. In 1931 she founded the Society for Spiritual Art. St. Denis continued to dance well into her eighties, and also taught dance at Adelphi University in New York. Her autobiography is *Ruth St. Denis: An Unfinished Life.*

SANDERS, Marlene
1931-
American television producer

Sanders was born in Cleveland, Ohio, attended Ohio State University and had a year at the Sorbonne in 1950, before she decided to go into the theater. She worked in summer stock and off-Broadway before she turned to television. She was a production assistant to Mike Wallace on *Night Beat* (1956-58), and was later appointed public affairs director of WNEW. In 1972 she became the first woman to co-anchor the news for ABC, where she later became the vice-president for news. While there she also produced the first of her award-winning documentaries, which include *Children in Peril* (1972) and *The Right to Die* (1974). In 1973 she produced *Woman's Place*, the first documentary to examine the question of sex roles. In 1978 she joined CBS as producer of *CBS Reports*, which included the first documentary about parental care, *What Shall We Do About Mother* (1980). In 1988 she wrote *Waitingfor Prime Time*, about her experiences in television.

SANGER, Margaret
1883-1966
American social worker

Born Margaret Higgins in Corning, New York, and educated as a nurse, Sanger became a social worker who was deeply concerned about the number of unwanted children born to low-income families. She founded the American Birth Control League in 1917 and set up clinics in which she taught methods of birth control. Such activities were illegal in many states, but she challenged these laws despite several arrests and won a series of favorable court decisions whereby physicians were permitted to give birth-control information for the "cure or prevention of disease." She traveled widely and worked for birth control in other countries, including India. Her books include *Woman Rebel* (1914), *What Every Girl Should Know* (1916), and *My Fight for Birth Control* (1931).

SARRAUTE, Nathalie
1900-
French novelist, essayist, playwright

Since the publication of her first book *Tropismes* in 1938 (labeled the "first anti-novel"), Nathalie Sarraute bypassed conventions such as plot and character development and concentrated on the psychology of society as a whole.

Born Ivanova-Voznesenska in Russia and educated at Oxford and the Sorbonne, Sarraute practiced law until 1939. A founder of the New Novel movement in France, her novels include *Portrait of a Man Unknown* (1948) and *Martereau* (1953). In these and other writings, her detailed, slow fragments take apart communication itself to discover great emotional truths. An influential member of the literary scene in Paris, Sarraute's work challenges writers not only to use language in innovative ways, but also to reach deeper into real experience to unravel the terrible events of our time.

SAUNDERS, Dame Cicely Mary Strode
1918-
British physician

The pioneer of the modern hospice movement, Cicely Saunders trained as a nurse and as an almonder (medical social worker) before deciding to become a doctor in 1951, and earning her medical degree in 1957. In 1959 she began raising money to create St. Christopher's Hospice, which was opened in 1967. Saunders's experiences caring for the dying at St. Luke's and St. Joseph's hospitals in London had convinced her that a combination of pain control and spiritual support would ease the distress of terminally ill cancer patients. Saunders's philosophy included allowing patients to choose where they were to die and making it possible for them to live as fully as possible until that time, and providing family counselling. In the 1960s she began lecturing widely on hospice care, and hundreds of hospice units, and teams who work with cancer patients at their homes, now exist in Britain, the United States, Canada, and Europe. Saunders was created a Dame of the British Empire in 1980.

SAUVÉ, Jeanne
1922-1993
Canadian politician, journalist

Born Jeanne Benoit in Prud'homme, Saskatchewan, and educated at universities in Ottawa and Paris, she was National President of Jeunesse Etudiante Catholique in Montreal from 1924 to 1947, and worked for UNESCO in Paris in 1951, after her marriage. She had two renowned careers: that of a highly respected television journalist (1952-72), and as a leading figure of the Liberal Party. In 1972 she was elected Member of Parliament for Montreal-Ahuntsic and served successively as Secretary of State for Science and Technology, Minister of Environment and Minister of Communications. In 1980 she became the first woman to be Speaker of the House of Commons, and from 1984 to 1990 served as the first female Governor General of Canada.

She was known for her passion for women's rights, a unified Canada, and her deep faith in the power of young people that led to the creation of a $10 million youth foundation that would join young leaders from around the world.

SAYERS, Dorothy
1893-1957
British writer

Dorothy Sayers's mystery novels not only have enjoyed widespread popularity ever since *Whose Body?* appeared in 1923, they also were among the first of the genre to draw critical acclaim for their literary merits. Her witty sleuth Lord Peter Wimsey puzzles his way through 11 novels and 21 stories, with style, intelligence and social commentary. In later books Harriet Vane, a smart, independent writer much like Sayers herself, joins Wimsey in his investigations.

Born Dorothy Leigh in Oxford, she was among the first female graduates of Somerville College, Oxford, in 1920. She worked in advertising, gave birth to a son and then married in the 1920s, exploring London's social movements as she produced her first detective novels. After 1940 she concentrated on theological and literary essays, religious dramas including the radio play *The Man Born to Be King*, and verse translation. Her translations of Dante and essays on his work are considered some of the finest in the English language.

SCHIAPARELLI, Elsa
1890-1973
French fashion designer

Elsa Schiaparelli was born in Rome, the daughter of a professor of oriental languages. She studied philosophy at university, and moved to the United States where she worked as a writer of film scripts for silent movies. When her husband left her, she moved to Paris in 1920. She designed clothes for her own amusement until a black sweater with a white bow knitted as the pattern proved to be so popular that she received orders for it from an American store. This started her in business in 1929. Her designs were flamboyant and innovative. Perhaps inspired by the Dada movement, she used outrageous patterns and brilliant colors, such as "shocking pink" which became her signature. She was one of the designers of the time to re-establish the natural waist in clothing, and she introduced padded shoulders in 1932. Her clothes featured large buttons and zippers when most designers were hiding closures. She was also the first couturiere to use man-made fabrics. She opened a salon in New York in 1949, and retired in 1954.

SCHIFF, Dorothy
1903-1989
American newspaper proprietor

Dorothy Schiff was born in New York, where her grandfather and father were partners in the brokerage house Kuhn, Loeb. Dorothy went to Bryn Mawr College and became involved in social welfare after graduation. With her inheritance in 1939, she bought the *New York Post*, which had been founded by Alexander Hamilton but which, by that time, was debt-ridden. Schiff changed the format to tabloid to make it easier to read, increased the number of columnists, and added comics and other human interest sections. During the long newspaper strike of 1962-63, Schiff kept the paper afloat until the strike ended, making the *Post* the only afternoon daily that had lasted. In the 1950s she had written her own column for the paper, called "Publisher's Notebook", and then "Dear Reader", but she cancelled them when she took over the physical running of the paper, becoming editor-in-chief as well as publisher and president, positions she held until she sold the paper to Rupert Murdoch in 1976.

SCHLAFLY, Phyllis
1924-
American anti-feminist

Born Phyllis Stewart in St. Louis, Missouri, she went to Washington University and earned a masters from Radcliffe College. Famous for her attack on the Equal Rights Amendment on the grounds that women are inherently different from men and shouldn't compete, Schlafly positioned herself as a moral authority and built up a powerful lobby group whose Stop ERA campaign achieved its end. She has also organized attacks against divorce, abortion, extra-marital sex, and rights for gays and lesbians. The last is especially poignant, given the 1992 revelation that one of her sons is gay, yet still supports his mother's stands that homosexuality is immoral. Her writings include the books *The Power of the Positive Woman* (1977) and *Class Abuse in the Class Room* (1984), and a syndicated column for Copley News Service.

Elsa Schiaparelli commissioned such artists as Jean Cocteau and Salvador Dali for her fabric designs and accessories.

Beverly Sills as Manon in the New York City Opera production Manon of Spring.

SIEBERT, Muriel
1932-
American economist

Muriel Siebert was a student at Case Western Reserve University, and graduated in 1952. By 1954 she was a securities analyst for Bache and Company, a position she held until 1958, when she worked as an analyst for Unitilities and Industries Management, Inc. The following year she went to work for Shields and Company, and was licensed by the New York Stock Exchange to sell stock. She joined several firms as a partner in the 1960s before establishing her own firm, Muriel Siebert and Company, in 1967. That year she bought a seat on the stock exchange, becoming the first woman to do so. In 1977 Governor Hugh Carey named her Superintendent of Banks for the State of New York. As such she oversaw the billions of dollars in New York banks and ran the New York City Municipal Credit Union. She resigned from that position to run for the Senate, although she lost the primary.

SIGNORET, Simone
1921-1985
French actress

Simone-Henriette Charlotte Kaminker was born in Wiesbaden, Germany, and grew up in Paris. During World War II she married director Yves Allegret who cast her in *Les Demons de L'Aube*. She became a popular French actress and appeared in *La Ronde* (1950), and *Casque d'Or* (1951) for which she won a British Film Award as Best Foreign Actress. The same year, now divorced, she married Yves Montand. Her performance in *Les Diaboliques* (1954) brought her true international recognition. She won the Academy Award for Best Actress for *Room at the Top* (1959), as well as awards at Cannes and from the British Film Academy. Her particular combination of strength and vulnerability allowed her to mature into character roles in the 1970s, and she won a French Cesar for *Madame Rosa* in 1977. Her last film, *L'etoile du nord*, was released in 1980, and she wrote a novel, *Adieu, Volodia*, which was published the year she died.

SIGURDSEN, Gertrud
1928-
Swedish politician

Gertrud Sigurdsen began her career as Secretary for the Swedish Confederation of Trade Unions (1949-64), then became Information Secretary of the Information Division (1964-68). A Social Democrat, she was elected Member of Parliament in 1969, and served as Minister for Internal Development Assistance (1973-76), Member and Vice Chair of the Parliament Standing Committee on Foreign Affairs (1976-82), followed by stints as Minister for Public Health and Medical Services (1982-85), and Minister for Health and Social Affairs (1985-89).

SILLS, Beverly
1929-
American coloratura soprano

Belle Miriam Silverman was born in Brooklyn, New York, and began her formal training with Estelle Liebling in 1936. She made her operatic debut on tour in *The Merry Widow* in 1947, and again on tour in 1951, sang the role of Violetta more than forty times. In 1955 she made her debut with the New York City Opera in *Die Fledermaus*, and appeared in a series of productions that brought the City Opera into the first flight of opera houses. Her performances as Cleopatra in *Julio Cesare* and Elizabeth I in *Roberto Devereux* put her on the cover of *Newsweek*. She also sang Lucia, Manon, the three heroines in *Tales of Hoffman*, Maria Stuarda and Anna Bolena, among others for the City Opera. She made her Metropolitan Opera debut in *The Siege of Corinth* in 1975, the same role she had sung for her La Scala debut in 1969. She also made a series of full opera recordings, as well as art songs, and operetta. She retired from the stage in 1980, but as General Director until 1988 she promoted American musicians and broadened the company's repertoire. In 1994 she became the Chairman of the Board of Lincoln Center in New York.

SIMPSON, Wallis Warfield
1896-1986
American-born Duchess of Windsor

In *The Heart Has Its Reasons*, Wallis Simpson, twice-divorced debutante, told the story of her Romance of the Century to the heir to the English throne, the Prince of Wales who became Edward VIII. Forced to choose between Wallis or the Crown, he abdicated in 1936. After living in the south of France, and the Bahamas, they moved to Paris in 1953. Entertaining the famous, the rich, the titled and the brilliant, Wallis achieved a reputation as a grand hostess. The Duke bathed her in jewels, worth millions of dollars, and when she died she had the proceeds go to the Institut Pasteur to fight cancer and AIDS.

SIMS, Naomi
1948-
American fashion model, beauty entrepreneur, writer

Successful business entrepreneur and beauty advisor, this former gangling teen from Oxford, Mississippi, was the first high-profile African-American fashion model. During her six-year modeling career, she appeared on the cover of *Vogue*, was the first black woman on the covers of *Ladies Home Journal* and *Life*, and appeared in Virginia Slims cigarette advertisements. By age nineteen, she had achieved national and international acclaim.

In 1973, having been dissatisfied with the quality of wigs manufactured for black women, she patented a type of hair more similar in texture to real black hair. Her wig business evolved into a multi-million dollar enterprise.

She has published several books on beauty, including the best-selling *All About Health and Beauty for the Black Woman*, and created a line of beauty products.

SITWELL, Dame Edith
1887-1967
British poet

The eccentric, talented daughter of English aristocrats, Sitwell was born in Scarborough and raised in a Derbyshire manor. She and her brothers, Osbert and Sacheverell, formed a lively triumvirate among avant-garde writers in London. Her first book of poems appeared there in 1915 and she edited the vanguard poetry collection *Wheels*. Her jazzy, syncopated verse such as "Clown's Houses" and "Facade" were published in the more sedate *Georgian Anthology*. In 1923 she presented a popular public performance of "Facade" set to music by the composer Sir William Walton, whose modern style suited the quixotic rhythms of her poems.

Sitwell dressed in wild costumes of turbans and robes with huge rings on her hands, and associated with bohemian figures such as Virginia WOOLF and Dylan Thomas.

Aristocratic and eccentric, Edith Sitwell was known for her avant-garde poetry and bohemian friends.

SMEDLEY, Agnes
1890-1950
American journalist, novelist

From an impoverished childhood in Missouri and Colorado, Agnes Smedley picked up the causes of socialism and feminism to become an influential activist, journalist and novelist. In the 1910s and 1920s she participated in the Indian independence movement. After the collapse of a relationship with an exiled Indian nationalist leader, Smedley suffered a nervous breakdown. To ground herself, she wrote her autobiographical novel *Daughter of Earth* (1929), a powerful account of a poor woman's struggle to be free. In 1928 Smedley went to China, where she wrote prolifically as a correspondent for European, American and Asian newspapers, and published four books on China. As an interpreter of the cataclysmic events in China to the West she was unparalleled.

SMITH, Bessie
1895-1937
American singer

The "Empress of the Blues", Bessie Smith was a native of Chattanooga, Tennessee, where she sang with Ma Rainey's Rabbit Foot Minstrels when she was just eight.

From 1923 to 1933 Smith recorded 180 blues songs, receiving as much as $1000 a record in her heyday. Her 1923 song "Down-Hearted Blues" sold over two million copies. Her early accompanists were jazz pianists Fletcher Henderson, Clarence Williams and James Johnson, and she recorded with Louis Armstrong and Coleman Hawkins, among others.

After recording the movie soundtrack for *St. Louis Blues* in 1929 Smith went into a decline, suffering from alcoholism and the break-up of her marriage. The producer John Hammond arranged recordings in the 1930s with Louis Armstrong and Benny Goodman, but by then she was virtually penniless. After a serious car accident in Mississippi in 1937, Smith was refused admission to a segregated hospital because of her race and bled to death from her injuries.

Columbia Records issued a posthumous, four-volume anthology of her songs called *The World's Greatest Blues Singer*. Edward Albee wrote his first play, *The Death of Bessie Smith*, about her, and she had a profound influence on later singers, including Billie HOLIDAY.

S

SMITH, Kate
1909-1986
American singer

Best known for her popular rendition of Irving Berlin's *God Bless America*, Kate Smith parlayed her full-bodied voice and buoyant personality into a radio and television career that spanned five decades. She recorded over 3000 songs and was perennially listed among the most admired American women.

Born in Greenville, Virginia, she grew up in Washington, D.C. and entertained the troops stationed there in her youth during World War I. She attended nursing school but left to sing with Eddie Darling's revue in 1926. She was cast in George White's production *Flying High*, playing opposite Bert Lahr. About this time, Smith met Ted Collins, a song producer who arranged for her radio debut for CBS. On May 1, 1931 she introduced the song "The Moon Comes Over the Mountain", her trademark ballad.

Her increasing popularity led to a news and talk show for CBS-TV called "Kate Smith Speaks". Smith hosted and sang medleys for several television specials and variety shows during the 1960s.

SMITH, Dame Maggie
1934-
British actress

Margaret Natalie Smith was born in Ilford, Essex, and trained at the Oxford Playhouse School. She made her stage debut with the Oxford University Dramatic Society in *Twelfth Night* in 1952, and her London debut in a revue the same year. In 1956 she appeared in New York in the annual New Faces. She made her first film, *Nowhere to Go*, in 1958, and joined the National Theatre Company. In 1963 she played Desdemona to Sir Laurence Olivier's Othello, repeating the part in the film version in 1965 and receiving her first Academy Award nomination. An actress of great range, she has appeared in Noel Coward's *Hay Fever* and Chekhov's *The Three Sisters*, as well as the one-man show *Virginia* in 1980, and *Lettice* and *Lovage* in 1988, for which she won a Tony. She is best known for her Academy Award-winning performance in *The Prime of Miss Jean Brodie* (1969). She also won an Oscar for Best Supporting Actress for *California Suite* in 1978, and received a nomination for *A Room With A View* (1986). She continues to perform in films and on stage. She was awarded a CBE in 1970, and was created a Dame of the British Empire in 1990.

SMITH, Margaret Chase
1897-
American politician

A four-time senator, Margaret Chase Smith was the first woman to serve in both the House and the Senate. With her husband, Clyde Smith, a congressman for Maine, influencing her, she became a member of the Republican State Committee for Maine (1930-36), and also worked as his secretary. When he died, she not only fulfilled his term, but also went on to run for the Senate. Elected in 1948, she served four terms. She continued to be politically active, and has supported the draft for women with the proviso that they choose whether to engage in direct combat. She donated her home in Skowhegan, Maine, complete with film clips, personal papers and speeches to the Northwood Institute in 1981.

Senator Margaret Chase Smith (R-ME).

SMITH, Stevie
1902-1971
British poet, novelist, illustrator

Known for her disconcerting wit, Stevie Smith juxtaposed frightening and tragic elements with irony and pathos in her unusual poems and line drawings.

Born in Hull, Florence Margaret Smith grew up outside London with her mother and sister at the home of her "Lion Aunt", whose independence and humor left their mark on the young poet. While working as a secretary, Smith wrote her first volumes of poetry and *Novel on Yellow Paper* (1936). Despite good reviews, depression haunted her, and in 1953 she attempted suicide at the office, foreshadowed in her best known poem, "Not Waving But Drowning". She recovered, quit her job, and wrote extensively while performing her works to burgeoning fame. Her readings for BBC radio and in public drew huge appreciative audiences. Smith received the Queen's Gold Medal for Poetry in 1969.

SMYTH, Dame Ethel
1858-1944
British composer, suffragist

Born in London, Ethel Mary Smyth studied at Leipzig, where one of her works, a quartet, was given its first performance. Her *Mass in D Minor* was performed at the Royal Albert Hall in 1893. She was a great believer in English music and its potential. She also campaigned for a British National Opera while composing her own operas *The Wreckers* (1906) and *The Boatswain's Mate* (1916). Smyth was an ardent crusader for women's suffrage and was imprisoned with Emmeline PANKHURST for three months. It may have been at that time that she wrote the song of the Women's Social and Political Union, *Shoulder to Shoulder*. She was created a Dame of the British Empire in 1922 for her services to music.

SMYTHE, Pat
1934-
British equestrian

A four-time winner of the European Ladies' Championship in showjumping and the first female member of an Olympic showjumping squad, in 1956, Pat Smythe grew up riding polo ponies at Richmond Park outside London. At 18

English composer Ethel Smyth was also active in the women's suffrage movement.

she was the first female rider on a Nations Cup Team, winning the Prince of Wales Cup for England in 1952. In 1956 she was a member of its bronze-medal team at the Stockholm Olympic Games. Smythe paired up with fine horses such as Tosca, Prince Hal and Flanagan in international competition. Flanagan won the European Championship in 1961-1963 (which Smythe won also in 1957). The pair also won the 1962 British Jumping Derby.

Smythe retired after the Rome Olympics in 1960 and went to Switzerland with her husband Sam Koechlin, where she raised two daughters. She has written several books and a series of children's stories.

SONTAG, Susan
1933-
American writer

Susan Sontag's essays, novels, short stories and films burn with bold intelligence and moral outrage. A brilliant student, she graduated from college at 18, and received two masters degrees from Harvard before taking up writing at 28. Her early works *Against Interpretation, and Other Essays* (1966) and *Styles of Radical Will* (1969) established her reputation as a provocative, insightful cultural critic.

In 1976, Sontag was hospitalized for breast cancer. This watershed experience of fighting not only the disease but the blame attached to it is explored in *Illness as Metaphor* (1978), a theme she returned to in *AIDS and Its Metaphors* (1988). In 1993 she published *The Volcano Lover*, her first novel in 25 years. A member of the American Academy of Arts and Letters, Sontag has served as president of the American branch of PEN, the international writers' society.

SOONG, Ching Ling
1893-1981
Chinese revolutionary and stateswoman

Ching Ling was one of the three famous Soong sisters, about whom it was said, "One loves money, one loves power and one loves China." She loved China. Born in Shanghai, she was educated there and at Wesleyan College for Women in Georgia. She returned to China and met her future husband, Dr. Sun Yat-Sen, head of the Kuomintang and founder of the Chinese Republic, whom she married in 1915. She traveled with him as his assistant and secretary, and founded the Women's Institute of Political Training. Soon after his death, she broke with the Kuomintang because of their anti-Communist stance, and went to Russia. Returning to China in 1929, she never stopped speaking out against the takeover of the Kuomintang by right-wing elements that betrayed the promise of democratic rule. She headed the League for Civil Rights during the 1930s, and on her deathbed was made honorary president of China.

STARK, Dame Freya
1892-1993
British adventurer, writer

Freya Stark was born in Devon, England, the daughter of a sculptor. Her family moved to Asolo, Italy, when she was ten to manage a silk production factory. In 1921, she began studying Arabic with an Italian monk and earned a degree in the language from London University. In 1928 she traveled to Lebanon, and each year thereafter delved further into the Middle East – Baghdad, Iraq and Iran. Her pioneer expedition into the mountains of Luristan in Iran was documented in her bestseller *The Valley of the Assassins* (1934). *The Southern Gates of Arabia* (1938) and *A Winter in Arabia* (1940) described further journeys. Her keen insights and knowledge about desert tribes and Arabic dialects were invaluable to British intelligence forces during World War II.

She was created Dame of the British Empire in 1972 and in the same year, at 80, traveled to Afghanistan. Stark wrote a three-volume autobiography in addition to her travel books.

English explorer and writer Freya Stark at her home in Asolo, Italy, in 1957.

STEAD, Christina
1902-1983
Australian novelist, short story writer

Australian author Christina Stead was nominated several times for the Nobel Prize for literature, and is widely considered one of the finest twentieth century novelists. Nonetheless, her work drew little notice during most of her life. Her nine novels and two collections of stories are studded with sharp social commentary, embedded in unusual characters and a classic sense of humor.

Born in Australia to English parents, she lived in Europe and the United States much of her life, with American husband William Blake, a writer and economist. Her remarkable first novel *The Man Who Loved Children* (1940) is a semi-autobiographical work about a father who invents his own language to communicate with his children.

STEIFF, Margarete
1847-1909
German seamstress, toy entrepreneur

Margarete Steiff was born in Giengen on the Brenz in Germany, and contracted polio at 18 months. The disease paralyzed all of her body except her left hand and arm. She attended a local sewing school and became adept at many kinds of needlework, despite her weakened right hand. By 1872 she had started a dressmaking business that became so successful that she opened a factory in 1877. In 1879 she made her first soft toy, an elephant following a pattern in the fashion magazine *Modewelt*. By 1883 the animals made of felt stuffed with lamb's wool were available in several sizes. In 1893 she was joined by her nephew Richard, who began to design other animals. The actual credit for the design of the first Teddy Bear has never been established, but the Steiff catalogue of the period was producing them in sizes up to 21½ inches, which Margarete Steiff believed would be too expensive. When she died at the age of 62 she left the company to her nieces and nephews, but the company name is still officially Margarete Steiff GmbH.

STEIN, Gertrude
1874-1946
American writer

As important for her nurturing of modern artists and writers as for the work she produced, Gertrude Stein was born in Allegheny, Pennsylvania, and raised in Europe, California, and Baltimore, Maryland. Her father was an immigrant German Jew and she learned French and German as a child.

She attended Radcliffe College and briefly studied medicine at Johns Hopkins before joining her brother Leo, an art critic, in London. Together they moved to 27 Rue de Fleurs in Paris, where they established a salon noted for its avant-garde members who included Picasso, Cezanne, Hemingway and Sherwood Anderson. They purchased a sizeable collection of modern art from the dealer Ambroise Vollard.

Stein's lifelong relationship with Alice Toklas was documented in Stein's 1933 novel *The Autobiography of Alice B. Toklas*, later adapted for a Hollywood film. She also wrote a collection of short stories (*Three Lives*), a volume of prose poems (*Tender Buttons*), a history (the opera *Four Saints in Three Acts* with Virgil Thomson) and several plays as well as her memoirs, *Wars I Have Seen* in 1945.

Writer Gertrude Stein's home in Paris was a focal point for avant-garde artists and writers.

STEINEM, Gloria
1934-
American feminist, writer, editor, publisher

This freelance journalist, born in Toledo, Ohio, and educated at Smith College, came to national attention with the publication of an article in *Esquire* magazine in 1963 about her experience as a Playboy bunny. She founded and contributed to *New York* magazine in 1968; organized the Women's Strike for Equality with Beth FRIEDAN in 1970; and with Bella ABZUG and Shirley CHISHOLM founded the National Women's Political Caucus. However, she is best known for creating *Ms.* magazine in 1972.

A first in this genre, *Ms.* covered a wide spectrum of women's issues. It offered thoughtful articles on abortion rights, day care and pornography, and has been a sounding board for many leading feminists over the years.

A leading liberal feminist, Steinem has been a vocal opponent of Camille PAGLIA's views. She has published two collections of her essays and articles, *Outrageous Acts and Everyday Rebellions* (1984) and *Moving Beyond Words* (1994), and *Revolution From Within: A Book of Self-Esteem* (1992).

STEWART, Martha
1941/2-
American designer, entrepreneur

Martha Kostyra was born in suburban New Jersey, where her family taught her to cook and garden. She married David Stewart while still at Barnard College, after a career as a teenage model, and worked as a stockbroker until 1973, when she and her husband moved to Connecticut. In 1976 she started a catering business, which had a $1 million annual turnover within a decade. Part of this success was due to the success of her first book, *Entertaining*, in 1982, which along with recipes included suggestions for parties combined with beautifully composed photographs of carefully prepared food, designs for table settings that combined folksy yet chic decor, and Martha Stewart herself, to give it a sense of reality. Her subsequent books on weddings, gardening, interior decoration and even restoration were followed by videotapes, lectures and seminars. Her appeal was broadened by the initiation of a magazine called *Martha Stewart: Living*, and a well-advertised consultancy with K-Mart. Martha Stewart has parlayed her taste, creative flair, incredible energy and shrewd instinct into a tremendous and lucrative empire.

STONE, Ganga
1942-
American charity organizer

Ingrid Stone was born in the Bronx, the daughter of Hedley Stone, a labor organizer and one of the founders of the National Maritime Union. In the late 1960s she dropped out of college and became a follower of Swami Muktananda. Stone stayed in an ashram in India for two years, changing her name to Ganga. Returning to New York, she did volunteer work in the evenings, delivering food to housebound patients. She realized that some of these patients, especially those with AIDS, were too weak to cook for themselves. Although living close to the poverty line herself, in 1985, Stone established God's Love We Deliver, a charitable organization that provides complete meals to these patients. At first she funded the charity out of her own profits from a pastry pushcart, but later persuaded many New York restaurants to donate meals. She has also encouraged many other New Yorkers to donate their time in the charity's kitchen or driving the delivery van, donated by former mayor David Dinkins. More recently she has established My Sister's Keeper, a group that provides bodyguards for abused women.

STOPES, Marie
1880-1958
British scientist, writer

Marie Stopes was a gifted botanist and zoologist, but she is best known as a pioneer in the struggle to educate women about birth control and to make contraception available. Born in Edinburgh, she obtained simultaneous degrees in geology, geography and biology from University College, London, and was the first woman to join the science faculty at Manchester University, in 1904. Her unsuccessful marriage to Dr. Reginald R. Gates inspired her to write *Married Love* (1918), encouraging women to seek sexual fulfillment in marriage. This was followed by *Wise Parenthood* (1918), which advocated birth control in marriage to space out pregnancies and limit family size. Stopes and her second husband, Humphrey V. Roe, opened Britain's first free birth control clinic in London in 1921. Clinics were subsequently opened elsewhere in England and Scotland, and they were eventually united under the Family Planning Association.

Multifaceted actress Meryl Steep has won three Oscars for her work.

Feminist Gloria Steinem is best known for founding Ms. *magazine, in 1972.*

STREEP, Meryl
1949-
American actress

Mary Louise Streep was born in Summit, New Jersey, and majored in drama at Vassar College. She also attended the Yale School of Drama, and joined the Yale Repertory Theater before going to New York to work for Joseph Papp, appearing in his revivals of *Trelawny of the Wells* and *Secret Service*. She made her film debut in *Julia* (1977), and the following year won the Academy Award for Best Supporting Actress for *The Deer Hunter* (1978). Also in 1978 she won an Emmy for her role in *Holocaust*. In 1979 she won Best Supporting Actress again for *Kramer vs. Kramer*. She has played a Polish refugee in *Sophie's Choice* (1982), for which she won an Academy Award for Best Actress, writer Isak DINESEN in *Out of Africa* (1985), and an Australian mother in *A Cry in the Dark* (1988). She has an underused flair for comedy which did show up in *She-Devil* (1989) and *Postcards From the Edge* (1989). Her other films include *Silkwood* (1983), *Heartburn* (1986) and *The House of the Spirits* (1994).

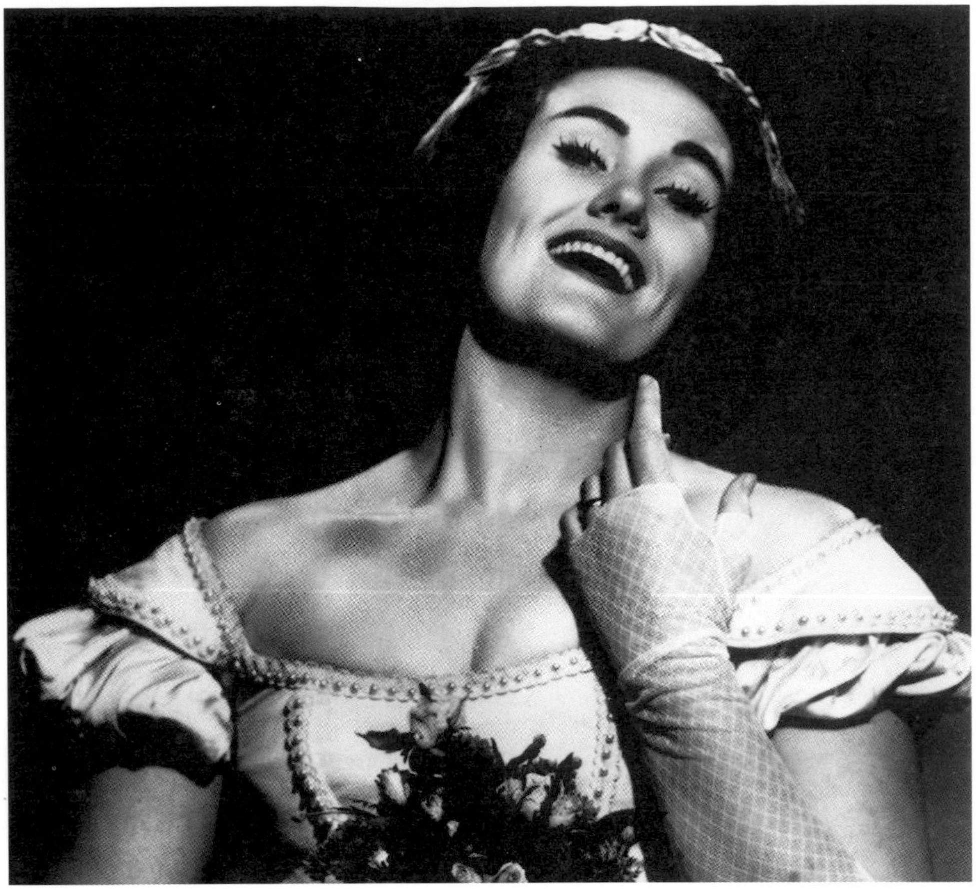

Coloratura soprano Joan Sutherland in Bellini's La Sonnambula, *a rarely performed piece which was revived especially for her at the Met in 1963.*

STREISAND, Barbra
1942-
American singer, songwriter, actress, director

Brooklyn-born Streisand sang in Greenwich Village coffee houses before her 1962 Broadway role as Miss Marmelstein in *I Can Get It For You Wholesale* launched her career. She played the lead in Broadway's *Funny Girl*, and won the Best Actress Award in 1969 for her film performance of the role. Her hit single "People" in 1964 won her the Best Female Vocalist Grammy, an award she also won in 1963 and 1965. She scored a huge box office hit with the film *The Way We Were* with Robert Redford in 1973, and her rendition of the movie's title song won a Grammy as Best Song of the Year. In 1977 she was featured in *A Star Is Born* and won a Grammy and a songwriting Oscar for its theme song "Evergreen". She has had more gold record sales than any other solo performer, with 21 top ten albums and an estimated 50 million records sold for Columbia Records.

She made her directing debut in *Yentl* (1983), in which she also starred, and followed this success with *Nuts* (1988) and *Prince of Tides* (1992). In 1994 she returned to the concert stage to sold-out performances.

SULLIVAN MACY, Anne. *See* **KELLER, Helen**

SUMMERSKILL, Baroness Edith
1901-1980
British politician

The severe but compassionate Baroness Summerskill of Kenwood was greatly influenced by her father's concern for preventive medicine, and strong feminist leanings. Born in London, she was educated at King's College, London, and Charing Cross Hospital. After qualifying as a physician in 1924, she became involved in the Maternity and Child Welfare Committee of her Urban District Council, which formed the underpinnings for her political career.

As a Member of Parliament from 1938 until 1955, she worked on preventive medicine which became the National Insurance and Health Service, and feminism. One of her most intense battles was for women to receive salaries as housewives. Although unsuccessful, she did succeed in legislative battles for women to have the same property rights as men. For her many achievements, she was created a Life Peeress in 1961 and a Companion of Honour in 1966.

SUTHERLAND, Dame Joan
1926-
Australian coloratura soprano

Joan Sutherland was born in Sydney and made her opera debut as Dido in Purcell's *Dido and Aeneas* in 1947. She went to London in 1951 to continue her training, and made her debut as the First Lady in *The Magic Flute* at Covent Garden the following year. She was one of the resident sopranos in that company for seven years, during which time she married a fellow Australian, the conductor Richard Bonynge. In 1959 Sutherland sang the title role in Donizetti's *Lucia de Lammermoor*, in a manner that harkened back to the voices popular a century earlier. She became an overnight sensation, and helped to popularize a great number of works that had fallen out of favor. She was equally at home in the standard repertoire. She made her Metropolitan Opera debut also in the role of Lucia, though she continued to learn other parts, and made her farewell performance in *The Huguenots* in Sydney in 1990. She was awarded a CBE in 1961, and was created a Dame of the British Empire in 1979.

SUTTNER, Baroness Bertha von
1843-1914
Austrian pacifist, writer

Born into an aristocratic but impoverished family in Prague, Countess Bertha Kinsky became a tutor with the von Suttner family where she met her future husband, Arthur. In 1876 she traveled to Paris to interview for a position as personal secretary to Alfred Nobel, but returned to Vienna shortly thereafter in order to elope with Arthur. The couple traveled throughout Europe acquainting themselves with the progressive thinkers of the time. Successful writers, they espoused the contemporary concepts of the day.

Convinced of war's futility, her 1889 anti-war novel *Lay Down Your Arms* was the Baroness's first contribution to the peace movement. Thereafter, she focused all her writings toward that end. Having maintained her friendship with

Alfred Nobel, she kept him apprised of the developments in the movement, and in his will he established the Peace Prize in her honor. In 1905 Baroness von Suttner became the first woman to receive the Nobel Peace Prize. She never lost her resounding belief in mankind's progress and growth towards "internationalization and unification".

SUZMAN, Helen
1917-
South African politician

For years Helen Suzman raised her voice against apartheid in South Africa, often finding herself isolated from other whites. Born Helen Gavronsky, the daughter of a Lithuanian Jew who emigrated to South Africa to escape pogroms in the early 1900s, she worked as an economics teacher at the University of Witwatersrand from 1944 to 1952. In 1953 she was elected to the Parliament, and formed the Progressive Party in 1959. For the next 12 years, she was the Party's only member.

Outspokenly anti-apartheid, she used her post to reveal abuses toward imprisoned black South Africans, and counts among her close friends President Nelson Mandela. Her awards include the United Nations Human Rights Award (1978) and the Medallion of Heroism (1980). In 1993 she published her memoirs, *In No Uncertain Terms.*

SYMBORSKA, Wislawa
1923-
Polish poet, editor

Wislawa Symborska is one of the most important contemporary poets of Poland, and perhaps the most innovative. Her delightful wit and use of stories in her poetry have gained her popularity with a wide audience, at the same time as her intellect and skill have won praise and prizes from the literary critics.

Criticized by the communist censors in the postwar period, Symborska had to simplify and politicize her poems to get them published. Her 1957 book broke new ground with a more lyric voice, and quietly questioned the participation of artists like herself in the creation of a drab Stalinist culture. In recent years, her poetry has grown in popularity and availability. Symborska is also the poetry editor of the weekly magazine *Literary Life* in Krakow.

Austrian pacifist Bertha von Suttner.

SZABO, Violette
1918-1945
French-British war worker, spy

Violette Szabo applied to join the French Section of the Special Operations Executive (SOE) after her husband's death in North Africa in 1942. She was a brilliant student and was selected to set up a network in Rouen to prepare for the Allied invasion. On April 6, 1944 she parachuted into Paris and traveled to Rouen to find that her chief's cover had been broken and his photograph was on posters all over Rouen. On June 6, 1944 Szabo set off for Limoges with the local leader of the Maquis, "Anastasia", to coordinate groups and alert them to action. After successfully completing one mission they ran into a Gestapo patrol, and Szabo, who had orders to protect "Anastasia", was captured while her companion escaped. She was sent to Paris for interrogation but did not reveal the identity of any of her contacts. She was executed in Germany on January 26, 1945.

SZOLD, Henrietta
1860-1945
American Zionist leader, educator

Henrietta Szold devoted much of her life to the Zionist movement. She was responsible for translating many Hebrew works into English and was editor of the Jewish Publication Society of America.

In 1889 she started a school in her native Baltimore that educated several thousand immigrants, and she is credited with saving over 100,000 Jewish children from the Holocaust by coordinating their emigration from Nazi Germany.

After a 1909 visit to Palestine she became interested in Zionism. In 1912 she co-founded Hadassah, the largest and most visible Jewish women's organization in America. Dedicated to improving health conditions in Palestine, its members first sent assistance there in 1912. She moved to Palestine in 1919 in order to personally direct Hadassah's work.

T

TAILLEFERRE, Germaine
1892-1983
French composer, pianist

Marcelle Germaine Tailleferre was born in Parc-St-Maur near Paris, and entered the Paris Conservatoire against her parents' wishes. She won prizes in harmony, counterpoint and accompaniment and also took a few classes with Ravel. While at the Conservatoire she met Georges Auric, Artur Honegger and Darius Milhaud. In 1918 her *String Quartet* was performed in a concert presented by a group known as the Nouveaux Jeunes, who would later be known as "Les Six". They were Auric, Honegger, Milhaud, François Poulence, Louis Edmond Durey and Tailleferre. They collaborated on a few pieces including *Les Mariés de la tour Eiffel*, with a libretto by Jean Cocteau, in 1921, but mostly worked on pieces independently. Tailleferre's music has been described as pleasingly, teasingly modernistic. Her other works include a piano concerto and the chamber opera, *Le Maître* (1961), with a libretto by Eugene Ionesco. She also wrote songs, comic operas and ballets.

TALLCHIEF, Maria
1925-
Native-American dancer

Maria Tallchief was born in Fairfax, Oklahoma, on an Osage reservation, and grew up there and in Los Angeles. As a child she wanted to be a concert pianist until she began to study ballet in high school. She later studied at the School of American Ballet in New York, and made her debut with the Ballet Russe de Monte Carlo in 1942. In 1946 she married Georges Balanchine, and the following year they both joined the newly organized New York City Ballet. Balanchine created a number of ballets to feature her, including *Danse Concertante*, *Apollo* and his revival of *Firebird*, probably her best-known role. She also danced Scheherazade and the Black Swan. She received great acclaim for her performances in Europe and the United States. Although she appeared with many other companies as a guest, City Ballet was her base and the company from which she retired in 1967 to teach. She was a recipient of the Capezio Award in 1965.

Amy Tan's semi-autobiographical novels The Joy Luck Club *and* The Kitchen God's Wife *have been bestsellers.*

TAN, Amy
1952-
American novelist

Amy Tan has touched millions of readers with her skilled storytelling. Born and raised in California, she lived briefly in Europe, following the tragic death of her father and brother in 1968. Despite her Chinese immigrant parents' hopes that she would become a brain surgeon and concert pianist, Tan opted instead to study English and linguistics. She found success, but not happiness, as a business writer. With a self-prescribed therapy of jazz piano and fiction writing, she began the mother-daughter stories that would become *The Joy Luck Club* (1989), an instant bestseller later adapted for film. Her second novel, *The Kitchen God's Wife* (1991), tells the painful story of Tan's mother, forced to abandon three daughters in China in order to flee a brutally abusive husband. She is also the author of *The Moon Lady* (1992) and *The Chinese Siamese Cat* (1994). Tan, her husband, and her mother visited China in 1987, and were reunited with her three half-sisters.

TARBELL, Ida
1857-1944
American journalist, writer

Born in Erie City, Pennsylvania, muckraker Ida Tarbell was dedicated to exposing political and industrial corrup-

Famous muckraking journalist Ida Tarbell's 1904 exposé of the Standard Oil Company led to federal action.

Actress Elizabeth Taylor holds the Jean Hersholt Humanitarian Award she won in 1993 for her work fighting AIDS.

tion. Her investigative journalism for *McClure's* magazine made waves, and her most sensational book, an attack on John D. Rockefeller and his oil monopoly called *The History of the Standard Oil Company*, led to federal investigations and the eventual breakup of the company.

She was also a member of the peace movement. After an interview with Benito Mussolini, she forecasted a rise in fascism in Europe. Her autobiography is *All In a Day's Work*.

TAUSSIG, Helen Brooke
1898-1986
American physician

One of American medicine's pioneers, Taussig studied at the University of California, Berkeley; Harvard Medical School; and Johns Hopkins Medical School, where she earned an M.D. degree in 1927. She began heart research in her student days, and during the thirty years in which she concentrated on pediatrics, she developed a surgical method for replacing the constricted pulmonary artery that caused cyanosis in infants labeled "blue babies". In 1959 she became the first woman to attain the rank of full professor at Johns Hopkins Medical School, and in 1965 she was elected the first woman president of the American Heart Association. Her most important publication is *Congenital Malfunctions of the Heart* (1947).

TAYLOR, Elizabeth
1932-
American actress

Elizabeth Rosemond Taylor was born in London, but was evacuated to the United States in 1939. Becoming a child actress, Elizabeth was cast in a number of films, including *Lassie, Come Home* (1942) and *National Velvet* (1944). She made the transition to adult roles in *Father of the Bride* (1950) and *A Place in the Sun* (1951). She was nominated for an Academy Award for *Raintree Country* (1957), but it was her performance in two Tennessee Williams plays, *Cat on a Hot Tin Roof* (1958) and *Suddenly, Last Summer* (1960), that made her name as an actress. She won an Oscar for Best Actress in 1960 for *Butterfield Eight*, but it was for her working and personal relationship with Richard Burton, her costar in *Cleopatra* (1962), that many people best remember her. With Burton she also made *Who's Afraid of Virginia Woolf* (1966), for which she won her second Academy Award. Founder in 1985 of the American Foundation of AIDS Research and of the Elizabeth Taylor AIDS Foundation in 1991, she was the recipient of the Jean Herscholt Humanitarian Award in 1993.

Te KANAWA, Dame Kiri
1944-
New Zealand operatic soprano

Born near Auckland, Te Kanawa, who is part Maori, received a grant to study voice in London after winning many prizes and awards in New Zealand and Australia. She made her operatic debut at the Camden Festival in a rare production of Donizetti's *La Donna del Lago* in 1969. She first appeared on stage at Covent Garden in 1970 in a minor role, but sang the Countess in *Marriage of Figaro* the following year to great acclaim. She made her Metropolitan Opera debut as Desdemona in 1974, substituting for Teresa Stratas. In 1981 she sang Handel's "Let the Bright Seraphim" at the wedding of the Prince of Wales and Lady Diana Spencer. In the 1980s, she broadened her repertoire by making recordings of quasi-operatic musicals, including *West Side Story*. She was awarded the OBE in 1971, and was created a Dame of the British Empire in 1982.

MOTHER TERESA (b. Agnes Gouxha Bejaxhu)
1910-
Albanian missionary

The daughter of Albanian peasants living in Yugoslavia, the future Mother Teresa became a nun in 1927 and was sent first to Ireland and then to Calcutta, where she taught in a girls' school for almost 20 years. Shortly after becoming head of the school, she had a spiritual experience in which she was called to devote herself to the people of Calcutta's slums. After a few months of medical training, she and two other nuns took up their ministry to the sick and dying in the streets of Calcutta. In 1950 she opened a Mother House for the newly founded Missionary Sisters of Charity, which now has several thousand sisters and brothers working all over the world. In 1979 she was awarded the Nobel Peace Prize. She has published *Heart of Joy* (1987) and *The Best Gift Is Love: Meditations* (1993).

Mother Teresa's Missionary Sisters of Charity, set up to help the poor in Calcutta, has become international.

T

TERESHKOVA, Valentina
1937-
Russian cosmonaut

The first woman to travel in space, Tereshkova orbited the earth 49 times in three days as a cosmonaut aboard the Russian space capsule Vostok 6.

Tereshkova was the daughter of a tractor driver and textile worker and was raised on a farm 250 miles from Moscow. An active participant with the Young Communist League, her interest in space travel was sparked by the exploits of the first Russian cosmonaut, Yuri Gagarin, in 1961 and she wrote to the space commission to volunteer for training.

Nikita Krushchev boasted that her exploits proved to the Western nations that women were not the frailer sex, and that Tereshkova had orbited longer than all the American astronauts to date at the time of her journey in 1963. As a member of the Soviet Praesidium she traveled internationally to lecture about her epic mission, and she became head of the Soviet Women's Committee in 1977.

TERRELL, Mary Church
1863-1954
American civil rights activist

Mary Church Terrell was born into an elite black family in Memphis, Tennessee. Well-educated, multi-lingual, and very fair-skinned, Terrell could have chosen to "pass for white". However, she elected to embrace her African-American heritage and fought to enhance the lives of black women.

In 1896 she founded and was the first president of the National Association of Colored Women (NACW). This self-help organization offered support to its members and created programs which addressed racial problems.

Her efforts soon moved away from black self-help to promoting integration and interracial understanding. She was praised for her intellect and wrote articles about the disenfranchisement of African-Americans. During the latter part of her life, she became more militant. She picketed segregated facilities and successfully instigated a court action in Washington D.C., against a segregated restaurant. She died two months after the landmark *Brown vs.the Board of Education* mandate, which desegregated American public schools, was passed.

Russian Valentina Tereshkova became the first woman in space in 1963.

THARP, Twyla
1941-
American dancer, choreographer

A witty and inventive modern dancer and choreographer, Twyla Tharp was born in Portland, Indiana. Dedicated to dance from an early age, she formed her own company in 1965 after working as a freelance choreographer and following her dance debut with Paul Taylor's Dance Company.

Tharp's come-what-may approach to dance welcomes bizarre and comic gestures. Her collage method synthesizes jazz steps, clowns' slapstick routines, athletic jumps and even roller skating, and her company will perform anywhere – in gymnasiums, outdoors, wherever their skills can be freely expressed.

Tharp's ventures into other fields include choreographing routines for the British gold medalist figure skater John Curry – she put on ice skates for the first time to get a feel for the difference in movement and rhythms. Tharp's best known works include *Eight Jelly Rolls* (1971), *Push Comes to Shove* (1976) and *Mud* (1977), and she continues to produce new works in the 1990s, including *Cutting Up* (1992) and *Waterbaby Bagatelles* (1994). Her autobiography *Push Comes to Shove* was published in 1993.

THATCHER, Baroness Margaret
1925-
British prime minister, politician

When Margaret Thatcher became England's first female prime minister in 1979, she represented Conservative ideals that had been present for quite some time, but that no one else had had the will to implement. Fiercely anti-socialist and anti-centralist government, she set about restructuring England's social welfare system, increasing the size of the private sector through privatization of formerly state-owned industries and breaking the power of labor unions.

Born in Grantham, Lincolnshire, the daughter of a retail grocer, she earned a degree in chemistry. Swept up in politics when she became a member of the University Conservation Association, then its president, she later studied and practiced law. In 1959 she was elected Member of Parliament, and by 1961 had become Joint Parliamentary Secretary to the Ministry of Pensions and National Insurance, followed by a position in the Cabinet as Minister of Education in 1970. Prime Minister from 1979 to 1990, she resigned and, being presented with a peerage, entered the House of Lords. Her book *The Downing Street Years* was published in 1993. The longest-serving British prime minister this century, Thatcher was a highly respected world leader.

THOMAS, Helen A.
1920-
American journalist

Washington correspondent Helen

Margaret Thatcher, former prime minister of Britain, was known as "The Iron Lady" for her firm policies.

Thomas has covered the front page and backstage at the White House through eight presidencies. Born in Winchester, Kentucky, she is the first woman ever named White House bureau chief for a major wire service (UPI), a post she has filled since 1974. She broke into the White House press corps in 1961, covering the Kennedy family. Her Watergate scoops and sharp observations of four administrations are included in her 1975 book, *Dateline: White House*. Thomas served as the first female president of the White House Correspondents Association and the formerly all-male Gridiron Club. Now in her 70s, she is still at the White House nearly every day.

THORNDIKE, Dame Sybil
1882-1976
British actress

Born in Gainsborough, Lincolnshire, Sybil Thorndike trained to be a concert pianist, but made her stage debut as a member of the American touring company of Ben Greet in 1903. When the company returned to England in 1907, she joined Miss Horniman's Repertory Company in Manchester, and the following year married Lewis Casson. She joined the Old Vic company in 1914, as Lilian BAYLIS began her complete cycle of Shakespeare plays. In 1919, Thorndike appeared in *The Trojan Women* and in *Candida*. George Bernard Shaw was so taken with her performance in the latter that he wrote *Saint Joan* for her. She returned to the Old Vic during World War II, and continued to appear on stage and in movies into the 1960s. She collaborated with her husband on a biography of Lilian Baylis. Sybil Thorndike was created a Dame of the British Empire in 1931.

TSVETAYEVA, Marina
1892-1941
Russian poet, essayist

Born to artistic parents, Marina Tsvetayeva published two volumes of poetry by the age of 20. These mythlike poems soon gave way to such themes as love affairs, motherhood, and immense hardships.

Married to poet Sergei Efron, Tsvetayeva had three children, one of whom starved to death in Moscow during the famine that followed the Revolution of 1917. In 1922 she escaped to Prague, and then Paris. In these years she produced her most innovative and influential works, including *Craft* (1923) and *After Russia* (1928), though her greatness was unrecognized during her lifetime. Her husband and son returned to the Soviet Union before World War II, and at her son's urging she returned to Moscow in 1939. There she found her husband had been executed, other relatives arrested, and her son had become a dogmatic foe of his mother's political and artistic independence. She committed suicide in 1941.

TUCHMAN, Barbara
1912-1989
American historian, political philosopher

A two-time Pulitzer Prize winner for her books *The Guns of August* (1962) and *Stilwell and the American Experience in China* (1971), Barbara Wertheim Tuchman is a remarkable commentator on national and world politics with a perceptive historical viewpoint. She was born in New York City and graduated from Radcliffe College in 1933. She worked as a research assistant for the Institute of Pacific Relations in New York and was a contributing writer to the political journals *Foreign Affairs* and *Nation*. She married Dr. Lester Tuchman in 1940.

Tuchman first received recognition in publishing circles for her 1958 book *The Zimmermann Telegram* which chronicled Germany's efforts to embroil Mexico in a war with the U.S. during World War I. In 1966 Tuchman produced *The Proud Tower*, a chronological tour of events during the quarter-century before World War I. Her later works included *A Distant Mirror: The Calamitous 14th Century* (1978), *Practicing History* (1981) and *The March of Folly* (1984). She was the first woman to hold the presidency of the American Academy and Institute of Arts and Letters.

TURNER, Tina
1939-
American singer, songwriter

Tina Turner was born Anna Mae Bullock in Nutbush, Tennessee, and chopped cotton as a little girl. She joined bandleader Ike Turner in a popular music partnership in 1956. They married in 1958 and produced a series of rhythm and blues hits beginning with "Fool in Love" in 1960. They had several successful singles and albums, including "Proud Mary" (1971) and the album *Feel Good*. Ike Turner was a cruelly abusive and alcoholic husband, and Tina Turner left him to go it alone with few prospects. She established a solo career by singing six nights a week in small clubs until Rod Stewart put her on his billing act in 1980, and she opened for the Rolling Stones in 1982. Her recording career revived with a version of Al Green's "Let's Stay Together" and she had a runaway success with the album *Private Dancer* in 1984. Three songs from the album became number one hits, and it won three Grammys and two American Music awards. After another Grammy in 1986, Turner went on tour in 145 cities in 25 countries. Her 1988 autobiography *I, Tina* was made into the popular film *What's Love Got To Do With It*.

TWIGGY (b. Leslie Hornsby)
1949-
British fashion model, actress

A pop icon during the late 1960s, Twiggy was famous for her stick-thin figure, doe-like eyes and promotion of Mod fashion.

Born Leslie Hornsby in London, she changed her name to Twiggy when she launched her modeling career in 1967. It was an immediate success. Through shrewd management and successful merchandising, she became "the look" for the time. She appeared on every major fashion magazine cover and posed often for photographer Richard Avedon. In 1971 she starred in the Ken Russell film *The Boy Friend*. She retired from modeling in the mid-1970s, and in 1983 made her Broadway debut in the musical *My One and Only*, co-starring with dancer Tommy Tune. She has since co-starred in the film *Madame Sousatzka* (1988) with Shirley MacLaine, and appeared in a number of cameo roles and in TV and cable TV movies.

Born Leslie Hornsby, Twiggy earned her name with her skinny figure in the Swinging London of the 1960s. The former model now is an actress.

Empress Dowager Tz'u-Hsi, the last of China's Manchu dynasty, reluctantly instituted reforms to modernize China.

TZ'U-HSI, Empress
1835-1908
Chinese dowager empress

The last of the Manchu rulers, Empress Tz'u-hsi was a ruthless leader who stopped at nothing to maintain her power. Originally a concubine to Emperor Xian Feng, she gave birth to his only son, Tong Zhi. When the Emperor died, she was able to gain control of the court, and never let go. Defeat by the Japanese in the 1890s called attention to her corruption and demands were made to lessen the power of the monarchy. She refused, crushing the resistance. Yet in 1901, the Boxer Rebellion compelled her to institute reforms, which included an end to foot binding, allowing state schools to admit girls, and the institution of a constitution. She died in 1908, and three years later the Manchu dynasty was no more.

U

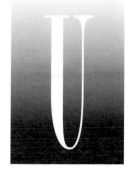

ULANOVA, Galina
1910-
Russian dancer

The daughter of two dancers at the Mariinsky Theatre, Ulanova was born in St. Petersburg and coached by her mother and later by Agrippina Vaganova. She made her debut at the Kirov Theatre in *Chopiniana* in 1928 and earned increasingly important roles. Her performance of *Giselle*, first danced in 1932, is considered the ultimate modern interpretation. Ulanova created many new roles as well, including Maria in Zacharov's *Fountain of Bakchisarai* (1934) and Juliet in Lavrovsky's *Romeo and Juliet* (1940). She joined the Bolshoi Ballet in 1944 and continued to interpret Lavrovsky, appearing as Tao-Hoa in *Red Poppy* (1949) and Katerina in *Stone Flower* (1954). She danced in Vienna in 1945 and in Great Britain in 1956.

Ulanova married the Bolshoi's chief designer, Vadim Rindin and gave her farewell performance in 1962. She became a ballet mistress for the Bolshoi Ballet, and her stylistic effect upon Soviet ballerinas has been enormous. She was awarded the Lenin Prize in 1957. Her autobiography *Ulanova: Her Childhood and Schooldays* was translated by Dame Marie RAMBERT in 1962.

ULLMAN, Liv
1939-
Norwegian actress

Liv Johanne Ullman joined the National Theatre in Oslo where she played young leads, including Juliet, St. Joan, and Nora in *A Doll's House*. She also made movies in Norway in the late 1950s. She met the great Swedish director Ingmar Bergman in 1965 while making her first Swedish movie. Bergman directed her in several movies that have become classics, beginning with *Persona* (1966) and including *Cries and Whispers* (1972). That same year she appeared in *The New Land* (1972), part of the great Swedish emigrant epic written by Wilhelm Moberg and co-starring Max von Sydow. Her later movies included *Scenes from a Marriage* (1974) and *Autumn Sonata* (1978). She made her Broadway debut in *A Doll's House* in 1975, and also appeared in the musical *I Remember Mama* in 1979. She has also directed two films, *Love* (1982) and *Sofie* (1992), which she also wrote.

Actress Liv Ullman made a number of memorable movies, including Cries and Whispers *(1972) with director Ingmar Bergman, and* Scenes from a Marriage *(1974).*

UNDSET, Sigrid
1882-1949
Norwegian novelist, poet

Sigrid Undset's powerful sagas of medieval life grew from her childhood, during which she became familiar with the ancient legends and ballads and artifacts which were the passion of her archaeologist father. Born in Kallundborg, Denmark, Undset converted to Catholicism in 1924, and this religious search for a moral compass runs through her fiction and essays. Her greatest work is the trilogy *Kristin Lavransdatter*, whose detailed descriptions and strong characters bring the Middle Ages alive for readers. Undset won the Nobel Prize for literature in 1928.

In World War II, she sheltered refugees, and so in 1940 was forced to flee Norway by Nazi occupation. She traveled the globe, seeking assistance for Norway and spreading Scandinavian culture, before returning in 1945 to a liberated Norway.

V

DE VALOIS, Dame Ninette
1898-
Irish-born choreographer, dancer

One of the founders of the Royal Ballet, Ninette de Valois was born Edris Stannus in Baltiboys, Ireland, the daughter of an Army officer killed during World War I. As a young woman she performed in pantomime, operetta and revues, and began using the stage name Ninette de Valois at her mother's suggestion. She became a soloist with Diaghilev's Ballets Russes in 1923.

She left his company to form her own Academy of Choreographic Arts in 1926. Lacking a theater for her dancers, she joined with Lilian BAYLIS in a small building in London attached to an opera house. Baylis and de Valois founded the Vic-Wells Ballet in 1931, and de Valois's program of classical and contemporary dance turned it into a national theater and first-class ballet. Only British-born dancers performed there (Alicia MARKOVA and Margot FONTEYN were its principal prima ballerinas) and de Valois employed a young British choreographer, Frederick Ashton, who now ranks among the finest in history.

De Valois also created 31 ballets, the best known of which are *The Rake's Progress* (based on John Hogarth's prints), *Job* and *Checkmate*. The company was granted a royal charter in 1954 to become the Royal Ballet Company. De Valois was created a Dame of the British Empire and married Dr. Arthur Connell in 1935.

VAN BUREN, Abigail. *See* **LANDERS, Ann**

VAUGHAN, Sarah
1924-1990
American singer

Born in Newark, New Jersey, "Sassy" Sarah Vaughan sang with her parents in the choir of the Mt. Zion Baptist Church at 7 and went on to study piano and voice during the 1930s. After winning an amateur contest at Harlem's Apollo Theater, her singing skills were noticed by Billy Eckstine, a musician with the Earl Hines Band. He hired her to be their lead vocalist and she made her professional debut at the Apollo in 1943. During the 1940s Vaughan sang bebop and jazz with Eckstine, Charlie Parker and Dizzy Gillespie, with whom she formed a partnership from 1946 onward. Her rich voice, with its unusual vibrato resonance, were notable on a series of hit albums, and single recordings such as "I'll Wait and Pray", "My Funny Valentine", "Tenderly", "A Foggy Day", and "The Summer Knows".

In the 1980s she recorded with such greats as Count Basie and Oscar Peterson. Nominated for a Grammy in 1983, she was presented with a Lifetime Achievement Grammy in 1989, the year before her death.

Fashion editor Diana Vreeland prepares the Balenciaga exhibit at the Metropolitan Museum of Art in New York in 1973.

President of the European Parliament from 1979 to 1982, Simone Veil is now France's Minister of Health.

VEIL, Simone
1927-
French politician, government official

"For women, power is action", says Simone Veil, the Minister of Health, Social Affairs, and Urban Affairs since 1993. A formidable woman successfully challenging France's growing disdain toward North African immigrants, she reminds France of the bitter cost of xenophobia, and their own war crimes during World War II. As a Jew, she and her family were deported in 1944 to Auschwitz. She survived, but never saw her parents or brother again.

Returning to France, she studied law, and became an assistant public prosecutor at the Ministry of Justice. Appointed Minister of Health in 1974, she pushed a bill legalizing abortion through the French Parliament, despite tremendous hostility. From 1979 to 1982 she was president of the European Parliament.

VIONNET, Madeleine
1876-1975
French fashion designer

Born in Chileurs aux Bois, near Paris, Madeleine Vionnet went to London in 1896 to work for the dressmaker Kate Reilly, and then returned to Paris and Callot Soeurs until 1907, when she joined Doucet. In 1912 she opened her own fashion house, which closed during World War I. She reopened it in 1918, and the following year designed the first of her tubular dresses, which slipped over the head. Vionnet claimed to be the designer who was responsible for models discarding their corsets. It was said that when she turned fabric on an angle that it gained elasticity, which was invaluable in the bias-cut dresses that became her trademark. She did not sketch her designs, but draped them on specially made mannequins, one-quarter life-size. When she had worked out any problems, the toiles would be cut full size. She closed her couture house in 1940, when the Germans came into Paris. She became a Chevalier of the Legion of Honor in 1929.

VREELAND, Diana
1906?-1989
American fashion journalist, museum consultant

Diana Dalziel was born in Paris, and returned to New York with her American parents at the beginning of World War I. Diana had a sheltered childhood, attending private school, making her debut, and marrying Thomas Vreeland in 1924. The young couple moved to London in 1929. When they returned to New York in 1936, Diana was hired by *Harper's Bazaar* to write a column, and produced the popular, semi-facetious "What Don't You", which was much parodied. However, three years later, she had become fashion editor of the magazine. In 1962 she joined *Vogue* as editor in chief, and turned it from a high-fashion speciality magazine into a society journal of widespread interest. She became consulting editor in 1971, the same year she became a consultant to the Costume Institute at the Metropolitan Museum. Under her guidance, the Met staged a series of outstanding exhibits, beginning with "The World of Balenciaga" in 1973, which brought costume into a prominent place in the museum world.

W

WACHNER, Linda
1946-
American business executive

Linda Joy Wachner grew up in Forest Hills, Queens, New York, and graduated with a BS in Economics and Business from the University of Buffalo. The first female chief executive officer of a Fortune 500 industrial company, Linda Wachner started in business as a buyer for a department store in 1968, moved up quickly in corporate management, and was recruited in 1978 to run the U.S. division of the Max Factor cosmetics company. The dynamic Wachner turned the money-losing operation around in her second year, but she left five years later, following her failed attempt to buy the company after a corporate takeover. In 1986, she and Los Angeles investor Andrew Galef won a hostile takeover battle for Warnaco Inc., a maker of lingerie and menswear, and Wachner became chairman, president, and CEO, and one of the highest paid women executives in the country.

WADE, Virginia
1945-
British tennis player

Virginia Wade's most memorable win occurred on a propitious occasion – she was the champion at Wimbledon in its centenary year which coincided with Queen Elizabeth II's Silver Jubilee, and the Queen was in the Royal Box to watch the 1977 women's final match. Wade had tried 15 times before at Wimbledon, and her victory for her home country was a fairy-tale triumph.

Wade won the first U.S. Open title in 1968, defeating Billie Jean KING. She won the Italian Open in 1971 and the Australian Open in 1972. Teaming with Margaret COURT in women's doubles events, the pair won the U.S. Open three times (1969, 1973, 1975), the Australian Open in 1973 and the French Open in 1973. Wade holds five titles on the Virginia Slims circuit from 1971 to 1977 and she was the 1977 WTA Player of the Year. As

America's first black millionaire, Madame C.J. Walker.

a member of the Wightman Cup team from 1965 to 1968 and the Federation Cup team from 1967 to 1982, Wade ranked number one for Britain for a record ten consecutive years. In 1982 she was the first woman elected to the Wimbledon committee.

WALKER, Alice
1944-
American poet and novelist

Alice Walker was the youngest of eight children born to Willie Lee Walker, a sharecropper in Eatouton, Georgia. She attended Spelman College in Atlanta and Sarah Lawrence College in New York. Her searing experiences as an activist for voter registration and welfare rights in Georgia, New York, and Mississippi spawned her early poetry, a volume called *Once* of 1968. The strength and perseverance of black women, and their bonds of family, humor and ethnic identity, are the essential themes of *The Third Life of Grange Copeland* (1970), *In Love and Trouble* (1973) and *Meridian* (1976). Walker won the National Book Award and the 1983 Pulitzer Prize for *The Color Purple* (1982), whose characters' volatile emotional and sexual lives are entangled with difficulties unique to the African-American experience. The book was made into a popular film by Steven Spielberg. *The Temple of My Familiar* (1989) and *Possessing the Secret of Joy* (1992) continue to explore the themes and characters' lives Alive Walker created in *The Color Purple.*

WALKER, Madame C. J.
1867-1919
American cosmetics entrepreneur, philanthropist

Sarah Breedlove McWilliams was born in Delta, Louisiana, and moved to St. Louis, Missouri, as a young widow. Concerned with her own hair loss, she began to develop hair care products, which she mixed in the washtub she used as a laundress. Her shampoo, combined with a "hair grower" pomade, vigorous brushing and a heated comb, became a system for straightening and adding shine to frizzy hair. As her business began to expand, she married C.J. Walker, a newspaper man with a solid knowledge of advertising and mail order procedure. Madame Walker trained assistants who sold the Walker system door-to-door. Her employees, easily recognized by their white shirtwaists, black skirts, and black satchels were also bound by contract to a hygenic regimen that anticipated later state cosmetology laws. Mme. Walker employed black women, for the first time, in jobs outside housework, and became the first black millionaire in the United States. She used her money to aid the NAACP, for scholarships at Tuskegee Institute and to support a salon in her house in Harlem, New York, where many of the poets, authors and artists of the Harlem Renaissance met.

Lila Wallace, editor and co-owner of the Reader's Digest, *in a 1954 photograph.*

WALKER, Maggie Lena

1867-1934

American social activist, bank president

Maggie Lena Mitchell was born in Richmond, Virginia. She taught school until she married in 1886, and then joined the Independent Order of St. Luke, an African-American insurance cooperative. By 1899, she had become Grand Secretary, and she soon increased membership through the formation of a department store, and a bank which aided blacks in obtaining mortgages. She encouraged children to save, establishing an educational loan fund for those that did. The bank which began as the St. Luke's Penny Thrift in 1903, making Walker the first female bank president, became the St. Lukes Bank and Trust and is now Consolidated Bank and Trust. In 1912, Maggie Walker also founded the Richmond Council for Colored Women, a charity which raised money for black programs.

WALLACE, Lila

1889-1984

American publisher, philanthropist

Lila Bell Acheson was born in Virden, Manitoba, and grew up in a series of midwestern towns where her father served as the Presbyterian minister. She attended the University of Oregon and worked with the YMCA during World War I. In 1921, she married DeWitt Wallace, and the following year they founded *The Reader's Digest*. At first they only published excerpts of works, but after 1933 they began to solicit for original pieces, by which time their subscription list had grown to over 200,000. They published the first foreign-language edition in 1938, and accepted the first advertising only in 1955. The reprints of fiction (later amalgamated into condensed books), and the regular features, especially the humorous ones, helped develop the firm into a major communications empire which now also produces books and films.

The Lila and DeWitt Wallace Foundation is a generous donor to many arts projects, including educational television and National Public Radio. It also supplies the enormous vases of fresh flowers in the Great Hall of the Metropolitan Museum of Art in New York.

WALTERS, Barbara

1931-

American news correspondent

Born in Boston, Barbara Walters attended Sarah Lawrence College and began her career in television as an assistant to the publicity director of RCA-TV. She was chosen to participate in a producer's training program, and then joined station WPIX as a producer of women's programs. She later worked at CBS and NBC, joining the *Today* program at NBC as a writer in 1961. She became a regular panel member in 1963, working her way from the "Today Girl" to a well-established contributing reporter. She was the co-host from 1974 to 1976, when she joined ABC-News as the co-anchor of the evening news program, the first woman to achieve that position. She became a co-host of the news magazine *20/20* in 1979, and began to host the successful Barbara Walters television specials in 1976. She was honored by a retrospective of her career at the Museum of Broadcasting in 1988, and has received several Emmy awards.

WATERS, Maxine

1938-

American politician

When riots broke out in Los Angeles in 1992 following the acquittal of white police officers in the beating of Rodney King, U.S. Representative Maxine Waters described the violence as a rebellion against racial bias. For 14 years in the California State Assembly, Waters had represented the people at the heart of the explosion. Now the second black female member of the United States Congress, she had an opportunity to attack more broadly what she saw as years of neglect of the inner cities. Born in St. Louis, one of 13 children, she moved to the Watts section of Los Angeles in 1961. After a series of low-paying jobs, she was hired by Head Start, which she credits with turning her to politics. First a volunteer worker in local campaigns, she became chief deputy to a city councilman, earned a BA in sociology, and in 1976 won a seat in the Assembly, where she was active in women's issues. Nationally recognized by the late 1980s, she swept a June 1990 Democratic Congressional primary and won against only token Republican opposition in November.

Barbara Walters has won a number of awards for her news reporting. A celebrity herself, she interviews other celebrities on popular TV specials.

With husband Sidney Webb, Beatrice Webb founded the London School of Economics and the New Statesman.

WATTLETON, Faye
1943-
American nurse, reproductive rights activist

Faye Wattleton served as president of Planned Parenthood Federation of America (PPFA) from 1978 to 1992. The first woman and African-American to hold that position, she brought endless energy and determination to PPFA.

During her 14-year tenure there was a resurgence of opposition to reproductive rights, yet she remained an advocate of choice and reproductive responsibility.

As a nurse, she had seen firsthand the consequences of unwanted pregnancies and illegal abortion. Thus, she devoted her career to "improving the health rights and well-being of women". In 1986 she received the Humanist of the Year Award.

WEBB, Beatrice
1858-1943
British social reformer

Born in Gloucester, Beatrice Potter was raised in liberal political and intellectual circles. Her work included advocacy of the poor. She participated in the Charity Organisation Society and published a study on London's East End in 1880. In 1889 she contributed to Charles Booth's social survey *The Life and Labour of the People of London*, and laid the foundation of the welfare state in a report she prepared in 1905 for the Royal Commission on Poor Laws.

Along with her husband, Sidney Webb, a lecturer at London University and a member of the Fabian Society, she set out to reform Britain's sociopolitical system. Members of the Labour Party, they published over 100 writings on labor conditions. They established the London School of Economics, and in 1913 established the left-wing weekly the *New Statesman*.

WEBER, Helene
1881-1962
German politician

A pioneering politician, Helene Weber campaigned effectively for women's rights. A schoolteacher for five years, she became involved in social work, and was appointed head of the school for social welfare of the German Catholic Women's Federation in Cologne in 1916. In 1919 she became part of the Prussian Ministry of Social Welfare, and focused on issues pertaining to youth. Until her dismissal by the Nazis, she was a representative of the Zentrum Party (1924-33). When World War II was over, Weber became a member of the neophyte Christian Democrat Party, and in 1945 was elected to the North Rhine Westphalia assembly, quickly becoming a leading figure representing women's issues in the Bundestag. In 1957 she was honored with the highest award given to a civilian, the Grosse Bundesverdienstkreuz.

WEIL, Simone
1909-1943
French religious philosopher

Exceptionally precocious and serious-minded as a child, Simone Weil was the daughter of free-thinking Jewish parents. She studied philosophy at the École Normale and became a teacher who was active in trade-union work. Her deep affinity with the poor led her to work as a factory and farm laborer, and as a Republican in the Spanish Civil War. In her thirtieth year, she had a mystical experience of the presence of Christ and would have converted to Christianity except for her reservations about the institutional Church. After the German occupation of France, she wore herself out in the service of the Free French cause in London and died of tuberculosis at the age of 34. Her major writings include *Waiting for God* and *The Need for Roots*, both published posthumously.

Pulitzer Prize-winning novelist Eudora Welty is a writer in the great Southern Gothic tradition in American literature.

WELLS LAURENCE, Mary
1928-
American advertising executive

Mary Georgene Berg was born in Youngstown, Ohio, and attended the Carnegie Institute of Technology, where she met and married Burt Wells. She began her career in advertising as a writer for McCann Erikson, and was head of the copy group from 1953 to 1956. She then joined the creative group at Doyle, Dane, Bernbach, and had made vice-president by 1963. In 1964 she joined Tinker and Partners, for whom she designed the innovative Alka-Seltzer campaign and the Braniff airlines campaign which involved the restyling of the airline, the painting of the fleet in wild colors, and the dressing of the stewardesses by Pucci. Wells later married Brad Laurence, the president of Braniff. In 1966 she became a co founder of Wells, Rich and Greene, one of the first ad agencies headed by a woman.

WELTY, Eudora
1909-
American writer

Eudora Welty was born and raised in Jackson, Mississippi, and has lived almost her entire life in the southern setting that is the source of customs, temperaments and tone for her short stories and novels. Welty received her BA from the University of Wisconsin in 1929 and studied advertising at Columbia. After her father's death in 1931 she returned to Jackson, writing for local newspapers, the radio station and the Works Progress Administration.

Her first collection of short fiction was *A Curtain of Green and Other Stories* (1941) followed by *The Wide Net and Other Stories* (1943) and the novels *The Robber Bridegroom* (1942), *Delta Wedding* (1946), *The Ponder Heart* (1954), *The Optimist's Daughter* (1972) for which she won the Pulitzer Prize, and *Morgana* (1990). Her memoir *One Writer's Beginnings* appeared in 1983.

WERTMULLER, Lina
1928-
Italian film director

Arcangela Felice Assunta Wertmuller von Elgg Spanol von Braueich was born in Rome, and was educated at catholic schools and the Academy of Rome. In 1951 she joined Maria Signorelli's Puppet Troupe, and later worked in the Roman theater and film industry in many different capacities. In 1962 she was Federico Fellini's assistant on *8½*. The following year she directed her first feature *I basilischi* (*The Lizards*). Her first film to make an impression outside Italy was *The Seduction of Mimi* (1972), followed by *Swept Away . . .* (whose complete title was almost as long as her real name) which also made an international star of Giancarlo Giannini. Her films, including *Seven Beauties* (1976), have been described as grotesque political allegories, but they are frequently breathtakingly beautiful. Her later films, including *Blood Feud* (1980), *Saturday, Sunday, Monday* (1990), and *Ciao Professore* (1994) have been more mainstream and have gained her a wider audience.

ABOVE: *Film director Lina Wertmuller on the set of* Romantic Comedy *(1977).*

BELOW: *"Come up and see me": actress and vaudevillian Mae West's risqué act was a major cause of the creation of the Hays Office in Hollywood.*

WEST, Mae
1893-1980
American actress

Mae West was born in Brooklyn, New York, and began working in vaudeville in 1906, although she had appeared on stage as a child. She made her Broadway debut in 1911, but it was the production of *Sex* in 1926, which she also wrote, which truly identified her. Her parts were always similar. She was the woman who frankly enjoyed sex and used it to get her way. It was a character that ran contrary to the accepted heroine, and it shocked and titillated audiences while it also amused them. Her other plays included *Diamond Lil* in 1928, which was filmed as *She Done Him Wrong* (1933). Her plots, delivery and use of double entendre led to censure, legal battles and perhaps to the establishment of the Hays Office, which became responsible for film censorship. Her other films, including *I'm No Angel* (1933), *Go West, Young Man* (1936) and *My Little Chickadee* (1940) made her the highest paid star in Hollywood at that time. In her later films, she seemed to play a parody of herself.

WEST, Dame Rebecca
1892-1983
British novelist, journalist

West was born Cicily Isabel Fairfield, daughter of a Scottish pianist and an Irish journalist. Educated in Edinburgh, she abandoned school for the stage at 16, taking the pseudonym Rebecca West from the radical feminist character in Henrik Ibsen's play *Rosmersholm.*

She wrote for the journal *The Freewoman* and a socialist weekly, *The Clarion*, espousing women's trade unions, suffragists' rights and free love for women. A 10-year affair with the English author and social reformer H.G. Wells produced one son, Anthony West, in 1914.

Her novels *The Return of the Soldier* (1918) and *The Judge* (1922) explore illegitimacy, motherhood, female sexuality and the flawed customs of marriage. Her prose discloses an acute awareness of men's disdainful attitudes toward women's intellect.

In 1930 West married a banker, Henry Adams, and lived in a country manor in Buckinghamshire and continued writing novels. During World War II she published *Black Lamb and Grey Falcon*, a journal and history of Yugoslavia. In 1959 she was created a Dame Commander of the British Empire.

The Age of Innocence (1921) made Edith Wharton the first woman to receive the Pulitzer Prize.

WESTWOOD, Vivienne
1941-
British designer

Vivienne Westwood was born in Tintwhistle, near Manchester, went to London around 1970, and attended Harrow Art School for one term. Her association with Malcolm McClaren, mastermind of the punk rock group the Sex Pistols, brought her into contact with a new influence on fashion. Her early designs, with rough edges and metal pins, were a rejection of all polite standards of dress. She designed clothes for rock groups such as Boy George and Bananarama, as well as for the Sex Pistols. In the eighties, she developed a new romanticism revealed in the flowing sleeves of her Pirate collection, which was adopted by rock's Adam Ant and Bow Wow Wow. She ended her partnership with McClaren in 1983, and moved to Italy to work with Sergio Galeotti, a partner of Giorgio Armani. She launched her "Mini Crini" in 1985. She was named Designer of the Year in 1990 and 1991.

WHARTON, Edith
1862-1937
American novelist, short story writer

The first woman to receive the Pulitzer Prize, awarded to her in 1921 for *The Age of Innocence*, Edith Newbold Jones was born in New York City. She was educated by a governess and traveled in Europe before marrying a proper Bostonian, Edward Wharton, and living among the American upper class in Newport, Rhode Island; New York; Boston; and Europe.

Talk show host and actress Oprah Winfrey is known for her business acumen and firm control of her career.

Wharton's first published efforts were short stories for *Scribner's*, *Harper's* and the *Century* magazines. Her first novel, *The House of Mirth* (1905), was a successful satire about a young woman imprisoned by social conventions. Wharton moved to Paris in 1905 where she met another expatriate author, Henry James, who became her mentor. She wrote *Ethan Frome* in 1911 and would produce almost 40 novels in her lifetime to become America's highest paid author.

During World War I she was awarded the Legion of Honor for her relief efforts on behalf of refugees in France. After divorcing her husband in 1913, she settled permanently in France. Her autobiography *A Backward Glance* appeared in 1934.

WILHELMINA, Queen
1880-1962
Dutch monarch

Daughter of King William II and Queen Emma, she began her adult rule when she was 18, at the start of the Boer War. In 1900 she married Duke Henry of Mecklenberg-Schwerin. Throughout her reign, she tried to preserve the Netherlands' position of neutrality, offering to mediate international disputes and provide asylum. When Germany invaded the Netherlands in World War II, she sent her daughter Juliana and her grandchildren to Canada. She herself fled to London. For the rest of the war, she was a symbol of the Dutch resistance, broadcasting messages to her people and developing political relations with Allied leaders. At war's end, she returned home in 1945, and giving up neutrality, joined the United Nations as a charter member. She relinquished the crown in 1948 to her daughter Juliana.

WILLIAMS PERKINS, Betty. *See* **CORRIGAN MAGUIRE, Mairead**

WINFREY, Oprah
1954-
American talk show host, actress, television producer

Oprah Gail Winfrey was born in Kosciusko, Mississippi, and lived with her grandmother, and then was shuttled between her mother in Milwaukee and her father in Nashville. While a student at Tennessee State University, she was hired by a local black radio station, WVOL, to read the news. In 1976 she found a new position at WJZ in Baltimore. In the early eighties she was hired by the ABC affiliate in Chicago to anchor their morning show, *AM Chicago*. In 1985 it was renamed the *Oprah Winfrey Show*, when her ratings overtook those of Phil Donohue. Also in 1985 she made her first film, Steven Spielberg's *The Color Purple*, and received a nomination for Best Actress. The following year she appeared in *Native Son* (1986). She has formed her own television production company, Harpo Productions, which was responsible for the critically acclaimed *Women of Brewster Place* miniseries. She also continues to host her talk show and has become a force in the entertainment industry.

WINTOUR, Anna
1949-
British magazine editor

Anna Wintour was born in London, and attended the North London Collegiate School and Queen's College, London. She entered magazine publishing working for the fashion editor of *Harpers and Queen*. In 1976 she moved to New York as the fashion editor of *Harper's Bazaar*. She was editor of *Viva* magazine from 1977 to 1978, and a contributing editor for fashion and style at *Savvy* from 1980 to 1981.

In 1983 she became senior editor at *New York*, and the creative director at *Vogue*. She returned to London to be the editor of British *Vogue* in 1986, and then came back to the United States as editor of *House and Garden* which was renamed *HG* in 1987.

In 1988, S.I. Newhouse, the owner of *Vogue*, hired her back as editor in chief of that magazine, hoping to attract a younger readership. With the establishment of a new format, clever covers, and articles aimed at that audience, by May 1989 *Vogue* was selling more advertising space than ever before, and Wintour had managed to increase the subscription list as well.

WOLF, Christa
1929-
German novelist, essayist

Christa Wolf's essays and novels stretched the limits of literature in the Eastern bloc, without rejecting the utopian hopes of socialism.

Born in Landsberg, Germany (now Poland), as a schoolgirl she belonged to Nazi organizations. She critically examines that era in *A Model Childhood* (1976). After the war, she was active in the Communist Party, but her greatest political impact has been as a feminist. Her first novel *Divided Heaven* (1963) created waves by addressing the East/West split. Her novels *The Quest for Christa T.* and *Cassandra* use an experimental narrative to capture women's unique voices, and at times for veiled criticism of the State. Her later works express growing disillusionment, particularly *Current Texts* (1990), written during the collapse of German socialism symbolized by the dismantling of the Berlin Wall. *What Remains and Other Stories* was published in 1993.

Elsie de Wolfe decorated New York's first women's club in 1905.

DE **WOLFE, Elsie**
1861-1950
American interior decorator

Born in New York to ambitious but not wealthy parents, Elsie de Wolfe was schooled in Scotland and presented at court in London at 17. In the 1880s she had a brief theatrical career, appearing in amateur plays at the Metropolitan Opera and at Tuxedo Park, New York. There she met Elisabeth Marbury, a well-connected theatrical agent with whom she began a long relationship. Guests to their New York townhouse included Edith WHARTON, Nellie MELBA, Ethel BARRYMORE and Oscar Wilde. In 1905 she decorated the Colony Club, Manhattan's first women's club, and in 1913 published *The House in Good Taste*. Henry Clay Frick commissioned her to decorate his townhouse which included over $3 million worth of art treasures. Her decorating schemes cleared away the fusty darkness of the Victorian era, adding chintz, stripes, white paint and ubiquitous lighting fixtures.

De Wolfe bought "Villa Trianon" in Versailles, France, and was a nurse on the front lines during World War I, earning the Croix de Guerre and Legion of Honor for her efforts. In her sixties, de Wolfe surprised everyone by marrying a British diplomat, Sir Charles Mendl. In the 1940s they left France and settled at "After All" in Beverly Hills, a house she named after her autobiography.

LEFT: *Virginia Woolf.*

WOOLF, Virginia
1882-1941
British writer

Adeline Virginia Stephens was born in London to a literary family. Her mother died when she was 13 and the event brought on the first of many episodes of mental illness. When her father died in 1904 Virginia moved with her sister and brother to 46 Gordon Square, which became the first meetingplace of the Bloomsbury Group, a collection of avant-garde artists, writers and philosophers which included the economist John Maynard Keynes, the art critic Clive Bell and the novelist E.M. Forster, among others.

She married Leonard Woolf in 1912, and in 1917 they founded the Hogarth Press, which published works by T.S. Eliot, Sigmund Freud and Katherine MANSFIELD. Woolf's first novel *The Voyage Out* was published in 1915. The realism of her early work gave way in later writings to an impressionistic technique which put her at the forefront of modernism. Her most highly praised novels are *Mrs. Dalloway* (1925), *To the Lighthouse* (1927), and *The Waves* (1931). A noted literary critic, Woolf also wrote numerous critical essays and biography, and she was a prolific diarist whose intelligent, witty letters have been published in several volumes. Her last novel, *Between the Acts*, was published posthumously in 1941. Earlier that year she had committed suicide by putting stones in her pockets and walking into the River Ouse by her home.

WORKMAN, Fanny
1859-1925
American cyclist, mountain climber

The daughter of a former governor of Massachusetts, Fanny Bullock undertook a series of cycling tours with her husband from 1895 to 1899 and wrote several journals of their journeys. They traveled extensively through North Africa, Egypt, Palestine, and Greece, averaging 40-50 miles a day. Workman wore sensible clothes and advocated women's suffrage along with her cycling pursuits, epitomizing the Victorian era's "new" woman.

After a cycling tour in Java, the Workmans became pioneer Himalayan explorers and together embarked on seven expeditions. In 1906, Fanny Workman set an altitude record of 23,300 feet climbing the second highest Nun Kun peak. Workman's later books were documentary accounts illustrated with fine photographs, including *In the World of the Himalaya* (1900), *Peaks and Glaciers of Nun Kun* (1909) and *Two Summers in the Ice Wilds of Eastern Karakoram* (1917). A Fellow of the Royal Geographical Society and a member of the Royal Asiatic Society, she was the first woman to lecture at the Sorbonne.

WU, Chien-Shiung
1912-
American atomic physicist

A graduate of Nanking's National Central University, Wu emigrated to the United States in 1936 and rapidly distinguished herself by her research in the field of subatomic particles. She earned a Ph.D. degree in physics at the University of California, Berkeley and taught at Smith College and Princeton University. During World War II, she joined the Division of War Research at Columbia University, where she achieved the rank of full professor in 1957. She devised a series of experiments to confirm the theory that in certain reactions involving subatomic particles they do not behave symmetrically, a thesis developed by Tsung-Dao Lee and Chen Ning Yang, who won a Nobel Prize for their part in this work. Wu was the first woman to receive the Comstock Prize from the National Academy of Sciences, in 1964.

Y

YALOW, Rosalyn
1921-
American medical physicist

A native of New York City, Rosalyn Yalow was the first physics major to graduate from Hunter College, in 1940, and was offered a teaching fellowship at the University of Illinois. There she met her future husband Aaron Yalow, a fellow professor of physics. During World War II, she studied the medical application of radioisotopes as a volunteer at the laboratory of Columbia University's College of Physicians and Surgeons. While teaching at Hunter College in the late 1940s, she was a consultant to the Bronx Veterans Administration Hospital, after which she began a 22-year partnership with Dr. Solomon A. Berson. It was their joint research that brought Yalow the Nobel Prize for physiology or medicine in 1977, although she grieved that Dr. Berson, who died in 1972, had not lived to share it.

YARD, Molly
1912(?)-
American social activist

The eighth president of the National Organization for Women (NOW), Molly Yard was born in China into a missionary family. Her father was forced from his position for his outspoken social activism, and the family returned to the United States when Molly was 13. At Swarthmore College she gained a reputation as a passionate activist and an effective organizer and orator. Yard helped form, and then headed, the American Student Union (ASU) in the 1930s. She became active in Democratic Party politics in Pennsylvania, and in California after her marriage to labor arbitrator Sylvester Garrett. In Pennsylvania again from the mid-1950s, she was defeated for a seat in the state legislature in 1964, but became deeply involved in the movement for national civil rights legislation. Active in the Pittsburgh chapter of NOW in the 1970s, Yard moved to Washington to head NOW's national Equal Rights Amendment campaign. She became NOW's political director in 1985 and its president two years later. Following a stroke in 1991, she was succeeded by Patricia IRELAND.

YEAGER, Jeana
1952
American aviator

The first woman to fly nonstop around the world without refueling (1986), Yeager was born and raised in Fort Worth, Texas, where her hobbies were skydiving and helicopter flying. Trained as an engineer, she had had 10 years of flight experience prior to her adventure in the featherweight aircraft *Voyager*. Yeager's copilot was Dick Rutan, whose brother Burt had designed the aircraft. It weighed less than a car (1860 pounds) and carried more fuel than a gasoline tank truck (9400 pounds). The cabin was only four feet high and seven feet long, and the pair endured tremendous turbulence and engine noise. The flight departed from Edwards Air Force Base in California's Mojave Desert on December 14, 1986 and landed there a little over nine days later after a record 26,000-mile flight.

Both Yeager and Rutan were honored by President Reagan for their feat with the Presidential Citizen's Medal, and the *Voyager* was placed on display in the Smithsonian's National Air and Space Museum in Washington, D.C.

YOURCENAR, Marguerite
1903-1987
French novelist, poet, playwright

The first woman elected to the French Academy, Marguerite Yourcenar's elegant language and intellectual depth add to a centuries-old French classical tradition. Born in Brussels, Yourcenar traveled throughout Europe as a child, steeped in the Greek and Latin classics. In 1939 she moved to the United States, teaching at Sarah Lawrence College until 1949.

She first gained fame with *Memoirs of Hadrian* (1951), a prize-winning love story drawn from the life of the Roman emperor. She is also recognized as a fine poet, dramatist and translator. Yourcenar's precise mix of modern and classical sensibilities is especially beloved in France, where despite the controversy raised by her having adopted American citizenship, she was admitted in 1980 to the all-male bastion of the French Academy.

ABOVE: *Rosalyn Yalow won the 1977 Nobel Prize for physiology or medicine.*

ABOVE: *Marguerite Yourcenar, the first woman member of the French Academy.*

Z

ZAHARIAS, Mildred "Babe" Didrikson
1914-1956
American athlete

A nonpareil in amateur and professional sports, Zaharias excelled in an array of fields: she was an Olympic track and field gold medalist, a two-time All-American high school basketball star and so skilled a baseball player she was nicknamed "Babe" after Babe Ruth. Yet she is best known for her records in golf.

Born in Port Arthur, Texas, Babe held three national track and field records before her 18th birthday. In the 1932 Olympics she won gold medals in the javelin throw (a world record of 143′4″) and the 80-meter hurdles (a record of 11.7 seconds). In golf, she won 17 tournaments in a row in two years as an amateur and was the first American to capture the British Women's Amateur Championship. She helped found the Ladies Professional Golf Association (LPGA) in 1948 and went on to win 31 LPGA events. She also won three U.S. Opens (1948, 1950, 1954). She was elected to the LGPA Hall of Fame in 1951 and was the first woman to receive the Bob Jones Award, a posthumous honor, in 1957. The Associated Press named her Woman Athlete of the Year six times.

ZETTERLING, Mai
1925-1994
Swedish actress, film director

Born in Västeras, Sweden, Mai Zetterling was educated at the Royal Dramatic Theatre School in Stockholm, and made her stage and screen debuts in 1941, the latter in *Lasse-Maja*. She considered herself an actress only at first, appearing in films made all over Europe, and acting with the Royal Dramatic Theatre. Probably best known for her performance as the simple girl in *Torment* (1947), she worked with such directors as Ingmar Bergman and Marc Allégret before directing her first film, *The Polite Invasion* (1960). Her directorial credits also include *Night Games* (1966) and *Doctor Glas* (1967). She later returned to the screen as an actress appearing in *The Witches* (1989) and *Hidden Agenda* (1990). At the time of her death she was completing a film, *The Woman Who Cleaned the World*, for which she had also written the screenplay.

ZHIRKOVA, Lyudmila
1944-1981
Bulgarian politician

Considered the second most influential person in Bulgaria (the first being her father, President Todor Zhirkov), before her untimely death Lyudmila Zhirkova was expected to be the first woman to head a state in the Soviet bloc. A lover of philosophy, history and the arts, from 1975 she headed the Bulgarian Committee of Arts and Culture. She envisioned creating a "new socialist man" that would combine Marxism, European philosophy and oriental mysticism. In order to make this a reality, she set up local cultural councils to encourage love of beauty and appreciation of their unique history and culture among the masses of Bulgarian people. In 1979 she was admitted to the ruling body of the country, the Politburo.

ZIA, Khaleda
1946-
Bangladeshi politician, prime minister

The widow of Bangladesh's first president, Khaleda Zia took the oath of office as Prime Minister on March 20, 1991, after her Bangladesh Nationalist Party emerged in the February general election as the largest party. The election ended 16 years of military rule, which included that of her husband General Zia ur-Rahman, assassinated in Chittagong in 1981, and the 10-year rule of General Hussein Muhammed Ershad, whom she helped unseat by fomenting street rebellions. In addition to consolidating parliamentary democracy in Bangladesh, her goals included economic reform, empowerment of women, and ending illiteracy. Begum Zia and the leader of the opposition, Hasina Wazed, the daughter of the nation's founder, engaged in a bitter personal rivalry during her administration.

Mildred "Babe" Didrikson Zaharias.

ZWILICH, Ellen Taaffe
1939-
American composer

Ellen Taaffe was born in Miami, and began piano lessons at the age of five. At Florida State University she was concertmaster of the orchestra, under Ernest von Dohnanyi. She married violinist Joseph Zwilich in 1969, and enrolled at Juilliard in 1972, earning her doctorate in composition in 1975, the first woman to do so. That same year saw the premiere of her *Symposium for Orchestra*. In 1981 she was awarded a Guggenheim Fellowship which led to the composition of *Symphony No. 1*, for which she won the Pulitzer Prize in 1993. Other works include *Tanzspeil*, a ballet written in 1987, and *Symbolon* (1988), the first American work premiered in the Soviet Union.

DATE DUE
